Blessed By The Best

MY JOURNEY TO CANTON AND BEYOND

Brian Dawkins

with
Michael Bradley

Camino Books, Inc.
Philadelphia

Manufactured in the United States of America
2 3 4   24 23 22 21

Cataloging-in-Publication data available from the Library of Congress, Washington, DC.

Library of Congress Cataloging-in-Publication Data

Names: Dawkins, Brian, 1974- author. | Bradley, Michael, 1962- author.
Title: Blessed by the best: my journey to Canton and beyond / Brian Dawkins,
    with Michael Bradley.
Description: Philadelphia: Camino Books, Inc., [2019] | Includes
    bibliographical references and index.
Identifiers: LCCN 2019012166 (print) | LCCN 2019019542 (ebook) | ISBN
    9781680980264 | ISBN 9781680980257 | ISBN 9781680980257 q(alk. paper) |
    ISBN 9781680980264 q(e-book)
Subjects: LCSH: Dawkins, Brian, 1974- | Football players--United
    States--Biography. | Pro Football Hall of Fame (U.S.)--History.
Classification: LCC GV939.D34198 (ebook) | LCC GV939.D34198 A3 2019 (print) |
    DDC 796.332092 [B] --dc23
LC record available at https://lccn.loc.gov/2019012166

ISBN 978-1-68098-025-7
ISBN 978-1-68098-026-4 (ebook)

Interior design: Jerilyn DiCarlo
Cover design: Mario Juliana, Vionet Graphics

This book is available at a special discount on bulk purchases for educational, business, and promotional purposes. For information write:

Publisher
Camino Books, Inc.
P.O. Box 59026
Philadelphia, PA 19102
www.caminobooks.com

Contents

CHAPTER 1

Blessed By The Best

There was no doubt I would head out onto the stage at Tom Benson Stadium in Canton for the 2018 Hall of Fame Enshrinement Ceremony in full bear crawl mode.

This was about me and ALL of my beloved fans. For most of them, we had been partners for more than sixteen years there, and I was going to do the same thing I did on game day. Instead of playing with great energy, I would be *talking* with great energy from my heart, and that's why I came out onto the stage in my Weapon X crawl. I was going to do it one more time for the crew that had helped me get to Canton. I was going to do it for the group that respected the man I am, not just the athlete. The "get knocked down and get back up again with a new fire lit" man that I am. The "every fall is an opportunity to learn and grow" man that I have become.

I said it before I went in: when I make it, we all make it. So those loyal fans were going into the Hall of Fame with me.

The night before, at the dinner where we were finally presented officially with our HOF Gold Jackets, I had lost my voice. I was so full that I was screaming, yelling and shouting as I gave thanks and praise to the Lord. The next night, I was sitting on the stage in the stadium, waiting to see the bust of me that would be on display in the Hall of Fame and to talk to all those Eagles fans and the rest of the football world. My wife, Connie, sent me a text telling me not to yell when it came time for me to speak. I hadn't been able to talk the entire day. I was sucking on lozenges that opera singers use to preserve their voices, provided by Pat and Samantha Waters, drinking tea, and doing everything I could to get ready. So, of course, after they showed me the bust, and it came time for me to address my fans and the world, what did I do? The one thing that I could to give the highest praise.

I shouted.

"First of all," I screamed. "HALLELUJAH!"

Sorry, Connie.

Before the ceremony, when I was backstage, I was unable to contain my energy, as I was many times pregame during my career. I was pacing and praying, praying and pacing—it was game day. I knew I was going to go out there and praise the Lord with the gifts He has given me. It was almost like there was nobody else but me and the Lord in the whole stadium at that first moment. So I screamed to give Him praise. To set the stage that this wasn't about me. Then, all the faces of my family and friends came into view. My coaches and teammates. And, of course, the fans. And it was time to pour out my heart.

I had a lot to say.

◇◇◇

I was blessed to play sixteen years in the NFL, thirteen of them with the Eagles and my last three in Denver. Two wonderful organizations. I have been blessed to have so many different people helping me along this journey. As my career moved on, my mindset grew with thoughts that the athleticism I showed on the field, and the numbers that my teammates and coaches helped me put up, might give me a chance to be in the Hall of Fame. As my career went from season 13 to 14, from 14 to 15 and from 15 to 16 in the great city of Denver Colorado, people started to call me "future Hall of Famer Brian Dawkins." And I began to think, "maybe it can happen." But nevertheless, I kept my head down, stayed focused and gave everything I had left to the last drop for the Bronco faithful.

That's how I played. I never quit. I kept fighting. No opponent could break my spirit. When I was elected to the Hall of Fame, the ante was upped in my mind. I wanted to use that gold jacket and the platform to bless people with life's possibilities. As I said during my speech, "It wasn't supposed to be me. It wasn't supposed to be Brian Dawkins."

But I had been blessed by the best. First, that means the Lord, who has blessed me with so much. It also meant all those people and things around me that I believe were the best for me at the time. Maybe they weren't the best for somebody else. Your best may not be my best. That's fine. Everything that has happened to me has been to bring out the best in me. Even the toughest, hardest times in my life were the best things for me. If I hadn't gone through them, I wouldn't be the person I am today.

You have to make the conscious decision to look for the best, the good, the right things. You had better believe I had people I could have hung out with when I was younger, who aren't alive today or are in the criminal justice system, or allowing where we came from to determine what they saw for themselves. Settling for life, instead of living life with a purpose. If I chose to be with them, my life would have been different. My career that has touched so many, would not be. My family, would not be. The lives my story will now bless, would not be. But, I chose to hang out with different individuals, and here I am to tell the story.

The elementary school I went to was within walking distance of my family's home in Jacksonville, Florida. But don't be fooled. That joker was about three miles away. We didn't take the shortcut through the woods, which made it even longer. When we were kids, we weren't supposed to go into the woods near my house or near the school. The majority of the time we would follow that rule. Maaaan, they might as well have put a sign on a tree at the entrance to the woods that said, "Right this way, kids." As kids, we did what kids do from time to time, we bent a few rules.

One day in particular was supposed to be a great day. It was October 13, my birthday. And I was in the fifth grade and excited about my prospects. The only snag was, it was Friday the 13th. And as we all know because of Jason Voorhees, that is supposed to be a cursed day, right? I can't remember everything that happened that day, but I do remember getting written up for misbehaving in school and being sent out of the class. That hardly ever happened.

My friend and I decided to leave school early before the bell rang to dismiss us, after I left the principal's office. One, to beat the crowd. Secondly, so we could bend a rule. So, which way do you think we took heading home?

That's right. As we were walking in the woods, out of nowhere it seemed, an older man started walking at a distance behind us. We didn't pay any attention to him, but all of a sudden, he yelled, "Hey, kids! Come here!" We started walking faster, and he yelled, "What are you doing back here?" and started running after us. We took off, running as fast as our little legs could go. All I can remember is that I was faster than my friend. He stumbled a bit, but we kept running toward the opening in the woods. I felt like that entrance was actually moving away. Like when you go deep underwater and head back up to the surface because you are running out of air? That's how scared I was. I made it out first, and my friend managed to get up and get out a few seconds after me.

We ran down the street and turned to see if the man was still there. He popped out of the woods like Jason infamously would do when he missed a victim. He stared at us for a couple seconds, and then walked back into the woods. To say the least, my friend and I were terrified! We moseyed back to the school, but that was the last time we took that doggone shortcut, Jack! It could have been a really bad situation, but I know without any doubt whatsoever, we were "blessed by the best" in that moment, and were able to be safe and to learn a valuable lesson. In that moment, life was teaching a lesson as it does every day to those who are listening, and you better believe I was awake sitting in the front row taking notes that day.

There is no specific blueprint or guarantee that says, "Do this, and this will happen. Do that and that will happen." But I do believe your chances to rise to the top increase when you surround yourself with individuals who help you live positively, who help you be the best by holding you accountable. A Blessed Pack is what I now call them. A Blessed Pack: a trusted few who you should invite into your inner circle. It may be two or three, but they are in your life to bring out the best in you, not standing by idly watching you hurt yourself. Do that, and you can achieve great things individually and collectively.

When you look at how I got to Clemson from high school, it wasn't really because of my work ethic or how I performed. It was mainly because of one of my teammates, Patrick Sapp. Clemson wanted him very badly. He was highly recruited, one of the top recruits in the country. He said that if he went to Clemson, I had to go, too. They said, "okay." You could almost hear the fans saying, "You're wasting two scholarships on one guy!" But I got to Clemson, and I worked to become a starter, then an all-ACC player. You see, it really doesn't matter how you get there; what matters most is what you do with the opportunity.

The Eagles didn't draft me until the last pick of the second round, with a supplemental pick, so it was really the beginning of the third. I was constantly told that I was a tweener. I could play corner and safety but wasn't "ideal." So I dropped in the draft to that spot. Thanks to people like Emmitt Thomas, Ray Rhodes, John Wooten, William "Willy T" Thomas, Mark Woodard, Irving Fryar, and Jim Johnson and Troy Vincent and many others, I became a starter and a Pro Bowler and an All-Pro, and finally a Hall of Famer. Now I've reached the Hall of Fame, I feel I have a responsibility to use that gold jacket to lift people up, because so many other people had lifted me up. They lifted me up so I could see higher. And higher is where I soon went.

A lot of people are going through things where they don't feel wanted, or they feel they don't measure up. They don't feel they are getting the accolades they deserve or the simple affection they need. Not everyone can be a Hall of Famer in football, but people can learn what their gifts are and how they can surround themselves with people who help them be the best they can be. That gold jacket is one of the brightest colors you can have, and I pray for people to see me in it and know through reading this book that they can be the best versions of themselves. And the best versions of themselves are waiting, as mine was then, and even now, because we should be forever growing in some area.

Because I had a good friend, Pat Sapp, who put in a good word for me, I WAS given the opportunity to grow and become who I am.

Because of what my father taught me, which was never to quit, I grew into the man I am today. (Finish what you start.)

Because of what my mother taught me, which was to keep fighting until they pulled you off the person, I grew to be who I am today. (Be a pull-back player.)

Because my basketball coach in high school, Coach Humphrey, couldn't break me, I grew to understand and believe no one can. (Mental toughness.)

Because Coach Black in high school showed me I was smart enough to learn if I did things a little differently, I grew to understand that I could make good grades consistently. (Take ownership of things.)

Because Troy Vincent showed me how to be a professional, I became an All-Pro in many areas. (Professionalism.)

Those are some of the "blessed by the best" people that you will soon read about, who showed me not just how to be better in different situations, but most importantly, to *think different*. So, when I found myself in the situations that followed, I was better. So much better. Gaining more and more confidence. I kept going and kept going. And growing and growing.

Till I found myself with a gold jacket.

◇◇◇

When I retired, the five-year wait before I would be eligible for the Hall of Fame seemed to be a long time. My first real thought after my retirement was that I could exhale, and do absolutely nothing. I had been playing the game of football since the age of twelve. I had been getting up for early workout sessions and staying late for extra work forever, it seemed. And so that is exactly what I did. EXHALE! I wasn't going to do anything, Jack. I wanted to sit around and watch Netflix and catch up on TV series. I felt I had earned it. I'm happy to say I got caught up on a lot of stuff.

But before long, my motor started to pick up. I began to hear a voice that I've heard in the past when I am settling or staying stagnant for too long. When I'm just existing and not living on purpose. When I'm surviving, not thriving. A voice that screamed, "You know you're supposed to be doing more than this, right?!" That was the Holy Spirit. On top of that, professional athletes are used to living every day on a schedule that's very regimented. At eight a.m., we're supposed to be here. At nine a.m., we're supposed to be there. That part of me also started to itch again, so I started working out and getting into the gym. I was hitting it pretty good. When I played, I purposefully didn't train like the average cat. The card that they gave us with our workout routines, I felt were more like suggestions. I was not only blessed to survive Coach Humphrey—you'll hear about him later. I was blessed to witness how intensity in your workouts will turn up the greatest result on the field. Especially in the fourth quarter.

I went at it a lot harder, continually, and still do. I was blessed to be able to spend more time with my son, Brian Jr., who was just starting high school at the time. I had the chance to work out with him, and he got a taste of what it's like to train with me. The intensity that I am accustomed to has been known, for cats that try it, to make them call Earl… you know, get nauseous to the point that some have thrown up—calling out EARL as their stomach contents come up. Which is a crazy rite of passage. I too would get nauseous the first time and subsequently other times when I started training at the intense level of the particular MMA cats that I was training with in J-ville back in the early 2000s. This is way before the popularity of the sport today. I was already someone who pushed the envelope—with them, I discovered another level for my kind of madness to go to.

I was blessed to be spending time with Brian Jr. I helped coach at Denver's Valor Christian High School, Brian Jr.'s school, where I worked with the defensive backs and helped with the game plan. I poured myself into that role. If you know anything about me, you know that I pour myself into the things I do. It was a blessing for me to be working there and to be close to him on a continual basis. Oftentimes I was not there for a lot of his things in my playing days. I felt blessed to be taking trips with him as the team traveled to play other schools out of state. Being around him a ton more and bonding, not being forced to go work another job, was a blessing. It was also a blessed time for me, being around a game that had taught me so much and given me so much. Now, I was able to give to young men that were all ears. It was my job then to break things down so that they could take ownership of the information. It wasn't always easy, to say the least, but I enjoyed the challenge of helping bring out the best that they had to give, as well as allowing them to see into my crazy mindset.

In 2014, I started a two-year stint at ESPN, and that was another blessing, because it brought me into contact with many quality cats including, but not limited to, Mike Cambareri and Gerry "G-Matt" Matalon. Both of whom would help me on my journey to find my voice on air. But it was the late John Saunders, one of the greatest sports hosts and commentators of all time, who would open my eyes and ears to find my voice. He wanted to open up an avenue for me that he felt was there, and took me to another magnitude when he talked about the voice and presence I was blessed to have. I had seen that I could reach my teammates when I spoke to them, but it was important to hear John talk about how I could reach others by improving my depth and articulation. I had already been working to become a better speaker, to do things like using "th" instead of "d" on words like "this and that." Not feeling like you have to finish an entire paragraph in one breath—to pace myself, to name a few. Hearing from John made me work even harder. You see, powerful things happen when those who have been blessed to earn a higher position, reach back and speak into the lives of people on the way up. He used the most precious resource we have, TIME, to nourish the gift, the seed that I had inside, with some powerful words of encouragement. Mr. Saunders was helping me prepare for that night on stage in Canton and beyond, when I spoke in front of the nation during my enshrinement speech. And when I speak in front of businesses on leadership, or to inspire and encourage in speaking appearances, his advice and investment pay dividends. Thank you, Mr. Saunders!

I hadn't been very comfortable talking on camera in studio to that point, because the mistakes you make there are so glaring—everybody can see them, so it seemed to me. I had been just as hard on myself about my work on camera as I had been during my career on the field. Because I had made some errors, I became robotic. One of the so-called laws to playing the game of football fast is to not be thinking and play fast. You must be able to flow with your talent, by anticipating and quickly reacting from a place of confidence to any and all surprises. You can't do that being a robot and thinking. I was also blessed by my good friend Hugh Douglas, to not treat this just like my playing days. As he put it, "You gotta learn to laugh at yourself, bro... Even on camera."

Mr. Saunders had also given me something to hang on to. "Live happens," he said. Meaning, during live shots, stuff happens. Just get your balance back and keep going. One time, I almost got up and left the set during a live show, because I felt I had royally messed up a couple things. I almost had a panic attack on air—that's how anxious I was. I got hot as fish grease, and it felt like a brick hit me in the chest, and I felt like I couldn't breathe—something that had never happened to that extent. But their advice would help me get through it, and finish with a bang and a forced smile.

Because of that experience and John's faith in me, things started to open up for me, a little at a time though. I had a bit of claustrophobia, so I wasn't too fond of flying in college, and that kept up when I first got into the NFL, but I fought and overcame it with God's grace. It was hard for me to get into the hyperbaric chamber I bought as a player to help me recover after practice, but I had fought to become comfortable with it. And an MRI was brutal, but again, I managed. But because of that panic attack I had on air, those familiar phobias came raring back. To the point that I would get hot and felt like I couldn't breathe when I had to fly back and forth from Denver to ESPN in Bristol. But as I worked on my ability to speak better and control myself on the set, I started to learn how to handle other anxieties, and to ward off ALL panic attacks.

I'd have to thank my lovely bride, Connie, for this one though. When she was pregnant with each of our four kids, we did Lamaze classes. One of the keys that I would take from that, was how powerful breathing can be. Or simply put, THE POWER IN BREATHING. The ability to focus on breathing and imagining your body relaxing is a powerful tool. The ability to feel the breath you are taking to loosen a tight muscle as you stretch it, or breathing through a deep tissue massage. I've adopted certain types of breathing for different things. And of course, when I am feeling panicky. Different breathing styles for different stressors, and they work wonders!

I became mentally stronger in these ways, and I learned that breathing was important and that meditating helped me slow down. It helped me stay away from the negativity. Which helped me get to positive conclusions sooner and more consistently.

Even as I got closer to being eligible for election to the Hall of Fame, I wasn't thinking much about it. I was working to improve my relationship with my son, especially because of the way I had behaved my last few years in the league, when I was at Denver. I was really beat up then, and I wasn't home a lot, because I pretty much lived in the training room, getting treatment, massages, chiropractic, Active Tissue Release (ART), acupuncture, and the list goes on. After I retired, I was able to see Brian Jr. fight his battles against ADHD, without even knowing he had it, before finally getting medicine that helped him. And going from that to learning he could focus without it, and now able to be good on his own. I had missed a lot of things as a player, sometimes out of selfishness, as I would prioritize things that were associated with the job.

I also had to "introduce" myself to my two youngest daughters, Chonni and Cionni. The Twins. I wasn't always in the best of moods. I could make the excuse that it was the way I left Philly. Maybe it was playing through the pain as I frequently had to do. Maybe it was dealing with the mounting losses that were happening in Denver at the time, with me having earned the privilege of being a leader and letting my actions and words both speak loudly. Perhaps it was the strain of doing Bible Study every week, as well as counseling both players and coaches as we dealt with so much drama, as well as the suicide of a teammate. Maybe it was all that combined? Nope. It was a selfish choice on my behalf, not to make it a point to choose to be what I am more of now. A more emotionally available husband and father. I hadn't been home a lot of those last few years, and when I was, I wasn't always in a good mood as I got older. I often felt my two youngest kids were afraid of me, or didn't know me. They had to learn who their father was. So as you can see, as I was building

my relationships with them, the Hall of Fame was on the back burn-
er. I thought, "If it happens, it happens."

But once the time came for that first ballot, in February of 2017,
my competitive juices started flowing. I wanted to be a first-ballot
Hall of Famer. People say that when you get in, you get in, and once
you're a Hall of Famer, you're a Hall of Famer. It doesn't have to
come on the first ballot. Because I'm a competitor, I wanted to be a
first-ballot Hall of Famer. I believe we all would.

The finalists all stay in the same hotel in the city that is hosting
the Super Bowl, which in 2017 was Houston. That way, Hall of Fame
President David Baker could come to your room to tell you that you
had made it.

I wasn't happy when I wasn't elected the first year, but what
made me furious were some of the things they did while I was waiting to find out if I had made it. The day dragged on too long. You're
supposed to get a call (if you didn't make it) or a knock on your
hotel door (if you did) within a certain time period. They went past
that period, and I was supposed to go to a reception that night for
all of the finalists. Well, I finally got the call that I didn't get elected,
and then they expected me to go to the event five minutes later.

I said I wasn't prepared to go to the event. I knew in that situation I wouldn't be in a good place. I went downstairs to congrat-
ulate those who didn't make it, but made it to be finalists as I did.
I had smoke coming out of my ears Tom and Jerry style. They asked
me if I wanted to go to the Super Bowl game, and I said No, thank
you. I got a call from someone I hadn't talked to before, telling me
where to get my plane ticket. I felt like a castoff. I didn't like all that.
It rubbed me the wrong way. I felt some resentment, some anger
and some wounded pride. All of that had to be removed from me.
Those impurities had been brought to the surface by the experience,
which tends to happen when the heat is turned up. So I had to pray
so that I would recognize them, repent and get rid of them. Those
were things that should not be in a righteous man's mind. But nonetheless, I had a choice as to how to deal with them. The Word says
be angry and sin not. So that is the example that I chose to finally
follow.

I try to be a humble man. I try to be that way as a man of God, but I won't lie. It was tough not getting elected. But then I started thinking that maybe the Lord wanted me to know what it feels like for those who don't make it or haven't made it yet, what it's like for those individuals who wait many, many more years than me. Like Steve Atwater, Darren Woodson or Leroy Butler. So I would later apologize for my behavior. There are things I may still not like about some things. But I only have control over me and my actions and reactions.

But I didn't have to wait. I knew what was coming, because I had seen it in a dream.

When I was waiting to learn my Hall of Fame fate that first time, I was so anxious and nervous that I took a fifteen-minute nap. While I was asleep, I had a dream that I received a phone call saying I made it. That was odd, because you don't usually hear by phone. You hear in person.

But I heard by phone that second year, because I wasn't in the same hotel with the other finalists in Minneapolis. I was in the hotel with the Eagles, who were getting ready to play in the Super Bowl against New England. I was working with the team as an executive and had traveled to Minnesota with the Eagles. Mr. Baker called to let me know, and my kids started crying, and Connie was screaming. It was a joyous moment, and I was so grateful.

But I was also so intent on the fact that the Eagles were playing in the Super Bowl the next day, that as thankful that I was, I was focused on the Eagles winning the Super Bowl. Going into the play-offs, I truly felt that I was going to get two rings (one for the world championship and a ring of Excellence from the HOF) and a gold jacket. I was 100 percent at peace about the fact that the Eagles were going to win. I knew that whatever problems and pitfalls came up on that game day, the coaching staff and the players would over-come them. I felt that way through the whole playoffs. I was blessed to be a part of it from the beginning. They grew as a team of tal-ent cats. A team that finally learned to hold themselves individual-ly accountable first, in order to then earn the right to hold others accountable. We often learn those lessons after losing. Because it's often difficult to have tough conversation with folk when you win. Especially when you don't have that culture built already in place to fall back on. I remember hearing Charles Barkley say this: "Winning is the greatest deodorant." Which is so true. A lot of stinky stuff is far too often covered up. But when you lose, I've found it gives you the ability to have tougher conversations with cats that may think they are not one of the problems.

I was so blessed that it all came to fruition. I was able to celebrate the Hall of Fame election with my family and to show great gratitude. And when the Eagles won the Super Bowl, I dropped to my knees and shouted, "Hallelujah!" And started crying the ugly cry, with snot bubbles coming out of my nose as I cried tears of joy.

◇◇◇

The Eagles fans blew Canton away. There were more of them than any other group of fans. There was green everywhere. For that to happen was tremendous.

When I came back to work for the Philadelphia Eagles in 2016, one of the things I felt strongly about was how many years people had laughed at and ragged on the fan base because the franchise hadn't won a Super Bowl. I saw the message boards and the memes, and heard the joke about how a female Eagles fan should never expect a ring. It all had a big impact on me.

When the Eagles pulled out the Super Bowl win, my thoughts rushed immediately to the fans. I was so happy for them. I had met so many fans during my time in Philadelphia, and I felt they deserved the championship. Before the win, I remembered back over the years, I had received so many letters from fans saying that one of their loved one's last wishes was to be buried in my jersey. After the Super Bowl win, I read about fans putting jerseys on relatives' graves. It was so freakin' powerful, and I believe the possibility for hope has increased in Philadelphia because of that win. I really hope that many more folk now think they can achieve the unachievable. It was so great to celebrate in Canton with them.

People who know me understand that when I would get ready for games, I would get so full of joy and energy. It's the same thing in my prayer life. When I let the Holy Spirit fully operate inside me, I can't contain it. In Canton, I wanted people to feel the joy and energy I had, not just hear my words.

When I gave my speech, I wanted to be so open and honest about some of what I had been through. It doesn't bother me to tell others about my life. If people think I shared too much, then my story isn't for them. I knew how close I had come to taking my life early in my career, and how the Lord has helped me before that, then, and ever since. My prayer is that others will experience that. I'm going to continue to love and have joy in my life, and to keep giving hope to people. That's why I said that the majority of the success in my life had come on the back end of pain. Pain pushed me to levels I had not known at the time.

There was a purpose to my pain. It increased my faith exponentially!

I didn't "write" a speech. When I prepare to speak, I write out some words or phrases that will get me going down a path. The folks at the Hall of Fame asked me for a copy of my speech, so that they could put it on the teleprompter. But I didn't have anything formal. I gave Troy the ragged piece of paper on which I had written down some notes, and he gave it to the people who put it on the teleprompter. That way, I could make sure I didn't forget to thank anybody. Which I'm embarrassed and ashamed to say I did nonetheless… HIGHLANDS JUNIOR HIGH in Jacksonville. The other being the DENVER BRONCOS (Pat Bowlen—Mr. B.) and their organization. They took me in as one of their own and welcomed me. And I absolutely apologize for that omission. SMH…

When it came time to speak, I would look at a name and go into my heart. I would look at a phrase and go into my heart. To make sure that the things that came from my heart are of the right stuff, I would have to be sure to cleanse it of all anger, hate, lust, envy, jealousy, or anything else. The Word of God tells us to guard our heart with all diligence, for from it flows the issues and springs of life (Proverbs 4:23). I wanted nothing but springs of fresh water to flow that night. So I thanked my coaches, teachers, doctors, trainers, massage therapists and family. I thanked my 100-year-old grandmother for showing me what a Christian really is. I thanked my mom for telling me to fight to the finish. I thanked my dad for making sure I honored all of my commitments to the fullest. I thanked Troy and Pat Sapp for being my "rabbits." They were the people I chased, the people I wanted to be like in many ways. I thanked the Eagles fans for loving me the way I loved them. Emotionally and crazily!!

And, of course, I thanked the Heavenly Father for blessing me with the sense to know that I didn't do it by myself.

Then, there was Connie.

◇◇◇

In the months leading up to the Enshrinement Ceremony, as I was praying and thinking about that night in Canton, I realized that I really, really, really wanted people to see how special a woman the Lord has blessed me with. Connie has been so instrumental in helping me become the man that I am.

I met Connie when I was in high school, and when I was growing up, there were some things that I had to stop doing in order to stay with her. Being from the part of Jacksonville where I grew up, I wanted to have some gold teeth. She and my mom both said, "I don't really like gold teeth." So there was no grill for B Dawk. Because of Connie, my eating habits even changed. I tried things that I would never think I would. There was no way I was ever going to eat sushi. Now, I eat sushi. A LOT. Being with her challenged the many norms I was operating under at the time. We are often only aware of that in which we are exposed to; she allowed me to be exposed to more.

More important than all of that is that I truly believe she was brought into my life to help me become the man of God that I am. When Connie was in high school, she went to a Holiness Church, and they stayed in church forever. The first time I went to a service there, it was my first time seeing the gifts of the Holy Spirit in action. People were speaking in tongues and shaking. I thought there was something wrong with them. I had been raised Catholic, and they don't do that in Catholic churches, Jack.

Connie inviting me to her church and me seeing the gifts of the spirit for the first time, opened my mind up to the possibility of a greater relationship with the Lord and the ability to understand His ways. It opened my eyes to things I never heard of, but yet here there they were in the world operating in full view. I would become more curious to see what else there was for me to understand for myself. Little did I know at the time, but I was in search of relationship, not religion. It was also the first time someone prophesied over me, at the age of sixteen. She said I would minister to thousands of people. At the time, I thought the woman had bumped her head. Now, not so much. As I am blessed to minister to many in messages on the different platforms available today. I have been used to minister to teammates, coaches and many others. But now I try to live my life a certain way. Respectfully bold! The greatest sermon I will ever preach, is the life that I live! I love that quote.

So, when I gave my speech, I wanted Connie to be center stage. I didn't just want the camera on her quickly with a headshot and the people to clap a little bit. I wanted her to get a standing ovation from the fan base, so she could feel what I did when I played. So she could truly enjoy what she too had helped come to fruition.

That's why the idea of giving her a gold wrap as her own Hall of Fame jacket was fitting. She is my Hall of Fame wife, and I wanted her to receive her just due. She deserved it. Early in my career, when I was fighting depression and flying into fits of rage, she could have packed it in. She could have taken Brian Jr. and headed back to Jacksonville. Had she done that, I wouldn't have made it to Canton. In some people's minds, Connie is just a housewife. Like being a Domestic Engineer is simple and straightforward. She is so much more than that. My love for her was one of the things that kept me out of the streets. My love for her is what helped me see past my own insecurities. I honestly thought growing up, that there was no way a girl like that would be interested in a cat like me. I am so happy I was wrong.

In my retirement, which often comes with more free time when I choose, I have been able to watch the plight of so many women as they give up so much of their dreams, and take on the greatest responsibility there ever will be: raising little ones. I chose to begin to really watch women as they struggle with strollers and car seats.

Many looking exhausted and disheveled. Then I looked at my bride, knowing that was probably her for many years. It has taken longer than it should have, but I truly honor and respect her for the sacrifices. And I've apologized for adding to her issues and not stepping up back then when I should have, to give her more breaks. Because as I have come to understand, a mom is never off duty!

When I asked her to stand up and had her wrapped in the gold fabric, she was extremely happy and totally shocked. I love her so much, and I am so blessed to have her in my life. I wanted to really do something different, to make sure she got a taste of the adoration I have received during my career.

Connie deserved every second of the ovation she received. She will always be my Hall of Famer.

◇◇◇

The toughest thing about the entire weekend was that we were under attack the whole time leading up to it. There was dramatic pressure coming from all areas—from one of the cars dying, to us trying to move and someone stealing from us, to uncertainty on where we were going to be staying when we moved, to some spiritual tension and spiritual attacks. We really felt the enemy was trying to take us out. Things were going wrong, and people were doing some underhanded stuff. Lies being told, and people not holding up their end of the bargain. Through it all, I kept feeling something special was supposed to happen that weekend. The more bad things that happened, the more I had to connect with individuals in my Blessed Pack for prayers and encouragement. And I did, often. Yet I did believe something HUGE was about to go down in Canton. And the heavy onslaught of attacks from so many different areas, I've come to understand was confirmation!

When we finally got to Canton, I was exhausted, but I was so at peace. I wanted to bless as many people as I possibly could. Which I was able to do with former teammates, coaches, teachers, friends and family. Most all of them never being blessed to go to Canton. I wanted to be around as many fans as possible, many coming from all over to come be a part of that moment. There are fans that spent their last dime to drive out from Philly. There are fans that told me they were there from Denver. Some using vacation time, on honeymoons, and everything in between. We all made it. In a sense, I had the same feeling I did during a game week. It was the same anticipation I had when I knew I was going to have a good game. When I knew the game plan cold and was all prayed up and ready to go. Spiritually, mentally and physically. Oh, my goodness. I felt like it was party time when I got on that stage.

Problem was, Friday night, at the Gold Jacket Dinner, I was giving praise and shouting "Hallelujah!" And because of that, the next day I couldn't speak. I literally opened my mouth to say a word and nothing came out. I had to preserve my voice for the Enshrinement Ceremony, but I still wanted to go to an event on Saturday afternoon where four hundred Eagles and Broncos fans would be. I wanted to share my joy with them. So, I asked my oldest daughter Brionni (Brian + Connie 4ever) to make up cards that said "Thank you," "I'm saving my voice," and "God Bless," so that I could interact with the fans by pointing to the cards, instead of talking. It was crazy. I even got on Instagram to ask for prayers from everyone that I would get my voice back. People had come hundreds of miles to share the day with me. Many were crying. It was a wonderful and powerful day, to say the least.

The ceremony was great, too. But as soon as I walked off that stage and got back to the hotel, my mom had a stroke. Everything was set up for me to panic, but I didn't. Even though everyone was telling me to run, and shouting "Hurry!" when I first arrived there, I walked calmly to the bus, where she lay stretched out in the front of the bus where she fell. I knelt next to my mom, and I started faithfully praying. I walked calmly next to her as they loaded her into the ambulance with my dad by her side, headed to the hospital.

I had just said on the stage that something was coming, and that I didn't know what it was. But I was prepared. Here it was. I had the Lord with me. I believed my mom would be all right. I thought about Romans 8:28:

"And we know that in all things God works for the good of those who love him, who have been called according to his purpose."

You can't see it all the time, but you have to have the mindset that if you are going through a trial, it's going to work out for your good. It was proof for me and those that were in the know and witnessed it, by the way I was led to walk onto the bus and encouraged everybody to calm down and prayed over my mom, telling her that "No weapon that formed against her shall prosper."

Get this, my mom "just so happened" to be sent to one of the top five hospitals in the US. They specialize in the area that my mother was indeed suffering. I for one do not believe in coincidences. Oh by the way, my mom had already had an episode when she flew into Charlotte on a connecting flight to come to Canton just two days before. She had to be removed by ambulance when they landed in Charlotte. They spent about two days there. No, it wasn't a stroke that time. If she had had that stroke in the air or in Charlotte—where they may not have had the same doctors or equipment as in Canton—who knows. My mother fought, like the fighter she is, and the fighter she raised me and my siblings to be, and she recovered. The Lord is with us. Even when we don't feel like it. Even in our pain. It was another moment on my journey with Him. A moment that will forever give me strength and a perspective far beyond my feelings. To see where my mom is today, from where she was on that bus, and even in the hospital? I'm gonna continue to trust Him above my emotions!

There would be more to come.

CHAPTER 2

Learning to Fight

I really don't know why they picked me back then. I certainly hadn't raised my hand or even looked at the teacher. As a matter of fact, I can almost guarantee I did what I usually did when the teacher asked a question I didn't know the answer to, or when I just didn't want to speak. I made sure to avoid eye contact, like my life depended on it.

But there I was, nervous as could be, standing all alone in front of a TV camera in the Channel 4 studio in Jacksonville, about to give Martin Luther King's "I Have a Dream" speech. Me. The kid with the stutter. The shy one. I was a young, tender first or second grader, staring into that camera's evil eye, with bright lights all around.

My teacher had told me, "Brian, you're going to give a speech on TV."

I don't remember a lot, but I do remember being so scared, and oh, so nervous. I didn't have a huge stuttering problem all the time, but the more nervous I got, the more I would stutter. You see, I had the feeling of being embarrassed. When I messed up a word or stuttered, I felt everybody had heard the mistake, and they were all waiting for me to make another. That way, they could mess with me later. It wasn't them; it was all me. I was real reserved, and it was difficult at times for me to express myself. Sometimes, when I would meet someone, I would think of two different greetings. Instead of choosing one, I would combine the two. Instead of saying, "I'm doing fine" or "How are you?" I would say, "I'm you" or something silly like that. It was so embarrassing, I can only imagine what the other person was thinking as they walked away. So, reciting that speech in front of a TV camera was almost torture. But my teacher taught me a trick to help me not to be afraid of the camera. She told me to find something else to look at. So, I stared at a clock above the camera for the entire speech. I had memorized the speech and I gave it. And what do you know? I was flawless. I even remember putting emphasis on the right words and all.

I certainly didn't know it at the time, but that had been my second real test. What was my first? Oh, it was the many solos my kindergarten teacher made me sing during our graduation. I had prepared—with help, of course. I had overcome the fear of speaking or singing in front of a large audience, and I had delivered. Not that I felt any sense of great triumph at the time. I was just so glad it was over. I could tell the knot in my stomach and the lump in my throat to go away. It was the end of a small chapter, and from there it was back to playing with my friends and doing the things kids do, without a care in the world. I hadn't wanted to give the speech, but I had agreed to it when my teacher chose me. My mom reminded me of the times she would take me to the library to sing Christmas carols. And how the people would stop in amazement as they stared at this curly-headed little cat with the part in the middle, that could sing like that.

It's not something I think about a lot, mostly because it was such an unpleasant experience. But I can't deny that I had done the job under some difficult circumstances.

And, what do you know, a few years later, there I was again, in the spotlight. I was older and more mature. I was a fifth-grader, chosen to sing over the school intercom for Black History Month. I wasn't in the choir, but I had sung solos in kindergarten and could hold a note or two. I could sing. They asked me to sing two songs, "Let There Be Peace on Earth" and "No Man Is an Island." This was sooo much easier, because there was no one in front of me, no camera staring back at me. Once again, they had chosen me, and this time I knew why.

Looking back, it's possible to believe that both situations were foreshadowing of what I was going to be doing in my life. I believe that the gift the Lord has given us can be seen early on in our lives. So, I would be the one delivering a message in front of large groups of people. I may not have understood back then why I was chosen, but when I was selected, I accepted the challenge. I stood up. And, by God, I killed it! These were early examples of the courage and the ability to rise up under pressure that the Lord had put inside of me.

Me? Volunteering? That was out of the question. But I had gifts that the teachers saw. Perhaps they saw that I cared about people. I cared about the feelings of my friends. I didn't want to be too harsh with them. If I saw one of them being done wrong, I would check to see if they were okay. Maybe the adults took those things into consideration and asked me to show others how the Lord had blessed me.

It's funny, but that's one of the main themes of my life. People have seen things inside of me that I didn't see or didn't want to show anybody else. They either challenged me to do something or just told me I was going to perform. And in those moments, things turned out pretty doggone well.

◇◇◇

The North Side of Jacksonville is a blue-collar area that is predominantly African-American. When I was growing up, it was the kind of place where neighbors looked out for you, and people grew close to each other because of it.

I was born on October 13, 1973, to Ralph Jr. and Patricia Ann (Pat) Dawkins, the youngest of three children and the second boy. My sister, Marian, was ten years older than me, and my brother, Ralph III, was three years older. My mother had two other, unfortunate pregnancies. One ended in a miscarriage, while another child was stillborn. My mother was Rh-negative, which means her blood lacked a key protein on the surface of her red blood cells. Because she didn't receive the necessary immunoglobulin injection when she was expecting Marian, her subsequent pregnancies were difficult. After Ralph III was born, my parents didn't plan on having another child, so I was a surprise. My birth was extremely difficult for my mother, who almost bled to death during delivery.

When I was a little kid, my parents would sing a little song, or I would hear music, and I would start scooting back and forth across the floor. So, they started calling me "Scooter." To this day, my dad and some of my cousins call me Scooter.

We lived in a one-story, three-bedroom, two-bathroom house on Wilton Avenue, near Yancey Park, where my football career began. (When I was born, we lived on Wrico Drive, not too far away.) My father said he and my mom bought the house because my brother, sister and I could get to the park in a heartbeat. As a matter of fact, I would climb up on the wall outside the front door. The wall happened to have bricks in it, and it was like a ladder to me. I used it as such. I wasn't supposed to. When I climbed up, I could see if there were any kids outside playing, especially on the basketball court.

We certainly weren't rich, but we had what we needed. Except for that second bathroom. As my dad tells it, the house sat on a septic tank, and because it would back up, we weren't able to use that second bathroom, except as a junk closet. Speaking of septic backing up, if you have seen that or—better yet—smelled it, it is horrendous. My dad was Mr. Fixit, though, and he would do things all the time around the house. To this day, I have to tell him to stop putting duct tape and the like on stuff to fix it. We can call professionals now to come and take care of it. But you can imagine that with five people using one bathroom, there were some tense times and some shouting. And you better have taken your shower early, or the hot water would be gone.

You won't be surprised to hear that Jacksonville was a hot place to grow up, but we didn't have central air. There was one AC unit that could cool the house somewhat, but when it broke, it was brutal. My parents had a unit in their bedroom, but they kept their door closed to make sure things stayed nice and cool in there. I thought that was jacked up, but it's not like we were going to make a big deal out of it. Not many others in our neighborhood were enjoying cool temperatures inside on a consistent basis, and frankly, we didn't know any better.

It drove our parents crazy—and that made it more fun—but we were always outside on the weekends, and especially in the summer.

We practically lived outside, coming in only to get something to eat. We would run inside and out, slamming the door, and we would hear my mom say, "Stop slamming the door!" or "Either stay inside or stay out!" That, of course, was when we were lucky enough to have the air conditioning working. It was only after I had kids of my own that I understood what "outside" smelled like. "You smell like outside," my mom would say. I have had the chance to experience what it smells like being a parent. And indeed, it is not a pleasant odor.

One of the greatest enemies in our neighborhood wasn't a person. It was a thing. And that thing was a streetlight. Most of the kids were under strict instruction to have their hips on the porch before those lights went on. When you are a kid, you lose track of time. So, the sun going down was just a thing that happens. But then we would hear the hum of the streetlight as it warmed up, and every kid would look up. It was like a track meet. On your mark. Get set. Go! We all darted through other people's yards to get to the porch before the lights came on. I was lucky, though, because the lights in front of our house were the last ones to go on.

Growing up in my neighborhood was a lot of fun for the most part. There were a ton of kids around, and we spent a good bit of time at our house. My mom didn't mind much, well, most of the time. When we were at our house, she knew where we were. But we made a lot of noise, and sometimes, she would tell us, "Y'all gonna have to take that somewhere else today."

To make it in our neighborhood, you had to show toughness. It wasn't like there was trouble all around all the time, but at some point, you would have to fight, to prove yourself, to make sure people respected you and to earn your rights. Sometimes, the older guys would force the little kids to square off. It wasn't an everyday thing, but you needed to establish respect, so you fought. They would pick you and another kid out, and say, "Either you two fight, or you have to fight us." That was the culture. I remember there was one guy, DB, and if he saw you, you were either going to have to fight someone else, or you better be ready to defend yourself, because at some point in the conversation, he was going to punch you. Here was the problem with knowing he was going to punch you: you couldn't flinch until he actually started the punching motion. If you did, he got a free punch. Not in the face, but that junk would still hurt!

The one thing about DB and the other older cats in the neighborhood was that they wouldn't let anybody from the outside hit us. Only they could hit us. So, we fought. Even if you lost, you had to attack non-stop to impress people. That way, word would spread, and people would say, "Don't mess with him." The biggest compliment I received after one of those scraps was, "He crazy!" That meant I wouldn't stop going at you, and as word spread about that, I didn't have to fight as much.

One day, I came home from school, and I had been in a fight. The first thing my mother asked me was, "Did you start it?" I said, "No, I did not start it." She was happy about that, but then she gave me the rules.

"You don't start a fight, but you finish it. And if that person is bigger than you, then you pick up something, and you knock the"—I'm not going to say what she said—"you knock the *heck* out of that person."

She was basically telling me not to stop until somebody pulled me off the other person. To go all in and all out on them. That when you get into a fight, it's on. My dad gave me pointers, too, without realizing it. He would be telling me and my brother stories about some of the fights he got into when he was younger. The stories usually had funny endings, because my dad is a prankster at heart. But while I was laughing, I was taking mental notes about how he attacked. Quick punch, then straight to the headlock. Then slam him, to choke him out? Got it.

I made sure, though, when I would have to handle some business, that I never challenged someone or threw the first punch. But if you came at me? It was on. I was coming at you with everything I had. Biting, punching, scratching and all that. By any means. Ironically, that's the way I approach my life. When I start something, I'm going to finish it. And I am going to fight full until someone tells me to slow down. I would call this being a "pull-back" person or player. That means you are someone others have to tell to slow down, not speed up or finish. This would go on to be one of my main reasons for success, on and off the field.

My dad was ultra-patient. My mom on the other hand? Not so much. When she yelled out a name, the whole house would get quiet quick. So, when she would yell my name, I would answer, "Yes, ma'am." Saying, "huh?" or "what?" or anything else would get you... let's just say it would get you. I walked to her room to see what she wanted. And nine times out of ten, she would ask me to get the remote or something. I would think to myself, "You called me way in here to get the remote?" Notice that I said that to myself. I was crazy, but not that crazy.

That was my mom. She worked as a physical therapist at times, but she didn't have the opportunity to work full-time, because she had to spend time at home with me and my brother. My mom played a boatload of Bingo though. Since my dad worked long hours, as well as odd jobs on the side, my mom didn't want us to be home by ourselves. There were times when I was a latch-key kid, with my own key to get in the house, but it wasn't often. It was actually my brother's and my key. We had a hiding spot and everything.

Speaking of hidden keys, I remember one day coming home and riding my bike up a couple steps onto our porch. I reached for the key, only to discover it wasn't there, and I was locked out. I was a teenager, and in our neighborhood, cursing was as common as breathing. I let out a bunch of choice words toward the person who hadn't put the key back, and all of a sudden, the door opened. It was my dad. Thank goodness. If that had been my mom, look out! All my dad said was, "Watch your mouth." He wasn't angry. He was more upset. But I learned a lesson: Be careful what you say when you think nobody is listening, because they just might be hearing everything you say. Or simply, always talk as if they are standing in front of you.

My mom had to grow up fast, because her parents separated when she was young. And then she had to help raise her siblings, because my grandma worked. She was always the disciplinarian in our house. She had a strong will, a strong mind and never backed down from battles. That's probably one of the reasons for that fire I have inside of me. She helped me develop the mindset about attacking. My mom isn't just a fighter. She's the ultimate fighter. As I write this, she has fought off breast cancer, for which she had to do chemo. She rang the bell! And she has survived three strokes. She still has strength, and she still is mobile. She still bowls with my Dad, and she will still let you have a piece of her mind. So, dig this, if my mom, who has lost so much weight because of the cancer and the strokes and other things, is still going, what excuse do I have? NONE! She told us before the latest stroke that she knew something was wrong, because she was feeling worse than usual. But to quote her, "There was nothing going to stop me from coming to your [Hall of Fame] enshrinement." She told me this from her hospital bed in Canton after the last stroke. Wow! So, depression, anxiety, panic attack and the like? Go sit down somewhere!

◇◇◇

Both of my parents loved playing cards—bid whist and spades—and there would be weekend card parties at our house with the neighbors. Cards. Cards. Cards! My dad had started building a patio that he never finished, but they would make do with lights and torches to kill the bugs. And there was a lot of music. Loud, loud music. They would play the Gap Band, Earth, Wind & Fire, Frankie Beverly & Maze, and much more. They were jamming. Well, I call it jamming now. Back then, it was just noise. So, we would be in our rooms with the TV up as loud as it could go to try to drown out their yelling about the games. The card games weren't always at our house. They would move around the houses of the friends of my parents, and since Ralph was usually out with his friends, and my sister was married, I would be home alone sometimes and have to find something to do, other than watch TV. Sometimes, my friend Tim would come over, and we would test our skills as DJs and MCs, with Jam Pony style being the thing. We would talk over a song, or turn down the music and make up our own rhymes. Tim even had a reel to reel machine we would make tapes on. Back then bass was king.

My father might have been the most patient man I've met in my life. He was patient almost to a fault. He was also extremely endearing and funny. It's so funny hearing him laugh at himself sometimes when he's telling a story. He had a quirky sense of humor. He would get things across at times by using sarcasm, which you didn't always want to hear when you were little, or even now. But he was so patient and understanding that it took us doing some of the dumbest things for him to get upset. That's something I'm envious of. I try to be as patient as possible, but I'm not as patient as he is. And I was blessed to see how he operated.

My dad was raised Catholic by my grandmother, who turned 102 years old in July 2020. My mother was Baptist, and we were given the choice of which church we wanted to go to each Sunday. Let's do the math here: Since Catholic Mass was an hour long, and the Baptist service was three hours, we chose Catholicism. My father considered it his obligation to bring us up Catholic, and he did. We went to Mass at either Church of the Crucifixion or Immaculate Conception. Though the shorter service was a big draw, an even bigger lure was that afterward, my father let us choose where we would go out to eat. We didn't eat fast food during the week. My dad told us that we didn't "have fast-food money." So, eating out was a highlight. Marian preferred Pizza Hut, Ralph III liked Burger King, and I was a Taco Bell man. My father continues to expose his family to the Church. His granddaughter (my niece) is staying with my parents now, and she has two children. My dad takes one of them, Taylor, to Mass each week.

My dad did a lot of different things to make money, but his number one job was working thirty-eight years for CSX railroad transportation, which is headquartered in Jacksonville. He started in the yard, doing manual labor, and moved into the mailroom. I remember going in there as a boy and watching him and the other men working. It was the first time I ever drank coffee—with a lot of sugar in it. It was tedious work, but they were having a good time doing it. My father could change the temperature in the room just by his presence. He would walk in, with his bass voice saying "Hello, hello," and just lighten the mood. You would see smiles on everyone's faces. I would come to know he did those things on purpose. But then he would pick someone he knew to mess with. He would say they owed him money, because they bet on a game.

My Dad was being a thermostat, not a thermometer. He was changing the temperature in the room, not changing to it. I try to do the
same thing with people. That's his gift. I learned how to treat people
from my dad. How to handle disputes, when to hold my tongue.
Even in conflict, he could hold himself back from getting too angry
and doing something he might regret later. He taught me how to
bring home the bacon, help others in need, to be a servant leader
and so many other things.

If you think *he* was patient, you don't know anything, Jack.
He was raised by the most patient person I have ever seen or read
about. That was my Grandma Dawkins. I have recently started calling her "Saint Dawkins," because of the true anointing that is on her.
When I needed a living definition of a Christian, all I had to do was
look at her actions and reactions. There was so much peace as soon
as you walked into her house. A peace that I pray my house brings
to those that enter. A kind of place where one feels they are escaping the madness outside, and enters a place where they can breathe
and think. It was almost like nothing else existed. A place where
they feel strengthened from being inside. Out of all the years I have
known her—and I have talked to my cousins and uncle and aunts
about this she NEVER lost control or flew into a fit of rage out of
anger. You won't hear a curse word from her. There is no yelling.
No screaming. She could be stern, but she was always under control.
She lived in a rougher neighborhood than ours, but everyone knew
her as Mrs. Dawkins, and no one would mess with her, because they
had so much respect for her.

I can remember walking with some of her kids and grandkids,
and the old heads in the neighborhood would be cursing up a storm
until they got in front of her house. She wouldn't even have to be
outside, and they would stop. There was such a peace when you
walked into her house. She walked around singing, baking cookies,
cakes and brownies. You would see her frequently reading her Bible.
And when she left the house, she was spot on with her outfit. She
never missed Church on Sundays, and she sang in the choir in an
opera-like voice. She recently sang a few hymns for us at her 100th
birthday celebration. And her voice is still powerful. The greatest

thing I can say about her is that she expected you to be the very best you could be, and she wasn't about to let you settle for less.

My father did a lot of other odd jobs, but mostly I remember him helping other people in the neighborhood, yes, but especially family members. He would come home from work, and if someone in the neighborhood needed help raking his yard, my dad would help. Or he would cook, even after working all day. My dad is outstanding on the grill. Unbelievable. He creates his own barbecue sauce by adding a dab of this or a dab of that, and it's outstanding. Seriously, it's outstanding. I keep telling him that he should have marketed that stuff.

So, at Thanksgiving, my mom would handle the macaroni and cheese and the beans, the dressing and some of the desserts, and my dad would handle the hearty stuff, like the turkey, the glazed ham. It was delicious.

My father was also a coach, and his experience in athletics had a huge impact on me. He coached football and baseball, but I think he loved baseball the most. He played in a softball league until his mid-thirties, but he messed up his knee and also had to work some other jobs, so he couldn't play anymore. He joined the Astro Jets, an organization designed to help keep young people out of trouble, at Scott Park in northwest Jacksonville. I learned a lot from how he handled players and parents, just by sitting there as a batboy, watching him. He often reminisces about those times when I talk to him. It was tremendous to see him handle the situations, and it taught me conflict resolution. Even in the most heated discussions, he had the ability to bring it down calmly. That's such an important talent to have, and it's something I have worked to do, following his great example. Be that blessed thermostat.

◇◇◇

Our neighborhood was sports crazy when I was growing up, and while I was usually up for a game of anything, I had other ways of occupying my time. One of my favorite shows was *The Fall Guy*, which ran for five seasons on ABC during the early 1980s. I loved the main character, Colt Seavers, who was a stunt man but also a bounty hunter. Yeah, I know he didn't do all his own stunts, but that's what

I thought. Now, I also loved cartoons, everything from Looney Tunes to superheroes like ThunderCats, He-Man, and the Silverhawks, and anyone who knows my Wolverine on-field character can figure that out. Can't leave out Tom and Jerry, DuckTales or Transformers. But I really enjoyed watching *The Fall Guy* and then trying to be a stunt man myself. I was a daredevil, in a lot of respects, and I have scars on my body from things I used to do when I was a kid to prove it. You know, battle scars.

I noticed that whenever Colt Seavers hit the ground during one of his stunts, he would roll. I figured that was all I had to do to escape serious injury. So, I would climb to the top of a swing set at the playground and do a backflip off of it. Or I would get up on the house, get a running start and jump. The key was to roll when you hit the ground. Crazy thing is, it worked. And crazy thing is, the ability to dive and fall gracefully would help me in my career. If someone was building a ramp near my house, I would be the one to test it. I ran around and jumped into things at home. I was always doing wheelies or cat walks, as we called them, on my bike. When my brother and I were younger, my parents bought us Big Wheels, and we would ride them down the hill behind our house and collide with each other. It drove my parents crazy. On the weekends and during the summer, we were outside all the time, but, like I said, we had to be home before the streetlights came on. If we didn't make it, we would get the strap.

One simple rule we had was not to talk to strange men. We heard that plenty.

One evening, another boy and I rode our bikes to a store many blocks away from the park to get some chocolate candy. We were riding and talking, talking and riding, and I didn't realize how far I was from home. I didn't know this boy too well. My new friend lived around the corner from the store we were heading to though, and I still had to get home before the lights came on. I was pedaling like my life depended on it, and as I saw light after light come on, I was crying my eyes out, because I knew the light in front of my house was one. My mother sent my brother Ralph to the park to look for me, but I was nowhere to be found. She called the police, who came drove her around looking for me. Get this: They even brought in a chopper to light the park. My brother told me it lit up the park like it was daytime. So of course, I was dead, right?

A police officer saw this little boy riding fast and crying. He turned on his lights and drove up behind me. That made me cry even harder, because not only was my mom going to kill me, but I must have also done something wrong, because the policeman was shining his light on me. Oh, Lord! Just take me now! I remember him telling me how worried my mom was, and all I could think of was the spanking that would be coming. When I finally got home, she just scolded me and hugged me and kissed me. I remember her asking me what happened, and when I told her, she said, "Didn't I tell you not to go off with strangers?" I said, "You said 'Don't go off with strange men. This was a kid.'" She couldn't do anything but laugh. Then she said, "From now on, you don't go with a strange man, woman, boy, girl, dog, cat, horse or anything else!" I realized that she was terrified. Now that I am a parent, I can understand why. My bad, Mom.

I had a lot of energy that I was trying to let out. So, into the woods we would go—the same woods I was not supposed to go into? Yep, those woods. In those woods I learned to flip or tumble, as some would call it. There were huge sand dunes. So that was heaven for the daredevil in me. Back handsprings. Back no hands. Backwards twists, I could do it all. And I learned it all in those forbidden woods. I would come home with a head full of dirt. At the scalp at least, because I feverishly tried to brush all the other evidence off.

In those same woods, we would build forts out of old lumber others would throw away. We would make slingshots out of metal clothes hangers and rubber bands. That was another thing I loved about my dad's job in the mailroom, besides the coffee with all that sugar and creamer: all the rubber bands I wanted. And the good, fat ones, too. Now, the favorite game for us to play was War. We would pick teams, build forts and start shooting rocks at each other. Dumb, right? Dumb, indeed. We would later graduate to BB guns—pump only, no gas guns. One pump is all you were allowed to use. And I know what you are thinking. "You'll shoot your eye out, kid!" Did anybody ever lose an eye? Almost. I shot my friend in the forehead. The BB lodged inside his forehead before we plucked it out, but he would go on to have that dent in his head forever. And that was the end of War. Well, that kind of war anyway.

We were in the woods a lot, but we spent a lot of time in my house, too. Although I was more of a homebody than Ralph—he was always on the go—I still had a lot of energy that I was trying to let out.

And a lot of anger.

I don't know what I was angry about. At first, it was just an overabundance of energy that wasn't being utilized properly. If I wasn't playing sports or doing something organized, I had a need to be moving around at high speeds, to be doing something. I built ant farms, or fed ants to spiders that lived under the roof of the building at the park near my house. I would get agitated easily. I was a good kid, but I had a mean streak. Later on, I discovered that I had anger issues that I had to address. But fortunately, when I was younger, I had sports to play to keep me from getting too worked up. On top of all that, I'm actually introverted in a lot of ways. So I'm cool with being around folk, just not all the time.

Sports were big for my family—going back generations. My father played high school football. He turned down a scholarship so he could start supporting his young family. He still tells stories about being an undersized middle linebacker. He used to say, "I was tough, aggressive, and boy, could I tackle." According to him, his nickname today would be "Hit Stick." Somehow, I believe him 100 percent. The apple doesn't fall far from the tree, right? His father, Ralph Sr., was an excellent golfer. As a matter of fact, he was the first African-American golfer to win a tournament in Florida. He was also great at making golf clubs. He made me a set or two when I was younger. He told me I was a natural, and tried to convince me to take lessons. But golf was too slow for me. My father had a cousin, Harold "Buster" Hair, who played baseball in the 1950s for the Kansas City Monarchs and the Birmingham Black Barons of the Negro Leagues. In '58, Buster Hair led the league in hitting with a .423 average. He later coached football, basketball, and baseball at Raines High

School, my alma mater. He was the first African-American baseball coach at Raines, and earned a Coach of the Year award for leading the team to a regional title. My mother and father enjoyed going to Florida A&M and Bethune-Cookman football games as well. They used to go every year for years.

Although my father was partial to football and baseball, my first love was basketball. But my neighborhood was football crazy, and guys would play the sport with anything they could find, from a ball to a pinecone. I couldn't stand to watch football on TV. I didn't like baseball much, either. My father wanted me to pitch, and I had a strong arm, but I wouldn't do it. I played basketball whenever I could, but since football was king where I grew up, I had no choice but to play. We played tackle on the grass and touch in the street, although if you got too close to the curb on the grass, you could get thrown into the street. Yep, intentionally.

The Pop Warner field was right around the corner from my house. Ralph had already established himself as a player in the park, so when I was eleven, I started to play football, mostly because a lot of my friends had started.

I had a great first year. A lot of kids signed up, so the park decided to have two teams in my age group. I chose the new team, and it was clear we were the misfits. From the hand-me-down gear, to the way we were treated when both teams were playing or practicing in the same place at the same time. Coach Willie Atkins let me play quarterback since I could throw the ball with zip. When we scrimmaged the other team in the park, I noticed my line struggled a great percentage of the time. To be fair, a lot of those guys were new to organized ball, like I was.

So I asked if I could move to running back. My thinking was it would give me the ability to make a move with more space. They let me do it. And do it well I must say I did. I was blessed to lead the team in rushing and TDs. I was also one of the leaders of the team. I would even switch jerseys often to help on defense. It was an extremely fun year. I was so happy that I played. Yancey Park was electric on Saturdays. It was filled with positive energy—and concession stands. I even got my frugal pops to buy me some towels with words on them. Not really. I had to make them from cutting and taping. I wrote out words in black tape: "I'm bad" and "With the Quickness." You couldn't tell me nothing, Jack. Yep. Life was good… that first year, at least.

The next year, my newfound love almost broke my heart. Well, it wasn't football. It was a coach. You remember that coach that I decided NOT to play for that first year? Well, because Coach Atkins could not coach that next year, I had to play for the other guy. Now, I was the starting QB/RB/LB of the other team. Captain. Leader of youngsters. And in the other coach's view, I was best suited for center. CENTER! Are you kidding me? I just knew he was joking. I was one of the fastest players on the field. I wasn't very big. And he put me there? So, of course you know I was not happy. I asked first if I could try another position. He said no. So I asked my dad to talk to him. I figured that would do the trick. Nope. My dad said that the coach thought I was good at center, and my dad didn't see him changing his mind. But here's the issue: before I signed up to play, my dad had asked me, "Are you sure?" I said yes. He said, "There is no quitting once you start. And you will give everything you have." So, I had to play center. Because no matter how much I hated it, I could not quit.

I would find out later that my pops went through something very similar. He had played split end as a youngster, as he tells it, but when he got to Stanton High, the team had people at that position. So, get this: He actually "volunteered" to play center on the JV team, and the coach kept him there for two years. He asked the varsity coach his eleventh-grade year if he could try out for a different position, and the coach granted his wish. So, there I was, hoping my dad was an advocate for me. And this joker actually didn't see anything wrong with the move, because he had done it. He wound up playing middle linebacker, because he could as he put it, "hit hard, boy." Yep, runs in the family! He would eventually wind up where he wanted to be, but not until he spent time somewhere he really didn't want to be. That stuck with me. Even to this day.

All that being said, I didn't like playing center. So with that anger that was already in me, combined with the anger and chip that was coming from this new coach, somebody had to pay. The now-head coach at Raines was a year younger than me, and he was one of the guards on that team. He wasn't that big, either. Get this: these two "linemen" would go on to play safety and cornerback in college at Louisville and Clemson respectively. I used to take out all my anger in one-on-one drills, scrimmages, warmups, even laps. I was also trying to show the coach I should be somewhere else. No luck.

After that first season playing center, the next year I decided I was going to show those coaches that there was no way they couldn't put me in the backfield. I worked hard at practice and was convinced I had proven to them that I deserved to play somewhere else.

And they put me at center again.

I was angry, but the experience taught me a lot. It humbled me, first of all. It taught me to respect my teammates better, my offensive linemen. It also helped me to channel my anger a little better. Because you better believe I was hot every game. Everybody else is celebrating and here I am, one of the fastest dudes on the team, and I've got to play center every dadgum snap. So I was going to take that out on somebody.

It taught me about leverage, which is huge to playing football. I used leverage when I played defense. Playing center taught me about tenacity, conditioning of my body, all those things at an early age. I wasn't big, but I was able to utilize my speed and my quickness to get myself in positions to deliver killer blocks. I was able to be physical but not just using brute force. I could work angles and leverage and hit somebody the best way I could.

I learned that I loved and thirsted for contact, and that shaped my brand of football dramatically because I was in the trenches for two straight seasons. But those two years weren't a story about football. They were about how my dad shaped me into an individual who won't quit. My mother taught me that when you are in a fight, you do not start it, but you finish it with extreme brutality until someone pulls you off. My father gave me the desire to finish whatever I start. And not only was I going to finish it, I was going to give it my all. It's one thing to see something through to its conclusion, and another to do so while putting out maximum effort and making a complete commitment—even if you don't like it. As the saying goes, it's not what you go through, it's how you go through it.

◇◇◇

I really didn't like playing center, but school was even lower on my list of favorite things. And because I didn't devote much attention to my work, I paid a pretty big price.

It didn't start that way. I enjoyed kindergarten a lot, because of the woman who ran it, Mama Moats. It was Mama Moats' kindergarten, and they showed such love in that place.

Mama Moats was a heavyset African-American woman who was very caring and endearing. She was patient. Growing up, I had a bed-wetting problem, and during those times when I would struggle with that, she would be patient and accommodating to help me through it. To help me gain confidence. I was terrified of taking naps, because I had a lot of energy, but also because I was afraid I would wet the bed. She treated us like we were her own kids. The kindergarten was in a rougher part of town; as a matter of fact, it was right around the corner from where my wife Connie grew up. There was a big fence around it, but nothing bad was going to come into that place with Mama there. Because Mama also had that other side. Nobody would even think about messing with her.

After kindergarten, I went to Harbor View Elementary School, which is now Martin Luther King Elementary School. It was within walking distance of my house, and I remember pretty much the whole neighborhood walking together to school. There were a whole lot of kids, and it was great. It was the innocence of walking with your friends and not having anything to worry about except a test or a pop quiz or somebody messing with you a little bit. Looking back on it, we didn't have a lot of bullies, especially when you could fight.

I enjoyed going to school, but I was not a big fan of doing my homework. It was like poison. I hated it. I did whatever I could to avoid doing it. And a lot of times I could get away with it, because my mom wasn't home, because she was out working some odd jobs, and my dad was still at work. I would come home, throw my books in the room and run out to play. Since my parents didn't always check to see if I did my homework, it was easy to skip it.

And keep skipping it. Until at the end of fourth grade, I had done so poorly that I had to repeat the grade. I told people that my mom held me back, but that wasn't the case. I failed. It woke me up for a few years, because my attention to do the things I needed to do increased. And it was embarrassing. I was going to the same exact school as my friends, and they knew I was in the other class-room, instead of being up there with them. The first day of school was awful. They all walked one way, and I went the other. I was still down there in the last grade they had finished.

It was a learning experience for me, but it didn't teach me for long. Still, it makes me think. What if I had done the work I was supposed to do and didn't have to spend two years in fourth grade? Maybe I wouldn't have met Connie and married her. Maybe I did what I was supposed to do by failing.

Fifth grade was much better because of Mr. Hooks. He taught us just about every subject, and he was very stern, but he had a huge heart. It was hard sometimes to tell where you stood with him because he wasn't someone who smiled a lot. That same thing hap-pened to me from time to time in the past. People would see me, and I have an intense look on my face, and they think I'm angry, so they get uneasy. If you're not part of my family or a friend, you might think I'm mad. It's just that I don't smile all the time. But now that I think about it, he didn't smile most of the time. Even then, when he looked at you in the beginning, you would wonder what you'd done wrong. But once we got to know him, we could tell when he was in a good mood, and we could mess with him a little and play around.

The biggest thing about Mr. Hooks was that he used vocabulary and a type of speech that was at a different level than the broken English my friends and I used in the neighborhood. He opened up an entirely new level of communication for me. To be honest with you, it was a whole different way of speaking. He would use terms like "thoracic cavity" and "gluteus maximus." His being an Afri-can-American man meant that I heard someone speak at another level than what I heard near where I lived.

I believe he was doing his best to help us understand that you're going to have to be, and you are capable of dealing with more complicated language and ideas to be successful in the world. We could go outside and play at recess and after school, but when it was time to work in the classroom, we went to work. He passed away a long time ago, but he was definitely a teacher who made a big impression on me. It was a seed planted in me, in my fifth-grade brain, that there was a life outside of my community, and a way of communicating that goes with it.

Mr. Hooks in his unique way painted that seed in fifth grade, but things got a little shaky after that. I went to sixth grade at S.A. Hull, which was named for a former president of the Florida NAACP who donated the land for the school. I spent seventh grade at Oceanway and then went to Highlands Middle School for eighth and ninth. After failing fourth grade, I became a pretty good student. I was doing my homework and trying my best to learn and to do the things I needed to do to pass. But my mindset remained twisted. A "C" was like an "A" to me. That meant I passed.

Still wasn't digging school. It did not come easy to me, and it took repetition after repetition after repetition for me to learn things. The problem was that I had a different way of learning than others did. Back then, people didn't understand the concept of visual learning as much. Teachers would say, "Here it is" and expected you to learn it. I didn't learn that way. I had to break things down into picture form to be able to truly grasp them. I didn't know that then, so I was trying to learn things in a way that didn't work for me. Someone else was forcing me to use a different method, and I couldn't do that. Instead of working according to the way my brain operates, I was working against myself. So school was brutal at times.

I did pretty well in sixth grade and enjoyed the experience. But when I got to seventh, that's when things started to change. It was also the first time I truly saw racism's ugliness for myself. I had heard family and friends talk about being called the N-word before, but that was about it. Because Oceanway was a more integrated school, and I would lean that it was majorly white, there was the chance for more trouble.

I remember one time, a truck filled with teenaged white broth-ers and sisters—I call everybody my brothers and sisters, so they were my white brothers and sisters—was sitting outside the school. The people were throwing bottles at us and calling us the N-word. We were kids. I was like, wow. It blew me away, because I guess I hadn't been paying attention to a lot of things that were going on in the world at that time. My mom and dad did a good job shielding us from a lot of things, and I guess I protected myself, too. I didn't watch a lot of the negative stuff. When I was a kid, I just watched a lot of cartoons.

And my parents didn't have the news on all the time, either. So, when I saw that, it was another side of humanity. Because I was so young at the time, it put a real divide inside of me. It began to separate things in my mind, like an us-and-them type of thing. I now understand that these things are taught. As kids, we played with whomever. But seeing how family members and those closest to them in the neighborhood talked about someone of a different skin color or ethnicity, we might start separating out. Not because the other kid was bad, or into a lot of stuff. No, simply because they were different. They would get rewarded when they reacted the way that the others wanted, and scolded when they did not. And that is the way you train anything. Rewarding them. The more they hated, the more adoration and laughter came their way. So guess what they kept doing? Exactly.

That's a horrible way to look at life, just horrible. We're blessed to be on this planet together. God created one race, the human race. I could have given my blood to save one of those individuals who were throwing things at me, and if my blood matched, it would save them. But we have classified ourselves and separated ourselves. That was something that separated me from them. It was time to protect my own and to look out for them. What a horrible way for an eleven or twelve-year-old to be thinking. That's not the way the Lord created us in this world. So this was often a struggle for quiet me.

Because I was so shy, and because of my stutter, I didn't feel comfortable discussing my feelings about this with anyone else, except with my friends. I didn't go to my parents with it. I'm pretty sure my dad would have done a good job breaking it down for me if I had, but it was just so shocking. And it was not a common thing for us to just sit around and talk about things, other than sports. Thanks to my young mind at the time, I could put it away and move on with my life. I didn't forget it, though; it was always entrenched there, but thankfully it didn't change the way I treated people. It changed how I thought about them, but it didn't change how I treated them.

I wasn't going to stay away from white students, because you have to do something to me for me to avoid you. Until you showed a bad side of yourself, I wasn't going to ostracize you. I'm not just going to push you away for no reason. But I was certainly looking at people more closely and was more conscious of what they were doing.

That was how the experience of life met up with the messages from home. I had always been taught to stand up for myself and to finish what I started—and not just go through the motions. I was supposed to give my best at all times. And I was expected to treat others the way you would want to be treated. That isn't always easy. But it's the right way. It's the Lord's way, and it was my parents' way.

It became my way.

CHAPTER 3

First Gridiron Steps

The pain was excruciating. I had been off to a great start in my eighth-grade season at Highlands Middle School, scoring two touchdowns in each of my first two games and piling up a lot of tackles. I was playing both ways, as a receiver/running back on offense and a middle linebacker on defense.

I had done my best to show the coaches I wasn't going to back down at all. When we did the "bull in the ring" drill—in which one player stands in the middle of a circle of teammates and hits whoever runs at him, from whichever direction—all the extra energy I had—and, yes, anger—just fueled me. I was trying to destroy people. I don't care if it was a bigger cat or whoever, I knew leverage is king. I wanted to show the coaches what I could and would do to any chump that stepped up. I remember being nervous as all get out, as this was the first time I was going to be playing football in a place that wasn't Forest View, my Pop Warner team at Yancy Park. I was moving up, you know, getting older.

On a running play during the third game, I planted my left leg to cut, but the defender hit me directly on the knee and hyperextended it. It cracked a bone near my growth plate, so surgery wasn't an option. Doctors put me in an immobilizer and sent me home with a bunch of pain meds. It cost me the whole season, and I was crushed. I sat at home, miserable, and my mom wondered whether I would ever play football again. The pain was unbelievable. I was away from school, friends, and my teammates. And on top of that, I couldn't run, jump, dive or do anything mobile.

I also couldn't go to school, so teachers sent home packets of work. I did some of it and sent it back, but I didn't do it all. I was lazy. Believe it or not, there is a laziness to me sometimes. And because I didn't do all of the work and was out of school for two months, I was afraid I wasn't going to move on to ninth grade. But somehow I passed, and I would be heading to ninth grade. You might be saying "high school, right?" Nope. Highlands was a seventh- to ninth-grade school. Junior High as it were. I wasn't a great student when I came back for my ninth grade year. This would come back to bite me later. But on to high school I went.

The real story was about to begin.

◇◇◇

William Marion Raines was forty years old when he came to Jacksonville. He had already attended five different colleges, including Columbia University, and had established himself as a man of letters. He spent twelve years as principal of Matthew W. Gilbert Junior and Senior High School, which had opened in 1928 as Franklin Street Public School, an all-African-American institution which in 1970 became Matthew Gilbert Middle School.

In 1964, the leaders of Duval County decided to send the growing African-American population in Jacksonville to Jean Ribault High School, an all-white school. But faculty and students at Ribault rejected the idea, and the city's school board decided to solve the issue by spending $2 million on a new school. In January 1965, School No. 165 opened on Clarkson Avenue, and students were treated to a state-of-the-art facility that featured air conditioning, distinctive architecture, sharp landscaping and science labs that had the best equipment. The African-American community took great pride in the facility, and its first principal, thirty-five-year-old Andrew Robinson, recruited a first-rate lineup of faculty, administrators and coaches. Students were happy to go to the school, which was named for Raines in June 1965.

Robinson walked the halls at Raines, raising expectations of his students and motivating them. If someone fell short of a goal, he would say, "Next time, we'll do better."

Robinson later became interim president of the University of North Florida (1980-82) and had an elementary school named for him after his death. The science wing that opened in 1990 at Raines was dedicated in his name. He wanted to instill excellence during his four years as principal, and helped set Raines students on journeys to achievement.

Raines' first football coach was Earl Kitchings, and in his first season, the Vikings went 8–1–1 and won the conference title. The quarterback on that team was Ken Burrough, who went on to be an all-America receiver at Texas Southern, and a two-time Pro Bowl receiver during twelve seasons (1970–81) with New Orleans and Houston in the NFL. Former Eagles great Harold Carmichael, a member of the NFL's all-1970s team, played football—and the clarinet—at Raines, as did eighteen other future NFL players played there, including my former Eagles teammate, Lito Sheppard.

In 1969, Freddie Stephens came to Raines as a physical education teacher and defensive coordinator. By 1978, he was the head coach, and before he was fired in 1996, Stephens compiled a 140–64 record. His teams won ten district titles and reached the state playoffs eleven times. His teams were built on defense and special teams and ran the triple option, which allowed for long, clock-eating drives or some big plays with the many outstanding athletes that played quarterback and running back at Raines.

One of those great backs was my brother, Ralph III. He had great mobility, could cut on a dime and accelerate quickly after he made a move. Ralph and I had something of a sibling rivalry type of thing growing up. To me, he was the big brother, and he didn't want me hanging around, so he would do his thing, and I would try to go with him. He wouldn't let me, so I would watch from a distance and try to imitate the things he was doing. When I was old enough to go places on my own, he couldn't tell me I wasn't allowed to be there. But I watched him and tried to imitate what he did.

One of the things he would do was to put on a plastic sweatsuit in the heat of the summer and work out to lose weight and get in better condition. We didn't know how dangerous it was back then to do that, but Ralph needed to lose weight, and later on, I would do it to feel the full brunt of the work I was doing. I was crazy, but I thought it was the right thing to do. Besides, it forced me to push through being uncomfortable. I wonder if this kind of mindset would help me out further on in my life?

When Ralph was a tenth grader, playing on the JV, his coaches told Coach Stephens that he was an excellent back who would help the varsity when he got there. But Coach Stephens had a favorite ballcarrier, Dominique Ross, to whom he gave the lion's share of the carries and who ended up playing in the NFL. It's crazy that two backs from the same team would end up playing pro football. When Ralph reached the varsity, he showed quickly that he deserved to be a featured back, and coach Stephens gave him the ball—some. Ross was still his favorite, and although Ralph gained 1,000 yards each of his two years on the varsity, college recruiters didn't pay much attention to him. In fact, as the story goes, my mom had to go to the local paper and make sure the writers knew about Ralph.

Ralph was recruited by Louisville and signed to play for Howard Schnellenberger and the Cardinals. Ralph played four years for U of L, from 1990 to 1993, and gained 2,159 yards and scored 17 TDs. His best season was his sophomore year when he rushed for 622 yards and caught 44 passes. He was also a pretty good return man for Louisville, too. Ralph wasn't drafted, but the Saints signed him and sent him to the World League of American football, where he played parts of six seasons with the Amsterdam Admirals. A torn ACL prevented him from reaching his pro potential, and although the Saints activated him in 1995, and he saw some time on special teams, he never carried the ball in an NFL game.

When I got to Raines in tenth grade, I was not a big person. I was 5'8" or 5'9," and I burned weight fast. I couldn't keep it on. I could lose ten pounds in a game easily, and I didn't have it to lose. My son, Brian Jr., went through the same thing. I used to get full-body cramps, and though I drank water, I wasn't getting enough potassium and sodium, so I cramped all the time. I was always lean. Since I wasn't a big-framed kid, I had to rely on my heart. The one thing that they will never be able to do, is measure a person's heart, and willingness to do whatever it takes to have success. My want-to, as I call it, was off the charts. I did not want to fail. I hated losing. I would do anything necessary to succeed. If they wanted me to guard the other team's best player while on the basketball court, I would be the defensive stopper.

Ralph provided a lot of help. He paved the way for me by cutting through some of the minutiae you have to endure to get to the next level. The coaches knew another Dawkins was coming, but they didn't call me Brian or "Scooter," my nickname growing up. I was "Little Ralph." I appreciated it, because it was a tribute to my brother, but to be honest, I got tired of living in his shadow. I got tired of people calling me Little Ralph or Lil Dawk. And that just added to the anger and angst and the energy that was already bottled up inside me. I had to prove that I was my own cat. I thank Ralph for setting the stage, but when I got to Raines, I wanted to make my own name.

When I was on JV in tenth grade, I was a starting running back and middle linebacker. I wore number one. I wasn't leading the team in rushing, but I was up there. I was scoring touchdowns, I was laying that unadulterated stank on folk and I was having fun, playing both ways and being with my friends. Because I was playing so well, I got called up to the varsity. It was exciting. I couldn't wait to play on the big team. So I thought!

Instead, I was a doggone tackling dummy. I was watching my friends having a good time on JV, and here I was, just doing scout team work. It wasn't fun at all. But I learned the defense. I learned about what it took to play on the varsity, the speed. It was all part of a grander purpose, though I could not see it at the time. That's the thing about perspective a lot of times, it's finally recognized in hindsight, though it was there the entire time. And I think now about what my mom taught me: "You keep on fighting." And my dad said, "You can't quit." I had to give my all. And so, while I was with the varsity that year, I gave everything I had. And it prepared me for the speed and contact on that level so that the next year I knew what I was doing. At the time, I didn't know or understand that, but there was a purpose to all of it. I was being prepared to excel the next year.

That's what we have to understand in our lives. Even during times when we are being tested or forced to do things we don't like, we are being prepared and primed for something greater. We have to understand that the Lord is going to get us ready. Get us ready to serve. Get us ready by allowing us to survive difficult times. Get us ready to be better people. As a tenth grader, I didn't know what was happening when I was getting pounded on by the older cats during varsity practice, but I know now that the work I put in then would help me later on my football journey. And on the path of life. And another thing. I begin the process of earning the respect of my older teammates—some of whom would vote me in as a captain two years later.

◊◊◊

As my father says, basketball was my heart. I could really jump and had great explosion. When I got in the air, I was able to float. You know, hang between floors for a cup of coffee. Even though I was only 5'8" 5'9" in ninth grade, I could dunk a soccer ball all the time, and a basketball sometimes. I could shoot some, and I was not going to let someone get the better of me physically.

In fact, it was the basketball court that shaped me into the football player I became. That might not make sense to some, but thanks to the lessons learned while playing for James Humphrey, I developed the desire and work ethic needed to succeed at any level. "Humph" took over at Raines in 1988 after running the program at two other Jacksonville high schools, Gilbert and Andrew Jackson. In five years at Raines, he was 85–42 and won the 1991 state title. He was a great player, too, at Bethune-Cookman, and is in the school's athletic Hall of Fame.

I had enjoyed my JV season at Raines. We played run-and-gun ball, and it was a lot of fun. My teammates and I jacked up three-pointers, went at the rim with dunk attempts—successful and failed—and threw alley-oops while trying to outscore the other team. We went undefeated, blew out a bunch of teams the first couple of games. But my days were numbered. As you might guess, I was pulled up to varsity again. This time because a lot of the older players that played varsity quit. Yep, they quit. LOL. And I would soon find out why dudes I knew that loved to hoop, decided Hump was not for them.

Coach Humphrey? He was something else, Jack. I didn't find this out until later, but the man was a willing disciple of Bobby Knight, the chair-throwing, wild-screaming coach of Indiana (and later Texas Tech), from afar. As he read and it felt like, memorized Bobby Knight's book. I don't think I ever heard Coach Humphrey hand out one single compliment. I am not exaggerating. He was going to get you to do what he wanted with "negative reinforcement." He ignored the good a player did and overemphasized his mistakes. Even if you did something minor wrong, he would blow up. And act... like Bobby Knight!

As you might imagine, that approach wasn't too popular, especially with those football players who already had scholarship offers and were just playing basketball for fun. Some of them quit, so he needed some guys to fill out the roster. Just like on the football field, I received an early promotion to the varsity. If I missed the JV on the gridiron, that was nothing compared to how much I wished I was still on the junior varsity on the basketball court my tenth-grade year. My favorite sport became a horrible drudgery. Humph's practices were like mental warfare. I take that back, they *were* mental warfare. We would do drills until someone messed up. Then, he would tell us to put the balls down and start running laps around the court. He didn't want us to do five or ten. It was more like 50 or 75. If somebody cut a corner, he would make us start again. "Oh, we got somebody who wants to cut corners?" he would ask. "Go back to number one." It was hard to tell who we were angrier at, the guilty party, or the drill sergeant dishing out the punishment. And he liked it.

We ran laps before practice, during practice, and after practice. Sometimes, practice would be nothing but laps. And Coach Humphrey would stand there, with his hands behind his back, whistling a tune. He had a pleasant look on his face, which was half-covered by thick glasses. Worse, he and his assistants watched everything we ate in the cafeteria. If he caught us with a chicken wing, we ran laps. Ice cream? Laps. Anything that wasn't good for us in his book brought a sentence of running before practice. We would get to the gym and see a list posted of our dietary sins and the corresponding punishment. When I got to Clemson, coaches were surprised to see that I was paying attention to what I put in my body. That was because of Coach Humphrey. As you can imagine, the strict rules and the over-the-top conditioning wasn't popular with too many people. And it made some of the upperclassmen leave the team.

But it did wonders for me, even if the bottoms of my feet were on fire, and I had to put Band-Aids on my nipples like marathoners did to protect me from chafing. I never quit. Maybe I would try to trim off some of the laps when he wasn't looking, but I wasn't about to leave the team because things were too tough. The natural urge in some athletes may be to sulk and loaf, but I couldn't let myself surrender to that. I was going to stay in it, no matter what.

And it paid off—in a number of ways. First, I was part of a state championship team in 1991. Second, I learned about how important it is to be in the best condition possible. You may not imagine that you can go another step, but then you do. And in the fourth quarter of a big game, when the other team was dying, we were strong. We played entire games employing 1–3–1 traps at full speed. I was a defensive stopper, and I would run the baseline, anticipate passes and lead opposing ballhandlers into the bodies of my bigger, beefier teammates, like 6'-4", 230-pound Patrick Sapp and 6'-6", 260-pound Derrick Alexander. Both of them played pro football, both would go on to play in the NFL as well and both of them delighted in intimidating—and sometimes beating on—other teams.

We had a "no easy layup" policy on defense. And one time, I hit a guy in the head so hard trying to block his shot, his mom almost came out of the stands and jumped me. She yelled, "You didn't have to do my baby like that!" We were on the road, and I needed my teammates to act like bodyguards around me after the game. Ahh, the good ole days.

Because we were in such amazing condition, other teams couldn't keep up. By the fourth quarter—and in some instances, the third—they were gassed. Playing for Coach Humphrey taught me how mental toughness and superior conditioning could cause others to check out mentally, and even better for me to see, they would tap out physically. I was already a physical player, and my endurance was at a peak. I wanted to compete more than anything. But now I was learning how it was possible to make the other guy quit. Sometimes, we beat opponents before the ball was tossed up, simply because of our energy during warm-ups and the threat of our high-tempo style and physical brand of ball on the defensive end of the court. Not that Coach Humphrey ever congratulated us for our efforts. He would find one thing, like a teammate who spent a few seconds bent over, grabbing his shorts while someone else shot a free throw, to prove that we weren't in good enough condition. We were trying to look smooth, imitating Michael Jordan and other basketball superstars, who grabbed the bottom of their shorts to look cool. He would insist that we were tired. "I guess we aren't running enough," he would say. So, off we went. Even after a convincing win, we would run.

After a while, it became normal. We were so conditioned to believe that nothing we did was right and that practice was going to bring pain and misery that we actually started clapping and singing as we ran. Of course, Coach Humphrey wasn't too happy about that. "Oh, so this is so easy that y'all want to sing?" he yelled. That meant more laps. Or, we would have to run the stadium bleachers. As we ran—silently this time—he would bark at us. "Y'all going to run until I get tired! Bet y'all won't laugh and sing no mo'!" So much for trying to make the process seem less painful.

The goal of every player was to have Coach Humphrey not talk to him. That's right; the more he ignored you, the better it was. Since he only spoke to us when we did something wrong, if he wasn't talking to (or barking at) you, you were doing things right. I'm happy to say he gave me the silent treatment a lot. Not that I was perfect. One time, I missed a dunk during a game. The ball hit the back of the rim and flew out to half-court. When it happened, I thought he might see it as an aggressive play. Fat chance. From the bench, I heard, "Get him outta there!" Before the next whistle,

I increased my defensive efforts—if that was possible—and actually knocked the ball away from an opponent. I had to be back in his good graces, right? Forget it. He still subbed for me and gave me a horror-movie killer stare as I went to the bench.

Fortunately, with me out of the game, our defense became a little lax, and Coach Humphrey stood up and walked down to me. I expected him to rip me for missing the dunk. Instead, he put me back in the game with the unspoken directive to be as aggressive as possible. Get this: after we won the state? He wouldn't let us celebrate. He yelled at us to "sit down and act like you got some sense." After winning the state, our crowd of Viking faithful, including my girlfriend Connie, who had driven to Tallahassee to cheer us on, were going crazy. And there we were, sitting like we were in the military.

There was one time (ONE!) when he actually showed a little humor. As I said earlier, I was a great jumper. And I could glide through the air. I would take off, hold the ball behind my head or off to the side until the defender flew past, and then take the shot. After I did that in a scrimmage one time, he asked me, "Why do you do that?" I was a little afraid to answer, so I kept my mouth shut. He asked me again. I said, sort of sheepishly, "I like to glide, coach," you know, like Clyde "The Glide" Drexler. For a second, I could have sworn he cracked a smile, as he shook his head. My teammates thought I was crazy. I probably was, and not because I told the coach about my love of airborne activity. I was crazy because I had come to love the pain of his brutal practices. I had developed my competitive drive by pushing myself to survive the running and the drills and the psychological warfare. It was pain for a purpose, and I saw that. It would shape me FOREVER, even after I stopped playing football. Yes, those lessons helped me get to the NFL. I learned the ability to filter out what some coaches were saying. I took in the good and spit out the bad. I didn't allow the bad to stay too long and to prevent me from doing good things. Coach Humphrey also helped me to be accountable for things I wasn't doing. I wouldn't get angry if a coach corrected me or cursed me. I would take in the good and work to improve.

I still go to the gym regularly, and when I work out, I push myself. My weight fluctuates between 210–230 pounds (I played the majority of my career at 204, my heaviest being my last years in Denver when I was 210–15). I played at 190-195 the first four years or so of my career. I still don't know what it means to go to the gym and get in a "light" workout. I'm going to move some weight. Connie is always joking with me that we can't work out together, or she tells me that whenever we go in the pool, I must wear a flotation device, as I will sink otherwise. She says it looks like I'm fighting a crocodile when I swim. The main reason is that I don't talk much when I'm getting after it. Also, I'm pretty intense. I lose myself in my music and my workout becomes my best friend. That's just how I was when I played for the Eagles. I would get in the weight room, turn on some reggae, or some old school, or gospel rap and do work, Jack. No talking. No smiling. It was time to work.

Even now, with no game on Sunday, I'm still going as hard as I can.

Thanks, Coach James (Bobby Knight) Humphrey.

◇◇◇

I was never a full "slop dog," and that was a good thing. Newcomers to the varsity football team were hazed some and forced to do some demeaning stuff by the seniors, just to show them that they hadn't accomplished anything yet. JV was nothing once you reached the varsity.

Because of Ralph, I didn't have to go through very much of that stuff. Even though he was gone from school and at Louisville, he had let everybody know I was coming up. As I said, they called me "Little Ralph," which I wasn't thrilled with, but they didn't give me too hard of a time, because of my brother. That helped me. There were a few older players that were absolute blessings. One of the older players, a nose tackle named Minka Pryor, took me under his wing and made sure I was okay. He was only about 5'8", but he weighed 215–230ish pounds it seemed and was a real sparkplug. The other thing that really helped was my mentality that I wasn't going to back down from anybody or anything. Even though I wasn't the biggest guy, I was going to go hard at you, every time. So me and Minka hit it off. As he was a key reason we were so dominant as a defense, though he was the smallest cat.

I didn't think too much about that then. It's just who I was. My dad told me how to do that, and that's who I became. I was going to go as hard as I could. I tell people to be a "pullback player." That means, instead of someone telling you to speed things up, they should be telling you to slow down. To pull back. I never wanted anybody to say, "Finish!" or "Go hard!" or "Can I see more?" I wanted them to tell me to slow down, even when they were just teaching. That's the mentality I wanted to have in everything I did.

When I was in tenth grade, I was on the scout team on both offense and defense. It wasn't a lot of fun, but I was learning how things were done on the varsity level. Because of my work ethic and my desire to show people what I could do, I used to run through the defense on scout team and get them angry from time to time. I wasn't being disrespectful, but I truly love to go hard. They were trying to hit me, but I was still getting past them. Because of that, and because of Ralph's success, they thought I wanted to be a running back. But I liked defense too much, so before my junior year I asked one of the defensive coaches if I could play for him. He said I should ask Coach Stephens, and I did. He asked me if I was sure about it. He was really hesitant, because he had witnessed what my brother had done. He told me it was okay, and I thanked him. I also told him that I would help out on offense if they felt they needed me situationally. I ended up doing some return work, but I wasn't going to play offense full-time. I was still holding a grudge from the Pop Warner coach who made me play center, I guess.

I played safety in eleventh grade, after they used me as a corner when I was on the scout team as a freshman. I loved safety so much because I wasn't limited. When I played cornerback, I could only have an impact on one side of the field. Being a middle linebacker or a safety, you can go to both sides, if you read the play correctly. So, I was basically a deep middle linebacker. I was going to read something as quickly as I could and come up and blast whomever I could. That's what I did, a lot of times. I had the ability to range across the field, to see it from the vantage point of the back line. I became a little more vocal and let people know what I saw, even back then. I wanted to help my teammates out. That leadership in me began to come out a little bit more, and I was more confident in who I was. I was becoming B-Dawk to my teammates.

And our football games were great. We were like a black college. We had a killer band. Our band director was the brother of the director at Florida A&M—Dr. William P. Foster—and if you have never seen the Rattlers' "Marching 100," back in the day, you missed out on a treat. In 1992, *Sports Illustrated* voted them the Best College Band. They represented the state of Florida in Bill Clinton's inauguration parade. They performed at Super Bowl XLI in 2007 with Prince, and even though they're called the Marching 100, they have more than 300 musicians. They step fast and have great moves.

Our band did that, too. Their routines were outstanding, and each halftime would basically feature competitions between Raines and the opponent. It was a great atmosphere for the fans. Even though we were usually in the locker room when they played, we got a chance to see them perform at pep rallies, when they would play. We even had step shows. It was great to be a part of that, and even better to be fully part of the team as myself, not as someone's little brother.

After that year, it was no longer "Little Dawk." It was no longer "Little Ralph." I had earned the right to be myself. To be "B-Dawk." And that felt wonderful, to have my own identity.

◇◇◇

I owe it all to Maurice Huntley, Bernard Ward, and Marlin Stewart. I really do. I was one shy dude. I would make it a priority to walk down the hall that Connie Kerrin's classroom was on, knowing full well it was out of my way, and I would have to then run to make it to class on time daily. But that's what I did. Every day. Just to make eye contact with her—I didn't have the courage to ask her out. She made me feel like Jim Carrey in Dumb and Dumber when she stuck out her tongue at me early on in the process though: "So you're telling me there's a chance."

I had seen her for the first time when I was in ninth grade at Highlands. We were playing a basketball game against Jean Ribault Jr High School, one of our big rivals, and Connie was a cheerleader for Ribault. When I saw her, I thought she was a vision of loveliness.

In tenth grade, we were both at Raines, and I would try to see Connie every day when I was jogging down the hallway. Maurice knew I wasn't going to ask her out, so he went up to Connie and asked if she knew who I was. She knew. So, he asked if she would meet me. She said she would. Later that day, I was shooting hoops in the gym, and he came up to me. Me, Maurice and Marlin spoke through a cracked gym door that was locked with chains. (Picture Lean On Me.)

"Hey, I've got good news for you."

I said, "What's up?" He asked me if I knew Connie, and I said I did.

Maurice told me she had agreed to meet with me. I wasn't too happy that he had spoken for me.

"Man, what do you mean?" I asked. "What did you tell her? Why did you do that? What did she say?"

"She'll meet you out in front of the guidance office," he said.

He said it wasn't a big deal, but I was so nervous. I practiced over and over what I was going to say to her, how I was going to say it and what I should wear. It was a huge thing for me, because I'm a stutterer, remember, and when I get nervous, I stutter more. I was afraid I would mess it up, and look like an idiot.

I don't remember what I wore, but she had on a purple shirt and a pair of white pants. That was our introduction. After that, she let me have her number. More accurately, her dad let me have her number. It was a while before I could call her, though. She was only allowed to speak to one boy at a time, and she had a friend that she would talk to on the phone. I could hear The Biz Markie singing, "But you say he's just a friend." She wasn't dating him, but her father said she couldn't have two boys calling her. She had to tell him that he couldn't call anymore, and then she gave me her number. We started dating, and the rest is history.

Connie's father didn't trust me at first, because I was so quiet. He thought I was sneaky, instead of just shy and introverted.

I was still not a fan of school, mostly because things did not come easily to me, but I really enjoyed going to school because of her. I used to tell Connie this all the time, and she would blush, but I just loved being around her. No, it was not because she had a car that her father had bought her, a little red Fiero. Which was awesome. It was because she had the kind of heart that would have her get up really early, come get me, and we would go to school together. Get up like 5 a.m. early, as school started at 7:25 and I lived 20 minutes away from her, and about 25 minutes from Raines. The anticipation of getting into the car with her and just being around her then, and during the school day for different segments, was great. Except for when it would rain, as there was a leak in the sunroof so we had to put up a plastic bag. But it was still all good. Sure, my friends would give me a little trouble for spending so much time with her, but I didn't care.

When I think about it, if I hadn't repeated fourth grade, I wouldn't have been playing on that basketball team, and I wouldn't have met Connie. We never know why things happen, because the Lord doesn't reveal his plans to us. Our job is to accept His Way and to do our best to serve Him. Going to fourth grade a second time was embarrassing, but it led me to my beautiful wife and family. That's a dadgum good tradeoff.

◊◊◊

Even though I was trying to be the best athlete I could be, I didn't stay away from some of the things I was supposed to avoid. When I was a teenager, I was drinking a lot of beer. One night, my friends and I got crazy drunk, and I tried to sneak home without getting caught. The older kids told me the plan: "Don't go straight to bed. Walk into the kitchen and look like you're trying to find something to eat. Talk to someone. Then go to bed." I had it down. Of course, I was naive. It's just like with my kids now. They're upstairs and are supposed to be going to bed, but they're jumping up and down and dancing, and they don't think we can hear them.

I executed the plan perfectly. Or so I thought. What I didn't know was that my parents could smell the beer on me. My father, being the person he was, didn't say anything that night. He just woke me up the next day and said, "I want to talk to you." He didn't punish me. He didn't yell. But what he said was a lot more difficult for me to hear.

"I am thoroughly disappointed in you."

That hurt me to the core. I could see tears in his eyes. I said to myself, "I can't. That dude has done too much for me to hurt him like that, so I'm not going to hurt him like that again. I'm not going to do that."

My dad also said that if I wanted to do the things I said I did, as an athlete, I shouldn't be drinking. First of all, I was too young. Second, I was putting myself in harm's way by drinking. I could get arrested. I could get involved with the wrong people and end up in trouble—or dead. I decided I wasn't going to drink anymore. I was going to make sure the things he heard about me were good things. I wanted to get away from all of that. I wanted to separate myself from that crowd and no longer indulge in the things they were doing. I wasn't going to be judgmental, because I don't believe in that. So, when people asked me whether I wanted to drink, I would say, "Nah, I'm good." That was my standard line. If people wanted me to go out. To go somewhere that might lead to trouble. To do something that would possibly upset my father. "Nah, I'm good." It became one of my favorite lines.

It wasn't about myself. It was my father. I didn't want to disappoint him. But it was also about protecting myself from some things that were going on in my neighborhood. I lost three friends from my neighborhood, and it still hurts to talk about them.

One was R., and he was my brother's age. He was driving another friend, B., who was around my age, and he was drinking. The car ran off the road, and R. drowned. B. survived, but he told the story of hearing R. calling for help before he drowned, and that was brutal to hear.

Another was G., who was my age. He was a good friend of mine. I'm talking about the kind of friend where I would stay around his house a couple of nights during the summer and he would basically stay at our house the rest of the summer. We played football and basketball together, but he had some people in his family who had issues. Some of his brothers were in jail, and others were into some bad stuff. G. started selling drugs, and that wasn't something I could be a part of. We separated, and he began to sell even more drugs and get more involved in other things. As the story goes, one day, someone robbed him, and G. was going to retaliate. He and some other guys were in a car looking for the robber, and there was a gun that went off. He was in a coma for a couple months before they pulled the plug.

And finally, there was K. I learned from my mom that they found him dead in the street. They said he had been robbed. I had hung out with him from eighth grade after high school, and he was always into something. He was the type of guy who could talk you into things. Connie did not like K., so I had to make a choice whether to stay with Connie or keep hanging around with K., I decided to stay with Connie. I remembered seeing K. one summer in high school, and I asked him, "What do you do?" He said, "Well, you know, I get by." I figured he was hustling, selling drugs.

I believe The Lord allows things to be put in my life as options. I could have chosen to sell, for instant gratifications. There was some "easy" money to be made there, so it always seemed. I could have started dressing better, having nicer things. That would have been one way to go. Or, I could have stayed on the athletic path and stayed with Connie. There were choices to be made, and there were always people in the neighborhood—the "old heads"—who would try to get you to do the wrong things. Thankfully, I was able to make the right choices and avoid big trouble. A lot of that was my father. A lot of that was Connie. All of that was the Lord. There something to be said for choosing delayed gratification over instant.

And a lot of that was me.

CHAPTER 4

A Tiger's Tale

I wanted to be a Florida Gator. It made sense, right? I grew up in Jacksonville, and the UF campus was a 90-minute drive from my house. I knew I was going to be there, and there was no way you could tell me anything different. It was my dream, and as I played my tenth and eleventh grade years at Raines, I was focused on that—and Connie. I had even mastered the Gator Chop celebration.

That was a problem. Instead of worrying about my schoolwork first and then playing ball, I was all about football. Even though I had gone to summer school when I was in junior high, sometimes because I just wanted something to do, I had let my grades slip. My GPA was a 1.6, and because I wasn't a big-time recruit, Florida coach Steve Spurrier sent Coach Ron Zook, who told me he couldn't and wouldn't hold a scholarship for me while I got my grades in line.

I'll never forget the day he came to Raines and sat down with me and told me that because of my GPA, the Gators weren't going to offer me a scholarship. Wow. There was really nothing I could do about it. They were taking the offer away, and it wasn't coming back. I was crushed. As far as I was concerned, the world was over. It would be the first time I would cry on Connie's shoulder. It was awful. To make things worse, my teammate Anthone Lott, who was my partner in crime at the safety position, was offered and accepted a full scholarship to be a Gator. As I think back on it, I believe they took the scholarship I was offered and gave it to him. I was so happy for him though. I felt it was my fault anyway.

I was low, and at that point I didn't know if I could have success on and off the football field in college. But I was determined to prove that I could.

A couple other schools recruited me: South Carolina, Louisville. I have no idea why Michigan was interested in me. It was more of a feeler. The problem was that because I wasn't big, I didn't fit the classic safety profile. South Carolina offered me a scholarship. So did Louisville, but that was more because of my brother, I felt. I didn't want to go through that again, having to go up there and make my name all over again. And I didn't want to go too far from Jacksonville either, because of Connie.

South Carolina would have been okay because I could have traveled back and forth to see her. Okay, so that was cool. And as we were getting close to Signing Day, I was ready to go to school at South Carolina. Then the calls stopped. The contact ceased. As a matter of fact, I called all day one day, trying to reach someone. I called coaches and the office, who took my messages. I even talked to a coach's wife briefly, I believe. Still, I got no call back. Nothing. I didn't know it, but I was no longer one of their targets. Since then, because I had a son who went through the recruiting process, I know that when the calls stop, the school isn't interested anymore. South Carolina wasn't interested. I was in trouble and didn't even know it. Thanks again, Gamecocks.

Thank goodness for good ole Patrick Sapp. One of the nation's highest prospects.

◇◇◇

Talk to football coaches about the best players, the guys who are really impressive, and they will call them "dudes." To many, that term may mean just another guy. But in football, a "dude" is big time. Now, there are levels of "dudes," and Patrick Sapp belongs at the top level. In Jacksonville, and all over Florida, people definitely knew who he was. They knew him in football. They knew him in basketball. He threw the shot put in track He's still big in Jacksonville.

Pat grew up pretty close to me. He was in Sherwood Park, and I was in Yancey (Forest View Park). We really got to know each other when we went to middle school, riding the bus together. When we went out for the middle school team, we got even closer. I don't think Pat believed I was very good when he first saw me, because I wasn't that big. That would soon change.

There was no doubt Pat could play. In high school, he was big, about 6'4", 215–225. He was fast, and he was a great athlete. He was the cat coaches always wanted to get off the bus first, because he had that presence. It's funny, and I don't think he knows this, but he was my rabbit. He was the guy I was chasing. Even though we were teammates, and I wanted him to be successful and the team to be successful, I still was going after him. I tell young people this all the time: You are who you hang around with. Pat had a lot of the same goals as I did, on and off the field, and that was good for me. Even if I thought about doing something I shouldn't, I could remember how I wanted to catch Pat, and if I did the wrong thing, that wouldn't happen. As competitors, we gravitated toward each other quickly, and we would work out together.

Sapp was a tough cat. Even though he played quarterback into his college days, he could and would still hit folk. And on the basketball court, he was especially nasty. He used to try to make somebody bleed early on with a hard foul or an elbow. Then he could settle down and play ball. He wasn't cocky. In fact, he was very down-to-earth. And he cared about his teammates. It was one of many things that made him such a good teammate. So, again, there were a lot of areas where I was chasing him.

Pat was a big-time recruit, and Clemson was recruiting him hard. So were Florida, Florida State, and Syracuse among many others. He told everybody he was going to take all of his visits before deciding. As it got closer to signing day, he recognized that I wasn't getting a lot of recruiting attention. He asked me where I wanted to go to school, and I said, South Carolina. His exact words were, "Don't go there. They don't send anybody to the pros on defense from there." He asked me if I wanted to go to Clemson. I said I did, so Pat called the coach who was recruiting him, Rick Stockstill, and told him that if he wanted Pat, he had to take me, too.

Coach Stephens sent some of my game film to Clemson, and he also made the sales pitch. Coach Stephens and Pat convinced them to take me. Then Coach Stockstill and Ken Hatfield, the head coach, came to watch me play a basketball game. Coach Hatfield watched me play defense, and he told Coach Stockstill to sign me. He liked how aggressive I was, and he was impressed by my quickness. He also appreciated the blue-collar approach I brought and my work ethic. Bottom line, they wanted Pat so much, they were willing to take a chance on me. The trouble was that I wasn't a big safety. Everybody wanted safeties who were over six feet tall and 200 pounds, and I wasn't close to that. I was 5'10½", 170 pounds, soaking wet, while standing on the balls of my feet. That's a huge contrast, in the eyes of far too many.

Even though Clemson was willing to take me, there was still the matter of my grades. In order to be eligible to play as a freshman, I needed to bring my 1.6 GPA up to a 2.0. That's when Kenneth Black, who coached the defensive backs at Raines, came into the picture. He taught woodshop and computer-aided design, but I didn't have him as a teacher. He had me come to his homeroom every day, and he would tutor me. There was a lot of pressure on me because if I didn't make the A/B Honor Roll every nine weeks, I wasn't going to get my GPA up high enough to play ball.

I started getting 3.6s and 3.8s during those periods, and I graduated with a 2.4. Even when I got an A on a test, I would ask the teacher what I could do extra. Of course, it didn't matter what I did as far as Florida was concerned. They were out of the picture. But I got my grades up high enough so that I could go to Clemson. More importantly, I learned my lesson about grades. I had to do the work. But doggone it, I did it. And I finally knew I could. Thank you, Coach Black!!

It may seem strange to some people who hear me talk about how hard I work, but schoolwork was different than getting into shape and handling my business on the field. I understood that and knew how to push myself to get better and better as a player. I could run those extra sprints. I could lift more and heavier weights. I could watch more film, which was reel to reel in high school. I had the physical tools and knew how to get better.

The problem was that I didn't know how to study. I felt that I couldn't retain information that was presented to me easily. It was a battle that I didn't know how to win. Get stronger? No problem. Memorize something? Huge problem. I have come to understand more than ever that my negative mindset about learning something, that was one of the main issues that I had. I had a closed mindset about my potential growth. I was limiting my ability to do what I would later find I could.

It was a constant problem for me, a constant struggle. Some of our children have had some trouble with this now, and it hurts me so much. It's so hard when you don't feel like you measure up, and you're struggling every day. You feel so stupid. I had to put in so much work to get those good grades my senior year. It never got to the point where it flowed as easily as it did with athletics. It was constant. Even at Clemson I lived with the tutors.

Back then, people were telling me there was only one way to do it. I have since found out I can and do learn differently. We all do in a sense. But the key is, we all can learn. Not all brains are the same. Yes, they are made from the same stuff, but just like a fingerprint, they're different. And we can now encourage our kids to learn differently. You're not dumb. You're not stupid. We all can learn, differently. As I got older, I began to realize that this wasn't so much about being visual for me. It's about having ownership of the material. I try to break things down to their least common denominators. I talk about it in fraction terms when I talk to myself, which I do quite often. I learn it from that perspective. Now, I can own it. It makes sense in some crazy way to me. I learned it so that when I saw it on a test, the feeling of ownership of that subject came back. Then, I can go into details on it, not just from memory, but with some feeling attached. Because I now own the info. It's a part of me. And because it's a part of me, I can even find ways to make it better.

Once I digest it, I can regurgitate it. If I'm just memorizing a list of numbers and stuff, forget about it. I'll often break the numbers up and use my former teammates' names to remember the number. A certain phone number is Don, Troy, Tra, Trott, and Boots. 108. It was the same thing when it came to football. If you just gave me a playbook and said, "I need you to memorize this," I wouldn't be able to do it. If I go out and experience it and break it into its basic parts—put it here, put it there—then I have it. That's why, for me, it was so tough to relate to people who got up on the board and wrote something and expected you to get it right away.

That wasn't me. When I got to Clemson, that was just part of my problem.

The whole experience was brutal.

At first.

◊◊◊

Clemson sits in the northwest corner of South Carolina, about a six-hour drive from Jacksonville. It's closer to Atlanta than to any other major city, including Columbia, home of the University of South Carolina. The university was founded in 1889 and has about 20,000 students. Without the university, the city wouldn't disappear, but it certainly wouldn't have much going on. It's no coincidence the city and school have the same name. The city was originally named Calhoun—after the owner of Fort Hill Plantation, on which the university was originally built—and was changed in 1943.

My first year there brought a huge culture shock. First of all, I was away from home, away from my family. Most importantly, I was away from Connie. My mother says I was a homebody growing up, so putting me 400 miles away from the place I was most comfortable wasn't a good idea. It's not like I had traveled very much before going to college.

Making the adjustment to the racial breakdown of the town and the college was almost as difficult as being away from home. Both were about 80% white and less than 10 percent African-American. I didn't know how to function in that kind of environment. Because of incidents going back to Oceanway in seventh grade, and others as I got older, I was very careful. To that point, communication with my—as I call them—white brothers and sisters was very guarded. There were things put in Jacksonville that let you know that in the higher-up minds, there was an "us and them" element at work.

On our side of town in Jacksonville, the Northside, we seldom saw any white people, because the area is predominantly black. And this is going to sound crazy, but many of the white cats in the neighborhood, I saw just like one of my other friends of mine who were doing worse than me and my family. So in my young eyes, we were all in the same boat. Fighting for everything we got!! But going to Clemson was quite a different experience for me. I felt like didn't know how to communicate with the folk there, and because I had so many racial incidents in Jacksonville, especially when we traveled outside of the Northside of town, my guard was up, even with some of the police officers I came into contact with in Clemson. And I was blessed to be a part of PAL in Jacksonville for a few years. So I had had blessed encounters with many great officers. But there was a way that "some" spoke "at" you in South Carolina, which made me very uncomfortable. They didn't know me, but they talked at me like I was the worst person alive. I was completely out of my element, and Pat was the only person I really knew there.

Worst of all was being away from Connie. She stayed home and went to University of North Florida that first year, and even though we talked on the phone a lot, it wasn't the same. Going through something as tough as my first year at Clemson without her was brutal. It's difficult enough to be a freshman, away from home for the first time, in an area with a culture that is alien to you. Doing it without the person who makes you feel the safest and the best about yourself is almost impossible. I did not want to stay there. I wanted to go home.

Connie and I talked on the phone all the time when we could. Remember that these were the days before cell phones, so the only phone we had access to was in our dorm room. I would be on that phone for hours. I was rooming with Pat, and he couldn't call girls or other friends because I was always using the phone. He was a single guy, looking to have fun, and I was serious with Connie. I'm sure it bothered him some because he wanted to hang out with me and have fun. We all went to high school together, so Pat knew Connie. But, I kept calling. And I kept talking. It made it possible for me to survive. And when I couldn't call? We wrote letters. Yep. With stamps and all.

Then there was the freshman hazing stuff. I had a sharp, high-top fade hairstyle. It was smooth too. It was a Kwame. My hair was always good, Jack. One time, my father gave me a haircut without checking with my mom, and she was not happy about it. But I came to Clemson looking good, and then the upperclassmen shaved my head. We weren't even allowed to wear hats around town. That was really tough. Not only that, they shaved one of my eyebrows half off. I would be spared a lot of the worst stuff because another lineman took a liking to me. This time it wasn't a smaller cat with a big heart. It was a huge, All-ACC cat with a big heart. Brentson Buckner, 300+ pounds. But it wasn't just my effort and play that would help this along, it was my love for reggae music that I spoke of earlier. And that fact that I could and would, often upon request from an upper-classman, big up. Buju Banton, Mad Cobra, among other popular hits from that time. I could sing close enough to the artist that it would get them hyped. So as you may have guessed, I would listen and learn more and more. Thanks, Buck!

Making things even more difficult was the fact that the Clemson defensive coordinator, Ron Dickerson, didn't seem to be too happy I was there. He hadn't recruited me, and I believed he had wanted someone—anyone—else besides me. I got the last scholarship given that year. Once the mind begins to perceive something, it's tough to make it stop, and the brain responds in kind, to generate those chemicals that lead to the corresponding emotions and reactions. Coach Dickerson may well have been fine with my being at Clemson, but because I was convinced he wasn't thrilled, it became my reality.

I did have some evidence to support my case. Mostly, it was the length of conversations I had with him and the other coaches. I would notice how they would talk to my other teammates, even the freshmen, and then how they would talk to me. They would smile with them and spend more time with them. With me, it was point-blank and pretty serious. "Do this. Do that." That was tough for me because I had been used to such good treatment at Raines. But also, every other safety who was there already and brought in as a freshman was 6'-plus and 210-plus. I was an outlier at 5'10", 170.

It was all one big mess. I was homesick, confused by the environment and the people there and just not happy. Again, what the mind perceives, becomes one's reality.

As a matter of fact, I was convinced I would be redshirted. Not that redshirting is not a good thing, but for me, it was not an option. We were doing a semi walk-through in a tackling drill; one of my hyper classmates went too hard, and we went knee to knee. I would find out that I had chipped a bit of my knee cap and had a bone bruise. I remember being in tremendous pain, trying to fight through. I went to one of the upperclassmen for advice. Lou Solomon was a junior backup QB, from New Jersey, no less. I was crying in his room, saying, "Man, they gonna redshirt me, what can I do!" Homesick, hurt, and looking for answers. He would talk me down of my ledge of emotion, so I could refocus my energy in a positive direction.

I wasn't going to quit. There was no way I could go home and say I couldn't handle college. I couldn't say that to my father, the man who told me when I was a little kid that I was going to play center, no matter how much I hated it. And I wasn't going to tell the woman who taught me how to fight to the finish, that a shaved head and some uncomfortable surroundings were stronger than I was. And I wasn't going to give satisfaction to some back in Jacksonville that I caught wind of talking about how I wouldn't last—that I wasn't going to keep my grades up, and even if I did, I wasn't that good. It was going to be others that would make it to the NFL. Not me! I threw myself into my books, my music (Bob Marley, Buju, Garnett Silk, Dennis Brown, Cutty Ranks and so many more), and I came out of the first semester with a 2.6. You may not be too impressed with that. But I had to stage a big rally at Raines to get eligible for college, and here I was away from my support system, not just passing but pulling some solid grades. I was jumping for freakin' joy. And I killed summer school with a 4.0.

As for the field, like I have said, that hasn't ever been a problem. I knew exactly what to do there. Outwork errbody!

◇◇◇

Clemson football began in 1896, when Walter Riggs brought the game to campus from what would eventually become Auburn University. A year later, he let the players vote on what the school's mascot should be, and they chose Tigers, because the Princeton Tigers had won the national championship the year before. Clemson had some impressive coaches during its early days, including John Heisman, for whom the famous trophy honoring the best college football player in the nation is named, and Jess Neely. Neely led the Tigers to a 9–1 record in 1939 and a 6–3 win in the Cotton Bowl over Boston College. It was the program's first-ever post-season appearance. Neely would go on to coach Rice for 27 years, winning four Southwest Conference titles and three Cotton Bowls.

The real legend of Clemson football is Frank Howard, who took over as head coach in 1940 after serving as an assistant under Neely. A colorful character who told fascinating stories, Howard won six ACC championships during his thirty years there. The school named the field after him in 1974.

The most enduring part of the Howard legend is the rock that sits on a pedestal above the east end zone of Memorial Stadium. Sam Jones, a Clemson alumnus, was driving through Death Valley in California in the early 1960s when he stopped and picked up a rock that was sitting by the side of the road. He gave it to Howard, who had taken to calling the stadium "Death Valley." Howard was appreciative, but he didn't know what to do with the thing. For a few years, it sat in his office as a doorstop, until one day in 1966 he told Clemson booster Gene Willimon to get rid of it. Instead of throwing it out, Willimon placed it on the small pedestal in the stadium. In 1967, the tradition of players' touching it before running onto the field began. Howard reportedly said to his players, "If you're going to give me 110%, you can rub that rock. If you're not, keep your filthy hands off of it."

That rock is a big part of what some people call "the most exciting 25 seconds in football." The team takes a bus from the locker room to the hill above the east end zone, and then the players touch the rock and run down into the stadium. It's an electric atmosphere. To be part of that and to get the engines revved up like that is perfect.

It is the best way to get ready to go out and play a physical style of football. It was just outstanding. It was exactly what I wanted.

Although Clemson is a charter member of the ACC and had plenty of success under Howard and during Charlie Pell's two years, the program didn't break through on the national scene until Danny Ford took over full-time for the 1979 season. Two years later, he had the Tigers on the top of the college football world. In 1981, Clemson went 12–0 and won the national title after beating Nebraska, 22–15, in the Orange Bowl. Although Ford captured four league titles, and his teams won ten or more games four times during his eleven years, Clemson was hit with two probation sentences by the NCAA as a result of violations that took place while he was coach. Still, don't try to tell a Clemson fan that the national championship is tainted. That won't go so well for you.

Ford left Clemson after the 1989 season, and Coach Hatfield took over. He had won 55 games in six seasons at Arkansas and had a reputation for being a straight shooter and for running a clean program. He won ten games his first year and nine the next, mostly with Ford's players.

In 1992, it was my turn to take part in Clemson's football tradition. It certainly wouldn't be boring. It was time to make my name.

◊ ◊ ◊

I might have been a starting safety at Raines, but Clemson already had a very good strong safety, Darnell Stephens, so there wasn't much of a chance I would be walking into the program and taking a spot with the first team. Plus, Clemson had recruited a couple of other safeties, Leomont Evans and Andre Carter, both of whom were like 6'1", 210+. There was only one thing for me to do, and that was to show how tough I was by going all out on special teams. My philosophy is simple. Wherever you put me, I will be the best there is now, and see who the best there was, and try to supplant them! I decided I was going to be the best special teams player on the roster, and that's what I was. They called me a "special teams demon," and I won special teams Player of the Week, week after week. I was just killing it. It got to the point where opponents were double-teaming me when I ran down on punt coverage and when I was on the kickoff team, and I was just a freshman. It didn't matter, because I was still making plays.

With a few games left in the season, Darnell got hurt, and I got the start, thanks to my special teams play. I showed them I could handle it. I made plays and even forced some fumbles. As bad as things had been for me with my homesickness and everything I had gone through trying to get comfortable at Clemson, the season had ended very well on the field for me. It didn't matter if you outweighed me by thirty pounds, I was going to beat you with leverage. Coach Hatfield has said that the coaches knew right away that I was going to be an impact player, because of how hard I worked and how much I liked to hit people. And plus, I had earned the respect of my teammates. I was once again BDAWK.

Another thing that helped me is that when players come to a program like Clemson's, they usually haven't experienced a lot of defeat or disappointment. They have always been the best on their teams. Big-time programs are filled with guys like that, so the newcomers can't just walk in and become stars. Some people can't handle that. Because I had played center as a kid, and because I had to fight my way out of Ralph's shadow, and because Coach Humphrey rode us so hard, with his version of hard knocks, I was able to handle things from a different perspective than some guys could. I was resilient. I was blessed. I was locked in. They were impressed by my work ethic, which was normal to myself and Pat. All of that, plus my desire to actually be unstoppable on special teams, got me onto the field that first year.

The team didn't have the best overall performance. We finished 5–6 and 3–5 in the ACC. We lost some close games, including a 24–20 decision to Florida State, who would go on to win the National Championship with Charlie Ward manning the QB position like a boss. We also lost to South Carolina, 24–13, in the annual game at the end of the season. That didn't go over too well with the fans. There was some pressure on Coach Hatfield, and after the season, the school gave him a one-year contract extension. That's not a big boost, but it was something. And the message was pretty clear: win some more games. Even though under Danny Ford the program was put on probation two times, he had won the national championship and a lot of other games, dominating the ACC along the way. That was the new expectation. We had to get better.

I still wasn't completely comfortable, but I was happy I had proved I could play, and went into off-season conditioning with a better attitude. One of the things that helped was that I was able to play a lot of pick-up basketball. We played so hard, they implemented a no-dunk policy for a while, because my teammates, myself and other folk playing with us were dunking so hard, we were tearing up the rims. I had the chance to play with some of my white brothers, who I met in class, and I was able to open up around them. I learned that a lot of them were just as nervous as I was about things. They were no different from me. They just came from different types of backgrounds. That was really positive. I was able to communicate and get out of my shell a little bit. I had allowed myself to withdraw, and that wasn't good. This helped me understand others better.

Coach Hatfield is a Christian man and a no-nonsense coach. He would be seen as the complete opposite of Coach Ford, who was giving players money and just about anything they wanted, so it was ruled on by the NCAA. That's why Clemson was on probation. There were some players on our team who had played for Coach Ford, and they were used to the old way, and they weren't getting any special benefits from Coach Hatfield. Some of them moved on.

Coach Hatfield was trying to raise young men to live wholesome lives, and that didn't go over too well with the fans, which is crazy. He was a little like Coach Stephens. He didn't curse, and he had a Swear Jar. If you cursed, even during practice, you had to put a dollar in the jar. It was almost like I was back at my grandma's house.

We went 8–3 during the 1993 regular season my sophomore year. It was better than 1992, but we still lost to Florida State, 57–0, in the second game of the season. North Carolina beat us pretty good, too, 24–0. Both of those games were on the road. We went 6–0 in Death Valley, which made sense because it's such a tough

place to play for opponents. We finished the regular season with a
16–13 win over South Carolina at their place. That's a big thing, for
sure. Tiger fans want to beat Carolina. But it wasn't good enough.
Remember that people expected the kind of results Coach Ford got,
even though we weren't breaking the rules. After the win over South
Carolina, Coach Hatfield asked for another year's contract extension, through the 1997 season, but he didn't get it. Even though he
went 32–13–1 during his four years there, a strong, .696 winning
percentage, he didn't feel supported, and the school wasn't willing
to commit fully to him. So, he left.

We played Kentucky in the bowl game, and Tommy West was
our coach. Coach West had been at Chattanooga, a Division I-AA
team (they're called FCS now), and had gone just 4–7. But he had
coached under Coach Ford for eight seasons, so the Clemson people
knew him and liked him. He led us to a 14–13 win over Kentucky
in Peach Bowl. One of the good things about Coach West was that
Rick Stockstill was his best friend, and he was the coach who had
recruited me. So, Coach West knew about me when he showed up
on campus. I felt so bad for Coach Hatfield. While I wasn't a fan of
the offense, what he represented, how he modeled himself, how
he expected us to treat others with respect and class, was something I was used to. And we were winning. But the worst is when I
heard he was getting death threats at his home. That should NEVER
HAPPEN!!

◇◇◇

Starting that whole '93 season and being blessed to grab three
interceptions. I quickly became one of the leaders on the team, and
my confidence began to rise. I could even see myself separating from
my teammates, in terms of how quickly I could recognize things and
how quickly I could get to the ball. My ability to hit was always
there. I can finish through a guy, no matter the size. I was beginning
to excel in each part of my game.

Bringing in Coach West was like trying to relive the Ford days.
But we didn't have the talent we did under Ford. Those guys could
just run through the opponents. We couldn't. But my sophomore

year was good overall. Connie had transferred up from Jacksonville, and having her there with me was tremendous because it gave me a sense of peace. We were able to enjoy things together. We could hang out whenever we could get money, and eat and just hang out. After such a rough start, things were starting to come together on and off the field.

And the best was yet to come.

CHAPTER 5

Walking the Walk

I had been christened in the Catholic Church, and baptized in the Baptist Church. My father was Catholic, and my mother was Baptist, and as I have said, I chose to go to Mass every Sunday because it was shorter than the Baptist service. I received the Catholic Sacraments—Reconciliation, First Communion, Confirmation—but at that point I was young and hadn't yet accepted Christ into my life. I was taking part in the rituals, but it was more out of habit than of true belief. I wasn't living the way I should have been. Hadn't gotten the understating of what I needed, or the knowledge of how to do so.

When I met Connie, she went to a Holiness Church. Holiness was completely foreign to me. Those folks stay in church forever. There is a lot of foot-stomping and singing. When I went to Connie's church, it was the first time I saw the Holy Spirit's gifts in operation. People were speaking in tongues and getting caught up in the Spirit. I was sitting next to people who started shaking and shuddering, and I was thinking, "Whoa, what's wrong with this person?"

But it expanded my mind. I began to question how much I knew about Christ, yes, but also and most importantly, did I really know Him, and whether there was more out there for me to uncover. I became inquisitive. But I was still not ready, I felt. It wasn't until after practice one day during my junior year at Raines when Coach Stephens brought a pastor/motivational speaker out to talk to us, that I really moved toward knowing Christ. The pastor asked, "If you died today, where would you go? Do you know?" That's when I decided how I wanted to live my life. I wanted to know where I was going. I didn't want to guess. But I was still very hazy on the details.

I would actually accept Christ in my life at least three more times at different points in my life. Once in an FCA basketball summer trip. Someone I will never meet paid for me to go. It was like nothing I had ever experienced to that point. I learned about praying, "making time" to read the Word, meditating on what I read, and listening. It's the first time I truly journaled. These have now become disciplines in my life that I do daily. I also accepted Him in my life at a church in Clemson that Connie and I attended. I remember when the Pastor got going, he would squint one eye and bug the other out real big. Oh by the way, if you don't know this, it only takes one time to ask Christ in your life. Then it's a lifetime of getting to know Him and getting to truly know you...

Hearing that pastor was when I started going to Bible study at Raines. But I had to do it quietly, I felt, because how would my friends act towards me? They would have given me a hard time about it for sure, or so I convinced myself. There was a guy at Raines whom we called "Rev." He acted a lot older than we did, even though he was our age. He's a pastor now, and he would have Bible studies. It began to build on the foundation of my walk with Christ. A foundation that was mainly based on some knowledge I had gained from going to Sunday school and church, and from watching Saint Dawkins (my father's mother) live it. I would sometimes spend extended times at her peaceful house during the summer, when she would send me to vacation Bible camps or to the YMCA near her house. So I could learn and be in a safe environment to play, learn to swim and so much more. I accepted Christ into my life in 1990. This was my choice. It was not something my parents, Saint Dawkins, or anyone else forced me to do. I felt it. I wanted it. And it quickly became something that helped me in all facets of my life. No, things didn't all of a sudden become calm and easy. But I had begun a walk with the ultimate guide.

Things started happening all around me that I couldn't explain. On the field, I was recognizing things before they even happened. It was happening on a regular basis for me. I know a big part of it was the work I had been putting in. It was also due to my mind being a little clearer, thanks to my faith. My relationships with other people improved, and I was more thankful for them.

I was trying to change my voice. I wanted to be a more positive force for others. Part of that was stopping my cursing. Today. That's why "doggonit" has become one of the things I say all the time. I had asked the Lord to help me with my cursing. Because as I've learned in the Word, no man can tame the tongue. I was really praying hard, because I cursed a whole lot. My goodness, I cursed like a sailor, as the saying goes. A sailor that drove trucks on the side. That's how it was in my neighborhood. That's how we talked. I wanted my words to have real power, and to do that, I had to stop using bad language. It wasn't easy, but I worked hard on it. I didn't want to judge how other people spoke, because in my neighborhood and on the field, guys were going to curse. It wasn't the right thing for me, especially as I became closer to Christ.

If you spend a lot of time around me, you'll hear me say "doggo-nit" a lot. I still get upset, and I still want to use some words to let people know how serious I am about something, but I would rather have them feel it in my intensity than in my bad language. Again, I want you to not just hear what I say, I want you feel it! I wanted to also begin to expand my vocabulary I use to orate on what's going on with me. Thanks, Mr. Hooks.

So, my walk with Christ has been evident in my life as I look back on it. He's been working and maneuvering things in me, so that I can be the man I am today and be able to share these things with you. I can see his work throughout my walk with Him. When I was a sophomore at Clemson, the coaches moved Darnell Stephens to outside linebacker so that I could start at strong safety. Things have fallen into place for me at times, but it hasn't been easy. I want to share the struggles and the triumphs. Through it all, the Lord has been right there, by my side, whether I knew it or not. No matter how difficult things were or how much pain I had to overcome, I now know the Lord was right there with me, guiding me to the next success and helping me overcome obstacles. And once you know that, believe that, you can receive an unbelievable peace, in the midst of storms. Which are inevitable.

◇◇◇

If you consider the idea of football practice these days, even at the college and pro levels, you have to think about protecting the players from too much contact. In the NFL, the Players Union has negotiated restrictions on how much time players can practice, how often they can wear full pads, and when they're allowed to have full contact. The goal is to protect the players from injuries, especially concussions, which come from the game's violence. It's the same thing in college, high school, and youth ball. The object is to protect the players, yet help them condition themselves in a tough environment. To help them grow physically and mentally. Toughness does not come from being in a comfortable situation. It comes when you are put in an uncomfortable situation and you have to push yourself and others to greater things. Things that were already inside of you. It's just like how most of us get a deeper stretch when we allow others to push us past comfort and through the initial pain of stretching, past the point where we may be just fine staying. We take that deep breath and breathe through the initial pain, to achieve more flexibility. Flexibility that was always there, we just needed to be pushed to gain it. But having good people in our lives who know how far to push, and when to, is essential. Coaches are that for a lot of athletes. Especially for those without a strong male role model in their lives. Someone I was blessed to have.

When I was at Clemson, Coach West didn't have too much concern about contact. It was a different time, before people knew about what shots to the head can do to people, and before the idea that rest was a good thing for the body, rather than something that people who weren't tough tried to get. I remember going through an entire practice without water in high school. Cats were pushing and shoving during a water break, and a coach got mad and knocked over the cooler. Wasting all that liquid gold. That's what it looks like when you are living and practicing in Florida in the hotter months, and are so thirsty you feel like you have cotton in your mouth, as there is no moisture to be found. We were also told at times in Pop Warner that drinking water makes you soft. Before my junior year, the first year of the Coach West era, I believe he was trying to show that there was a new sheriff in town and he did things different.

He sure did. We had three-a-days. That's right. With full pads on the first and last, with half shell in the middle. I thought he was trying to kill us. The heat was brutal, and people were cramping up, losing weight. Left and right. IV's were being given out like candy at a kids' party.

Sapp and I could handle it. Some of my teammates later would tell me that I made it look easy. That was because I had survived Coach Hump. I kept telling myself that if I can survive Coach Hump, I can survive anything someone else throws at me. He couldn't break me, and that meant no one else could. My mind was made up. I had convinced myself of this. No way, Jack. So, I was usually the guy that helped other people out. Because I had developed this form of mental toughness, because I had gone through those basketball practices, I could handle three-a-days. To this day, I'm still able to help people who are struggling, even when I myself am finding my way through. I can look outside of my pain and look for the pain in other people's eyes, to help them. And offer support and inspiration that comes from the reservoir of my past failures and success stories. When this is a part of your mindset, you tend to get more energy when you help others. Try it for yourself. This is one of the ways I continue to live a victorious life.

Thanks to the lessons I learned from Coach Humphrey, as well as me pushing myself to outwork others during conditioning to show the coaches I should be playing something other than center, I was able to lead the way when it came to conditioning and work at practice. The coaches didn't have to tell me what to do when it came to running sprints and lifting. They just lined me up and let me go. I wasn't going to be a rah-rah type when it came to that. Instead, I would just do my thing, and the others could follow me if they liked. Yes, I would encourage my teammates when I saw the need, but not all the time. No one was going to outwork me, and the coaches loved that. Because of that, I got the reputation as someone who could go all day. It wasn't just physical toughness; I was mentally tough, too. No matter how hot it was or how much we were doing, I would not allow myself to be knocked back or stay defeated. I was going to take on the elements, the opponents, the coaches, and anybody who wanted to stop me from getting what I wanted.

Some people say I had a chip on my shoulder, but I would say that a chip was an understatement. I had that chip and the rest of the block, Jack. When you constantly have people doubting you from the time you start out, and when you hear that some people were saying, "He won't make it at Clemson," it can provide fuel, if you develop the right mindset. There were those who thought I would end up right back in Jacksonville, because I wouldn't get my work done in the classroom. People would tell me what I couldn't do, and I didn't like that. At all! They would say, "Yeah, you're good, but you're not as good as your brother." Or Pat Sapp, or Derrick Alexander, or Anthone Lott... the list went on and on. I would hear that stuff, not constantly, but I heard it enough, to the point where I was retaining it and holding onto it. I was going to show them. I was going to show everybody. I was going to be the silent assassin. So as you probably see, I had a good mindset to grow, but I was not handling it the best way. So I became a more pent-up angry cat inside. As I found out in Pop Warner that I could take my anger toward one person and use it on another, I wouldn't make a lot of noise off the field, but when I put on the pads, I was going to be a different guy. I was going to bring constant intensity to the field, the meeting rooms, the weight room, and the locker room. The haters were going to become my elevators. As a matter of fact, that is just what they became. Don't ever let someone's opinion of you define you! Thank you, haters!

Football was not fun and games for me. I wanted to reach a different level of work and training than my teammates did, so that they could see what it took to excel, and so the coaches would understand they could count on me. Even if that meant looking at others who have done it. Like Ronnie Lott and Darren Woodson. Or even someone out of the sport like Michael Jordan. Guys who went about leading in different ways. They lead by example in practice, meeting rooms, and in mentality. I would hear about stories of them coming to the aid of teammates, pushing them, being an example of effort to them, and so much more. I was going to get the most out of my ability, and anybody who wanted to join me was more than welcome.

At the big-time college level, there are a lot of players with talent. Many of the ones who make it furthest are those willing to put in the extra time and to understand that excellence is not guaranteed. And that's what gets you to a certain level, and will have to be tweaked if you are to continue to grow. You must be open to changes in order to grow past the ceiling. I was going to be first in every drill I could. I was going to be more physical than anybody else. It got to the point where some of the coaches were afraid I would hurt myself. Nobody has a say in what their God-given abilities are. However, they can control their work ethic and attitude. I was going to make sure of that. Because in doing so, I was exercising my gift from a place of humility, allowing me to fan my gift into a bigger flame, creating bigger and bigger gains to be displayed.

My junior year at Clemson wasn't all that good. We went 5–6 and lost to Florida State and South Carolina. That didn't make people too happy. We were trying to be bullies, and we didn't have "bully" personnel. It really felt like some were just trying to survive in games at times. We held eight teams under 20 points and four teams to 10 or fewer, but our offense had trouble finding its rhythm. We were able to hold our own on defense, just lining up and playing. We were going to come get you. We struggled on offense, in my humble opinion, because we wanted to play Bully Ball like in the days of Coach Ford, but we didn't have the right personnel for that. They fought and fought, but scores were few and far between. And frustration was a-bubbling.

Defensively, we would get out there and do the best we could, and after a while I would keep my eyes open to cats showing frustration. It was tough for Pat Sapp, because he was playing quarterback, and they benched him. They wanted to try a couple other quarterbacks, but that didn't work, either. They ended up moving him to linebacker for his senior year, and he still got drafted in the second round. That's how good an athlete he was. I had thought there was a chance I would leave school after my junior year for the NFL, but I didn't have the season I wanted, even though I had a good year. Even being blessed to make First Team All ACC. So, I came back for one more year.

But I had convinced myself that the major reason for my return was that I wasn't a "big safety" or an "ideal safety." Had I been 6'1", 215 pounds, I would have been looked at differently with my junior year stats. I made a lot of tackles, but I only had two interceptions. In my opinion, it was good enough. But a lot of pro scouts still looked at me as a tweener. They didn't know if I was a cornerback or a safety or a slot man. You know, someone that's actually capable of doing multiple things well. Even play down in the box if need be. A chess piece. Like I was blessed to do for sixteen years in the NFL. They wanted to see me play another year. So I came back to get a better draft spot, so that I could support my family better. And once again, to prove the doubters wrong.

My senior season was going to be a three-month job interview. An interview that I was mentally and physically ready to kill.

◇◇◇

While I tried to get my college football career heading toward a great finish, Connie was struggling. It was great that she had come to Clemson. Connie was really struggling financially, and I was doing everything I could to help her. Thanks to the meal plan I had as a member of the football team, I was able to bring home food for her from the training table. It was a very stressful time because I couldn't stand to see her in a needy situation. I did the best I could, but because I wasn't allowed to work—due to NCAA regulations—it was tough. For two years, she was the breadwinner. She had to get jobs to help with our rent and groceries. At one time she was working in a place where oil was prevalent, making drill chucks. She would come home exhausted. Another job was a night-time thing. I felt terrible. There were times we didn't see one another except for brief moments. Then she got laid off. Which meant that the extra money, which wasn't a whole lot, was no longer there. That's when the worrying really began for me. I developed ulcers because of it. We made do with what we had. We lived off ramen noodles, rice, chicken parts, and canned goods. She sacrificed so much, including school. So when WE made it into the NFL I told her, she wouldn't ever have to work another day, if she didn't want to.

We may not have had the easiest circumstances, but we were so strong together. And I was beginning to pay more attention to my prayer life. Going to Bible study at Clemson. I took part in Fellowship of Christian Athletes events. Connie and I went to church together Sunday mornings. My walk of faith was growing stronger, and I was trying my best to live a more centered life. I was already thankful, but I began to recognize more clearly some of the gifts I was receiving. Things were happening for me, and my senior year, things were taking off. But I was still holding back things in my heart. Pain, regrets and fears.

Before my junior year, Connie and I had eloped. It was one of the dumbest things and also one of the smartest things I did. I knew I was going to be with her for the rest of my life, I knew that back in high school when she smiled at me in high school and stuck out her tongue as I jogged past her trying to make it to my class on time. But I had no plans and nothing in place for our future. We went to the Justice of the Peace in Jacksonville, and we were married there.

Connie's grandfather gave us $100 for the rings. We spent $49 on mine and the rest on hers. We still have them in a safe. The only two people who knew we were getting married were her grandfather and Pat. He drove us back to the justice of the peace for the wedding. He had a two-door car called "Blue Baby" which was an old model and had an exhaust problem. Our eyes would be burning from the smoke that came inside the car. We just kept putting Visine in our eyes to try to survive. Passengers were afraid to go to sleep because they thought they might die from the carbon monoxide. It was crazy.

Before Pat got his car, during my freshman year, we used to drive home with Jamie Trimble, who was our center. He had a hatchback, a two-seater. He and Pat would sit in the two seats, and I would lie in the hatch—there wasn't a back seat—with all the laundry and gear. I would travel from Clemson to Jacksonville lying down. But I wanted to get home so I could see Connie. It was dangerous and stupid, but one does strange things when he is in love.

When we eloped, my mom and dad were pretty good with it. They could sense I was extremely serious about Connie, because I was with her all the time. She was around the house so often, it was almost like she was another daughter to them. They figured it was going to happen. They just didn't want us to do it that way. Her dad was an angry and protective cat at the time, and he wasn't happy. Connie called him and said, "We eloped," and hung up the phone. She didn't want to get a tongue-lashing from him. That's basically how we did it. Knowing what I know now, I would have done things different. Like asking him for his daughter's hand in marriage only after I had a job, and had the capability to support Connie and my family. I was supposed to have everything in place before I talked to her father and asked for her hand in marriage. So in other words, we would not have gotten married in college.

That's what I will want for my daughters, and I will make it crystal clear in the conversations I have with them leading up to that moment. But we were young and foolish and didn't really know a whole lot. We didn't have a whole lot going on. We spent the summer on the pullout couch at Darnell Stephens' apartment after our marriage. We were really good friends with him and his wife, and he helped us out until the fall, when we were able to get our own apartment.

That summer, I was working 24-hour shifts on weekends at a plant. During the week I would take classes and work out with the team, but the weekends were mine. So, I made sparkplugs for airplanes at a factory. I would start working Friday night, and worked as many hours as I could until Sunday. I would take little breaks here and there, but it was tough, really tough.

My parents didn't make a lot of money, so they couldn't give us much. Connie was working and trying to go to school, and once the football season started, I couldn't work. So, we had to stretch every penny we made. We ate chicken all the time and a lot of ramen noodles. It didn't cost a lot of money to fill up our freezer with chicken, so we would head to the supermarket in Anderson, the next town over from Clemson, and buy as much as we could. We would get some canned foods and try to make do.

It was extremely stressful, and those ever-worsening ulcers my senior year were no joke. Connie couldn't go to school, and when she got pregnant with Brian Jr., she had to stop working. My goal was to finish the season, graduate after the fall semester and then get started with whatever team drafted me. A lot of people think college football players have it easy, but there are a lot of things going on that they don't know about.

Our difficulties off the field didn't mean I could take it easy at all in my workouts or during practice. It was time to get ready for the NFL.

◇◇◇

Three interceptions in a game are great. Three in a quarter are pretty amazing. But I should have had four.

It was Senior Day 1995, and we were in the midst of beating Duke, 34–17. I was blessed to pick off three passes in the second quarter, which is still a school record. It was one of those games where I was totally locked in, seeing things before they happened. But I should have had a fourth interception. I dropped one in the end zone. Right in my hands. When people say how great it was that I had three, I tell them I should have had four. They think I'm crazy, but that's the way I look at it.

We had a strong defense that year. Only three opponents scored more than 20 points against us in the regular season, when we went 8–3. We lost to Florida State, but we beat South Carolina. I was blessed to earn first-team All-ACC and second-team All-America honors. It was a great end to my Clemson career. Well, except for the bowl game. We played Syracuse in the Gator Bowl in Jacksonville, and in front of my friends and family, we got clobbered, 41–0. Some guy named Donovan McNabb threw for 309 yards and three touchdowns against us. It was raining, and we fell behind 20–0. Talk about a bad way to go out. But like I always say jokingly when he brings that up, I had good game.

But I had grown a lot during my time at Clemson, both on and off the field. I had gone from the guy who wasn't even recruited, the player who needed his friend to get him a scholarship, to an All-America player who intercepted six passes his last season. A guy who was blessed to come to Clemson running a 4.53, and worked his butt off to be blessed to run a 4.34 inside right before his senior year began. And a 4.41 on grass at the Pro Day at Clemson after my senior year. I still wasn't the "perfect size" to be a safety in some folks' minds, but I had proven to many in the college game—and, it turns out, to some NFL scouts—that I could play at a high level. One in particular, who saw something in me, way back then. As it turns out, all it really takes is for ONE to believe in you. That's all, ONE! What everybody else thinks or says, can be null and void. Or used as fuel.

I had become a much more confident person. I'd learned how to lead and to be a better teammate. Still, I wasn't all that comfortable speaking up in front of other people, but I was getting better. One of the best things I did was take a public speaking course. It taught me how to stand up in front of people and get them to be completely dialed in to what I was talking about, and anxious to hear what I had to say next. Anybody who watched my Hall of Fame speech knows that I have become much more at ease speaking in public.

At the end of the semester in that class, I had to do a project on someone who inspired me, and I chose Bob Marley. I respected the principles he lived by: love, positive vibes and the fight for justice. But I was most impressed by how he treated people. He did unto others as he would have had done unto him. That's the life he lived. He didn't care if someone was a senator or a dishwasher, he was going to inspire that person and help him or her along the way if he could. He was intent on sending positive vibrations by his music, his life, and his massages. So I did my project on him. And I'm so happy I did.

What I did was play music at the beginning and music at the end, and I gave my speech in the middle. This is of course before all the tech of today. so I had to time myself and put the music on a tape that played the entire time, with the music only being recorded at the beginning and at the end. If I spoke too fast, the music would come on too late at the end. If I spoke too slowly, the music would come on too early. It was perfect. I was so hyped. Focused in, yet so calm, and enjoyed every minute of it. I rehearsed that speech forever, and then I asked the professor if I could deliver it with a

Jamaican accent. I love reggae, and I can hold my own speaking in Jamaican tongue or dialect, until I would speak to "a couple of mi friend dem, born ah yard" (my friends born in Jamaica), that played on the soccer team. The way that flowed brought me comedically back down to earth. I'm not perfect, like someone who lives there, but I felt comfortable doing that. I didn't stutter, stumble or fumble. If I did, I would have messed up the music.

In the speech, I talked about how Bob lived, what the Jamaican people went through and the pain that he suffered. Being born the son of an older white man who didn't want anything to do with him and a young black girl, doing all she could to raise him. How he and his brethren used their gifts of music to champion a cause. Something that would not only bless Jamaica, but the entire world. How he rose from nothing to be one of Jamaica's—and the world's for that matter—most inspirational people. To this day, his music and the powerful messages in it, are not only still relevant, but alive today. POSITIVE VIBRATION MON. "One good thing about music, when it hits you, you feel no pain." (Bob Marley)

And just as I finished, the music came back on, and I got a huge ovation. The other students were smiling and so jacked up. The professor gave me an A-plus. It was great to get the good grade, but it was even better to learn that I could use my voice to inspire and captivate people. I understood the hard work that went into it and the passion that I had. That speech made me feel more comfortable speaking in front of people, and it led me to improve the way I spoke. I wanted to enhance the gift that the Lord had given me. And no, at the time I didn't know it was a gift, I thought that it was normal. But I now know better than that. I have been blessed to speak into the lives of people. My voice, combined with my passion, allows many to feel what I am saying.

Where I grew up, there is a certain way that we use the language. Parts of words are completely sliced off. Others are put together in interesting ways. I'd say I am "fixin' to go to dah store." I wouldn't pronounce my "th" sounds. I'd say "dese and dose," instead of "these and those." For some, they might say there isn't anything really wrong with it, but I noticed in more professional settings, in order to be able to captivate an audience, I must be able to speak so my audience can understand with clarity what I am saying to them. It's not so much about using big words or sounding intellectually astute, as it is about speaking with simple clarity. You won't be able to feel my words if you can't understand them. I have to use the language in a way that my audience can digest. That way, people can be focused on my point, rather than how I am saying things. The ability to communicate, orate and read your audience that way is huge, in my opinion.

I probably should have majored in Communications. Instead, I got my degree in Industrial Education and Human Resource Development, in three and a half years. That was in large part because of Coach Black, who had tutored me at Raines and taught shop. And what do I do now? Human resource development. I help inspire people to do bigger and better things. Some might say that's a life coach. They wouldn't be wrong. Some might say Minister, and they wouldn't be wrong. The same goes for encourager, teacher and counselor. No, I do not have a certificate or a title. Yet I've been blessed to do far more than what my degree says. If life is teaching, which it is, I'm listening, learning, and giving. I want them to see more inside themselves than they already see. I want them to find themselves. Not the person that they think they should be. But the one that the Lord has put them on earth to be. You see, you are more than your mistakes. You are more than where you grew up, more than what has happened to you. What you have inside you is worth the fight!

◇◇◇

When I was invited to the Senior Bowl in Mobile, I brought two pairs of shoulder pads with me. During the hitting drills, I wore the big boy pads. When it came time to run and cover, I put on the smaller version. I needed to show the pros I could hit, which I think they knew, but also that I could cover just as well.

There were a couple different All-Star games when I was playing college ball, but the most important one for me was the Senior Bowl. The teams were coached by NFL staffs, and all the scouts, GMs and personnel executives come to watch the players. They show the game on TV, but the most important part of the process is the week of practice. In fact, a lot of the people who evaluate talent leave on Thursday, so the most important work is done during the workouts. I was blessed to not only have the opportunity to play in the game and go through the interviews. I was blessed to come full circle when I was blessed to be an Executive of the Philadelphia Eagles for the 2014-2016 seasons. I've been blessed to see both sides of this hectic coin. What a blessing indeed.

I did well. I didn't give up much of anything in passing drills, and I showed I could run. I guess folks still didn't realize that I could do just about everything: hit, run and cover. The problem was that I wasn't big enough to look like a "real NFL safety." Yep, I know I've said this or versions of it many times already. Well, I'm going to be saying more times going forward. I want you to get as sick as I was from hearing it! I was a tweener. The teams wanted Kenny Easley, who played ball at UCLA, spent seven years with Seattle and was 6'3", 206. That's a safety. Scouts were saying, "We don't know if you can do it." When I went to the Senior Bowl, I knew I had to prove myself—again. I led the team in tackles, and I was kind of upset I didn't get the MVP award. I even played special teams and blew up a couple returners, running full speed. They even tried to double-team me on punts, in an ALL-STAR GAME! They didn't want me getting downfield. Didn't work.

That goes back again to my tenacity. I'm going to show you that I am better than you thought I was. Another philosophy I live by, give more than is expected. You have pegged me in your mind a certain way, and I'm going to show you that you are wrong, that I am much more than you thought I was. I think I did that in the Senior Bowl for a couple teams.

The Scouting Combine in Indianapolis did not go quite so well. I tried to put on weight beforehand to show that I wasn't too light to play safety, but I just couldn't do it. When it came time to run the 40-yard dash, I only ran a 4.5. My fastest to that point had been a 4.34, so I didn't show who I was and how fast I could run. When scouts came later on to work me out at Clemson, I ran a 4.41 on grass, so I was able to answer some questions. A 4.5 is pretty good, but that wasn't me. I felt I killed the other drills, and that was a good thing. It further verified what I had shown I could do on the football field.

That was one of the things that drew the Eagles to me. Emmitt Thomas, who was the defensive coordinator under Ray Rhodes at the time, thought I showed great leadership at the Combine. John Wooten, who was the Eagles' Vice President of Player Personnel, told Emmitt to watch me in Indianapolis. Mr. Wooten liked what he had seen of me, and he wanted to make sure his eye was true. Once he and Emmitt agreed, the Eagles went about trying to hide from everyone in the league the fact that they liked me.

Mr. Wooten was an NFL legend, thanks to his resumé as a player and a coach. He was a guard for the Browns from 1958-67 and for Washington in '68. He played in the Pro Bowl two times and was a member of Cleveland's 1964 NFL title team. After a brief career as a sports agent, he spent 17 years as Director of Pro Scouting for Dallas. He came to Philadelphia in 1992 to run the personnel department and stayed until '98. He finished his career with the Ravens. Mr. Wooten was the first NFL executive to believe in me. He is also an activist who stood side by side with the likes of Dr. Martin Luther King, Muhammad Ali, Bill Russell, Jim Brown and Kareem Abdul-Jabbar as they fought for the rights of minorities. He co-founded The Fritz Pollard Alliance, and he was very influential in the idea of the Rooney Rule and getting it adopted.

Others took a look. He brought me to Philadelphia.

Another man who had faith in me was Dick Daniels. He spent six years (1966-71) as defensive back with Dallas and the Bears and joined the Eagles in 1996 as Director of Football Operations. He spent the '97 season as the team's GM. I owe a lot to both of them for believing that I could be the player I became.

Emmitt and Ray didn't attend my Pro Day at Clemson, when I worked out for teams and was blessed to run the 4.41 40-yard dash. They sent Danny Smith, their special teams and defensive backs coach. NFL people get paranoid when they think they have found someone that others have missed. There was no social media back then, so the Eagles thought they could steal me. They didn't talk about me. They didn't mention me to the media. They didn't even interview me in person. So, I had no idea they had any interest in me. Meanwhile, they were out telling free agents they were going to take me. When they were recruiting cornerback Troy Vincent to sign with them, they said that having him, (cornerback) Bobby Taylor and me in the defensive backfield would help them beat Dallas. Troy said that Emmitt even called me a "little juggernaut." Emmitt told Troy I could be a special player once they got me under control.

The only team that came to visit was Kansas City. Defensive backs coach Kurt Schottenheimer came to Clemson and took me and Connie out to dinner. I thought they were very interested, but that could have been naiveté on my part. The thing that still bothers me about that is that they chose two safeties before me. Not one, TWO: Jerome Woods from Memphis and Reggie Tongue from Oregon State. It's one thing if you take someone at another position ahead of me. I'm cool with that. But you took people at my position? That means you're telling me you thought those dudes were better than me? Okay, I got you. Once again, logs for the fire. I couldn't wait to get out there and play.

Back in 1996, the NFL Draft lasted only two days. Since 2010, it has covered three days, with the first round Thursday night, the next two on Friday and the final three on Saturday. In '96, the first three rounds were on Saturday, April 20. My mom and dad threw a little party at the house in Jacksonville, and we had some close friends and family there.

It was very nerve-wracking sitting through all those picks in the first round. Once it got past Kansas City, which had the 28th pick (out of 30), and they didn't pick me, I had to go outside. I had to get out. I stood out there, dribbling the basketball, because I didn't know where I was going to go at that point. I was really stewing. Not only had Kansas City passed on me, the Chiefs had also taken a safety. A free safety. My position.

So, I stood out there pounding the basketball, trying to keep my mind off things. Then, the second round started. Pick after pick. The Eagles had the 54th pick in the Draft, and they took Jason Dunn, a tight end from Eastern Kentucky. Kansas City came up at 58 and chose Tongue, a strong safety. Another safety. I was hot. Hot as fish grease and grits this time. There was one compensatory pick in the Draft, and the Eagles had it. That's the one they used to take me. So, I was the last pick in the second round. People were telling me I should be happy to be chosen at all, much less in the second round. I took it as if I were the first pick of the third round, which is nothing to sneeze at, but I would have easily been in the first round, had I been "ideal.

I had gone from potentially the first round, from the impression I received from Kansas City, to the top of the third, because of my size. Jerome Woods, 6'3", 205, and Reggie Tongue, 6'0", 204. I was 5'11", 188. People didn't think I could do it. Once again, I was overlooked. Altogether there were four safeties before me. Even Pat Sapp, who spent one year at LB, went before me. Was and still am thrilled for him. At the time, I saw all that happen like a spicy gumbo before my eyes—I was seeing red. Twenty-nine other teams (there were only thirty in the NFL at the time) passed on me, twice the way I looked at it. I was going to show them they were wrong. That was my mindset when I went to training camp.

And I wanted to get to training camp as quickly as I could. I had finished my degree work during the first term, but I didn't walk during graduation. I just called the Eagles and said, "I'll be up as soon as I can get there." It was time to go to work. Looking back, not walking in graduation was another thing I now regret.

CHAPTER 6

Welcome to Philadelphia

As soon as the Eagles drafted me, I was ready to start working. I was extremely nervous, but I wanted to prove everybody who passed on me in the draft was wrong, prove to the Eagles that they got it right, and the best way to do that was to get to Philadelphia and start training ASAP. There was only one small issue for this cat from Florida. The fans, you ask? Nope.

The green. LOL.

Orange had been cool at Clemson, because I wanted to be a Florida Gator, and their colors were orange and blue. Highlands Junior High colors were the same, so I was used to putting orange on.

But those Eagles uniforms were tough. Yes, tough, because of the dudes that were rocking it. But it was something I would have to get used to. It wasn't so much the green, I could make that work. It was those socks with the two stripes. That was just killing me. How could I make that look sweet? How could I make that look smooth? It was going to be a challenge.

I decided I was going to wear the uniform with pride, whatever color it was. That I was going to engulf myself with whatever Philly had to offer. That meant that this Florida boy was also going to have to get used to the cold. The bitter, breathtaking cold. I would have to come to know what an ice scraper was. How *not* to get ice off your windshield. That you had to get up earlier than normal when it snowed, to dig your car out of the snow. I would have to learn what "jawn" meant. And all the wonderful ways it can be used. I would have to learn what ordering a cheesesteak "with" meant. I would come to learn what "youse" meant, and so much more. The good news was the team went from the Kelly green to the midnight green in 1996, just in time for me to put it on. The socks became all green. No more stripes. That was good news. But it took a few years before the socks matched the green on the jersey.

One of the other good things about the Eagles at that time was that the head coach and the defensive coordinator were both African-Americans. That took me back home, to be honest with you. When pretty much every coach that I had was African American. I had learned to be coachable, because of my father, yet there was something about having men that look like me, that really touched something deep inside of me. To see that African Americans can not only have success on the field but also be leaders as coaches and front office personnel. Which was an extremely powerful thing for a brown-eyed ebony young man, far, far away from home, to see. To not only see, but feel. And that's something I've been blessed to learn over the years: we are more likely to remember something that has a strong emotion attached to it. There were many more in prominent roles, including Mr. John Wooten, Director of College Scouting, and Mr. Dick Daniels, Director of Football Operations. Each one of them taught me things that I will never forget. And I'll always be thankful for. When I looked at them, I saw my dad, an uncle... I saw me! They were truly like uncles to me, and they quickly named me "Baby Boy."

Ray Rhodes had played seven years in the NFL as a wide receiver and defensive back for the Giants and San Francisco. Once he started coaching, in 1981, he began to build a tremendous reputation. Ray worked for the Niners from 1981–91, a period when they won four Super Bowls. From '89-94, he was a defensive coordinator for San Francisco (two different stints) and Green Bay, and he was recognized as one of the game's best strategists on that side of the ball. After the '94 season, when the 49ers won their fifth Super Bowl, the Eagles hired Ray, making him the league's second African-American coach—Minnesota's Dennis Green was the other—and only the fourth in NFL history. (Fritz Pollard and Art Shell were the other two.) The Eagles had offered the job to Dick Vermeil, but he turned it down and remained out of coaching until 1997 when he took over the Rams. Ray had won the NFL Coach of the Year award in 1995, his first season, because he led the Eagles to a 10–6 record, and to the playoffs after the team started the year 1–3. They had gone 7–9 in '94.

He was a tough guy who was brutally honest with his players. His Saturday night speeches were freakin' unbelievable. Coaches usually give their motivational talks the night before the game, so that they can give you something to think about as you get prepared. Ray's were almost like comedy routines that also got you very hyped. I remember one, before the Dallas game at the Vet my second year. He began by telling us all the things the papers had said about us and how they didn't know what they were talking about. They said the Cowboys were going to come here and kick our butts.

Then, he told us that the Cowboys wanted to come into our house, go to the bathroom on our new, expensive Persian rug and then clean themselves up with the fancy drapes hanging next to our windows. And not only that—and this is where he would get especially graphic—I choose not to add. Some of us were laughing. At one point, I looked over at Emmitt, and he had his head in his hand, just shaking his head, cracking up. But Ray was so passionate and worked up that he got us going, too. And you have to remember that this was a football team, and that the atmosphere in the locker room wasn't exactly suited for the church choir.

Ray and Emmitt got after me. Emmitt didn't let me settle for anything less than great. I have been blessed that throughout my life I have had people who have seen things inside me and have helped me bring them out. Emmitt was one of them. Emmitt knew all about overcoming obstacles. He went to Bishop College, an Historically Black College in Dallas that closed in 1988. Nobody drafted him in 1966, and Emmitt signed on with the Chiefs. He is still the team's all-time interception leader, and he was part of the Kansas City team that whipped the Vikings, 23–7, in Super Bowl IV—the last game before the old American Football League merged with the NFL. Emmitt had an interception in that game and he was elected to the Pro Football Hall of Fame in 2008. Even though he's seventy-five years old, Emmitt was still coaching, scouting and mentoring for the Chiefs till 2018. He was a legendary player, an outstanding coach and one of my most important mentors. I am proud to call him "Uncle Emmitt." He had that much of an impact on me.

It goes back to that teacher who made me do the Martin Luther King speech. I didn't know that I could do that, but the teacher who chose me to do it did know. Emmitt saw the player I could be, the Hall of Famer. I was just trying to make the team and do the best I could. I wanted to win a job and maybe be a starter. To be honest with you, I just wanted to survive my rookie year. Emmitt pushed me hard and held me accountable at all times. That was vital, because it is important to have accountability partners, people who will make sure you always do your best. He was an honest voice, but he also cared. So, when he chewed me out, I didn't think he was being nasty. He wanted me to be the best I could be. That's why I look at him with such respect and love.

If I made a good play, Emmitt said I should have made a better play. I could be doing more, and he knew that. So, he made sure I knew it. Back then, there weren't OTAs; you just worked out with the team. So, I was up at the stadium, working out and trying to learn the defense. And I was surprised by the facilities the Eagles had, and how much worse they were than what we had at Clemson.

Mr. Wooten would teach me something that I will never forget. I was at the back of an elevator with a few players, executives and the like. We were headed upstairs to the cafeteria to see what was edible. The elevator wasn't all the way full, and it stopped for a few more of my rookie classmates to get on. One was a happy-go-lucky, funny, country and extremely loud cat, who was Black. He saw me in the back and said, very loud, "That's Dawk! That's my N– – – – – r right there!" Not only that, he reached over and between folk to give me dap. As I said, there was a mix of players and executives in there. Some were my white brothers. I put my head down as I gave him dap in full-fledged embarrassment.

When we got to the final stop, Mr. Wooten told me and the other players to stay on. He then said the following: "I don't understand why you young folk use that word. It is one of the ugliest words there is. Do you know why they used it? To dehumanize your ancestors. Do you not understand or care that the last thing your ancestors heard before they were lynched, burned alive, drug behind a vehicle till they died, was that very word?" He went on to say some other things, but this is what hit me the hardest. When I allowed my mind's eye to think on what he had just said. And as I did with cursing, I decided to change that bad habit. I chose to use other words, because I can. It meant enough to me not to use a word that derived from so much hate and evil. Emotion and knowledge hit me at the same time. So I will choose to remember this till I leave this earth. Thank you, Mr. Wooten.

The weight room was like a box. It was about 15 to 20 feet by 15 to 20 feet. My goodness. And the locker room was rugged. The smells in the hallway were awful, because of the trash that was transported back and forth. There were cats in the ceilings. There were rats. It was bad. The meeting rooms were separated by these sliding doors, but you could still hear one coach yelling at his players in the other room, while you were trying to concentrate in your meeting. That's the first thing I recognized when I came to Philadelphia. Their facilities weren't nearly as good as what we had at Clemson. My learning curve in the NFL was going to be steep, and as I learned from the moment I joined the Eagles, it wasn't going to be comfortable, either. This was a whole new world.

◇◇◇

When teams have mini-camps today, they don't feature much contact. There may be a bit of hitting during drills, but the players aren't in full pads. We had much more physical mini-camps, and I pulled a hamstring early in my first mini-camp because I was still adjusting to how the practices were being run. It wasn't anything serious, and I was certainly ready to go full steam during training camp.

My first training camp sent me back to those Pop Warner days. In Pop Warner, we used to run a tackling drill, in which one player would stand with his arms out like they were forming the shape of a T, and another would run five or ten yards at him and hit him. It was crazy because you couldn't protect yourself, and the other guy could just run through you. In training camp, there were a lot of drills to get us ready for the contact and the collisions. Most of the time, we had two-a-days, in full pads, and there were a lot of drills where we would tackle to the ground. It was six weeks, away from home. It was brutal. But a part of me loved it.

I was all right with the physical nature of the practices, but it was hot, and we were working so hard that I couldn't keep weight on. I came to Philadelphia at about 188 pounds, and I wanted to get to 192. But in camp, I was dipping down to 180 or 182. And then there was the anxiety of trying to learn the playbook, because there were a lot of checks and calls we had to make before the ball was snapped. I was drafted in the second round, and people expected me to be a starter, so there was pressure on me to know what to do. And most importantly at that time, being a rookie, I didn't know how to study and I did not know how I learned best yet.

Emmitt wanted to get me on the field quickly, so he was always challenging me. All I knew was that I felt like I couldn't do anything right. That was extremely frustrating. On top of all of that, Connie had moved up with me, and she was pregnant. I was trying to make sure she was settled. It was a lot to deal with.

The veterans didn't do any physical hazing with me. It was more that they wouldn't let me go certain places. If they were there, they didn't want rookies around. That was all right with me. I just hung around with the other rookies, my classmates so to speak, until I could gain the respect of the older cats. But I quickly earned that, because of the way I practiced, how hard I worked and my willingness to strike fools.

There was a lot of anxiety. When I was at Clemson, it was the first time I was away from home, and I didn't know what to expect. I didn't know whether the team wanted me or the coaches liked me. They threw a lot of stuff at us, and it was difficult. It was kind of the same way with the Eagles. When I got to the NFL level, I heard all about the fans, the speed of the game, how much bigger the players were than those in college. I was wondering whether I could do everything. I had confidence, but there was a voice in the back of my head asking, "Can you actually do this?" I remember having some doubts about it. The good thing was that the other rookies, the guys in my "class," had a lot of the same feelings, so we could talk about them and laugh about things. I gravitated toward a couple of players in particular. Ray Farmer was a defensive back from Duke, and Tristan Moss was my roommate during training camp. He was a defensive back from Western Michigan—he ended up playing in the World League of American Football and the Arena League.

It also helped that one of the veterans, William Thomas, let me hang around him. "Willie T" had joined the team in 1991 and was a Pro Bowler in 1995, and I just started to cling to him. He helped me understand what was going on and how to deal with it all. I sure needed that. And Irving Fryar and Mark Woodard helped me a lot too. Irving was entering his thirteenth season and was still playing at a Pro Bowl level. He was also a Christian man who had fallen and gotten back up, becoming a Reverend in the process. He would give me a couple of extremely powerful things. The first thing was a vision of what I could do late in my career. Next, he told me "Rook… if you take care of your body now, it will take care of you later." Lastly, I saw in him a Christian man in my sport living respectfully, out loud with his faith in Jesus Christ, and killing it on the field with a vengeance. Mark Woodard was a second-year linebacker from Mississippi State, who would help me tremendously with my walk with the Lord by inviting me and Connie to spend time with him and his wife Deidre. As well as inviting us to attend their church and Bible study. Which would help me tremendously later on.

Everybody thinks that as soon as a football player makes it to the NFL, his financial worries are over forever. That certainly wasn't the case for me. In fact when I reached Philadelphia, my money problems were just beginning. My first contract paid me $750,000 for the first year, and after taxes and agent fees, I had about $400,000 left to work with. Yes, that's a lot of money, but there were a lot of people looking for some of it. I wanted to help members of my family out, but Connie and I had to get a place to live and set ourselves up. We found a townhome in Cherry Hill, NJ, near Woodcrest Country Club, and that was nice. But we needed to buy winter clothes.

We had to buy furniture and things for the baby. I had to get Connie a reliable car, so I bought her a Toyota 4Runner, because that was a bigger car. After I signed with my agent, Jim Steiner, I had bought myself a BMW convertible, which didn't make much sense, with a baby coming. I had to trade that in and get something else. Dummy.

We wanted to start building a nest egg, but some in my family knew that I had signed the contract, and needed and wanted help. They were definitely suffering in some areas, and we tried to help, but I couldn't keep giving them money to the level that I was doing. Being young and having money for the first time, I didn't fully understand how to save the money, because it was flying out of the bank account. I knew we couldn't continue the way we were going. Which soon became an issue. One of the biggest issues that come up for many rookies in sports, is money and family. I was a rookie and it was my turn to go through it.

There was a lot of pressure throughout the first season. I was disagreeing with some members of my family on finances. Meanwhile, I'm trying to learn how to be an NFL player. Little Brian Jr. had what seemed like colic, so nobody was sleeping. And we were still young newlyweds, trying to figure out how to be married and be parents. Everything was thrown into a big blender. It was turbulent, and It took a huge toll on both of us.

I was being ripped apart spiritually. I was being ripped apart mentally. I was getting pulled on the field. Pulled by family. Pulled by Connie and young Brian. At practice, Emmitt was really pushing me to learn the position so that I could play. I didn't want to make a mistake, because I didn't want the veteran players to get mad at me. When I came home, Brian Jr. was up every couple hours crying, so I wasn't getting rest. My family was calling. I had no idea what to do. And that's when the depression started to kick in.

I was basically walking around with a mask on, pretending nothing was wrong, pretending I was just fine. There was nobody I could talk to about this, or so I convinced myself, so it was eating me away from the inside. I started to drink a lot. I was a Corona guy. I drank some fancy beer at times, and when I was in college, it was the cheap stuff. But I also was drinking shots of whiskey and vodka and the hard stuff. When I got home, I was angry. I punched a wall once. I ran my head through it another time. It was a brutal time.

After I ran my head through the wall, Connie called Emmitt. And he said to me, "Baby Boy, you have to get some help with this." That wasn't easy for me to do, either, and I wouldn't have done it if they hadn't heavily and lovingly encouraged me to. I can only speak from where I'm from, and when you come from a black neighborhood, you don't tell your problems to someone else. It's not anything you ever heard about. People call psychiatrists "shrinks" and other names, but they aren't called "people who can help you." You don't go to your church. You don't go to your pastor. You don't go to anybody for help. What I perceived In my neighborhood was, you don't talk about your feelings. You're taught early on to "suck it up," "rub some dirt on it" and to "stop crying." "What goes on in this house, stays in this house." While I understand the premise, if something really bad happens, you're then telling kids that they have to deal with their pain, by themselves. Which is a recipe for a disaster, sooner or later. There are people in their adult lives that still have not learned to open up about things that happened in their homes as kids. And that pain causes many problems in this walk of life. Depression being a major problem that is plaguing the world!

When I started talking with the doctor, he told me to do things that I kind of already knew I should be doing, like talking things out with people and forgiving others. I had read it in the Bible, but I wasn't applying the words. I was being a hearer but not a doer. He was basically telling me Biblical stuff, just using other words to do it. He told me I needed to talk to people and be more open about things, which wasn't easy for me, because I had convinced myself by then that I was a shy person to begin with. But it helped. I was able to communicate with Connie a little better, even though it was still tough to show emotion and give away emotion. And he helped me deal with my anger. But I had a long way to go yet.

I had been going down a dark path, and that's a lonely place. It's a dark, lonely, demented place. I had been thinking about how to kill myself in a way that would allow Connie to get the insurance money. A lot of companies don't pay the beneficiaries if someone commits suicide within two years of taking out the policy. I began to take medication that helped me move away from the suicidal thoughts I was having. I believe the medication brought me down off that emotional "fight or flight" cycle I was constantly living in, and allowed me to think. It allowed me to focus on my thinking—to focus on how I could actually change my thinking. These were the beginning phases that led to where I am today. Trying to be aware of every thought that does not correspond with what could be positive outcomes. Or as the Bible says:

"We are destroying sophisticated arguments and every exalted and proud thing that sets itself up against the [true] knowledge of God. And we are taking every thought and purpose captive to the obedience of Christ." 2 Corinthians 10:5 (AMP)

Taking the medicine numbed me to "stinkin' thinkin'," but it numbed me in a lot of other ways, too. I didn't like that feeling. As a matter of fact, I hated it. It wasn't me. But what it did was pause me just enough to help me find another way to handle my anger and depression. The Word of God. Those seeds of faith that lay dormant inside me could finally get that living water. I quit the medication cold turkey, which you aren't supposed to do, but I was feeling like a zombie. Most importantly, I turned heavily to the Bible. Reading, studying for answers, journaling, listening and praying more consistently than I ever had till that point. I went cold turkey on the music I listened to as well. I did that for about a year. Then after that, I just couldn't go back to some of the vulgar things in it. I no longer felt comfortable listening to them. Since then it's 100% Gospel or Jazz.

It was then that I made the final decision to walk with the Lord consistently and live by the word. Since that time, my faith has increased exponentially. I started to seek Him as fully as I knew possible. I was influenced by the Bible story of Ananias and Sapphira, a married couple who lived during the earliest days of the Church, when all possessions of members were communal and those who gave away their wealth to the Church were praised by other members. Many who did that, like Barnabas, were not looking for the acclaim. They just wanted to help the Church. But Ananias and Sapphira wanted to be congratulated for their gesture, so they sold a piece of property and gave the Apostles—who were the leaders of the Church at the time—part of the sale's proceeds, while holding some back for themselves. They didn't necessarily say they were giving all the money they had made, but they gave that impression and were happy to receive the praise and status within the community that brought.

But Peter was able to figure out their scheme. When he confronted Ananias and said that he had not lied to men but to God, Ananias died instantly. Soon thereafter, Sapphira came to Peter and refused to be completely honest. She, too, died on the spot. Their sins of pride and self-importance were their downfalls. I made an oath to God to give away some things that I really enjoyed, if He would take that depression away, especially those suicidal thoughts. I wouldn't hold anything back like Ananias and Sapphira did. Or in my case, engage in certain things for personal pleasure again.

I decided to stop wearing an earring, because that was a sign of vanity for me. I thought it made me look good, so I stopped wearing it. I said I wasn't going to drink beer or the hard liquor I was drinking ever again. I will have a glass of wine with dinner on occasion, but I haven't had a drop of beer, or what I deem hard liquor, since that moment. I told the Lord I was going to walk his path completely. And by giving up some of those things, I believed he would reveal himself more to me. He did. Things weren't perfect, but because I was learning to talk about my feelings, and because I was walking closer to the Lord, I became stronger. And I do understand when it's all said and done, that oath was for me. When I give my word, I'm going to keep it. He gave me a better understanding on how and what to meditate on.

Finally, believers, whatever is true, whatever is honorable, and worthy of respect, whatever is right and confirmed by God's Word, whatever is pure and wholesome, whatever is lovely, and brings peace, whatever is admirable and of good repute; if there is any excellence, if there is anything worthy of praise, think on these things [center your mind on them, and implant them in your heart]. – Philippians 4:8 (AMP)

By confronting all of this and learning how to deal with it, I was able to help other people later in my life. If you haven't gone through something, it's hard to understand what it's like for other people who are facing it, to truly have empathy. Now, it's a lot easier for me to have empathy for those who are struggling with problems. I know what my version of being in a dark place feels like, and your place may be even worse than mine. By having experienced that, I can share that with other people. I can talk about what I felt and the panic in my mind. I was telling myself that I wasn't man enough to be married. I was just a boy. I should get out of the relationship any way I can. I should just end my life. Find a way that the money would still go to Connie and get out. I was telling myself I couldn't handle the situation. I had to start telling myself a much different message. Because I was slowly killing myself with the message I was constantly repeating.

If I can talk with somebody today about the tough situation I was in, maybe I can help them overcome their problem. It's about living life "on purpose." I want to have a purpose to what I do. And if tough things are happening, and I'm not particularly enjoying them, there is a reason. It is highly likely I will get some knowledge or experience that will help me or others sometime down the road. From my vantage point, we are either winning and growing or losing and growing. Either way, we are growing. For some people, life happens *to* them. I'm among the people who expect life to happen *for* me, BECAUSE OF ME! Because of my thoughts, because of my words, because of my prayers, and ultimately, because of my choices and actions.

When things don't go well, I ask myself, "What is the purpose of this failure?" What didn't I do in a certain situation? What did I do wrong? Asking those kinds of questions, and learning from them, will make me better for the next test coming down the road. If a situation doesn't turn out well, I can't let the emotions that come from that keep me staying down for too long. The Lord allowed some challenging situations to show up in front of me, and I expect that He will do that in the future. I have been given a better understanding now as to why He does that, and I want to grow from the experience. Nobody grows while comfortable. We only develop when we are challenged and when we work to surmount those difficulties.

It's like boxing. Sometimes a fighter gets really rocked, and his trainer tells him to stay down, to take the full eight or nine count. He can use the time to get himself together. We CAN do that in life. Sometimes, staying down means shedding a tear or two. Or praying. Taking deep, cleansing breaths. Yelling into a pillow. It's good to get some of that out and then stand up and move forward with a clearer look at the situation at hand. It allows me to make better decisions, to have the clarity I need, rather than allowing stress, panic, anger, and pain to cause me to make bad decisions that could have long-term effects. By taking a second to assess myself and the situation and to learn what's happening, I can be more effective for myself and others.

There have been times where giving myself a cut-off time has been the tool I used. I would allow myself to lick my wounds for a day or weekend. But when I went to bed that night before the cut-off, I had already made up in my mind that that issue was over with. And when Monday came, it wasn't completely over with, as that little voice tried to not only remind me of the event that I allowed to cause it, but it would try to get me to go down memory lane, so I could bring up more old emotions from my subconscious mind. You know, to pile on. But I will quickly take those thoughts captive, and literally say, "Shut up and get in line!" If that doesn't work, I meditate on what is worthy of praise, what is pure, what I'm thankful for, and soon after, the little voice gets its butt back in line.

Change is inevitable in our lives, and we have to choose how we're going to handle those new situations. There are four types of changes:

1. Change that happens TO us—we let it
2. Change that happens AROUND us—we watch it
3. Change that happens WITHIN us—we are conscious of it, aware of it
4. Change we MAKE happen—we make it. I know you might be thinking that a change that happens in us and a change that we make happen are the same thing. Just because a change happens inside of you that you are aware of, doesn't necessarily mean you will take the steps you need to make it happen.

By my being transparent as an individual in how I live and how I walk with Christ, I hope I can help people see that there is hope in dark times. Things we go through shape us; they don't end us. No matter how difficult things may be, if you make it through them, it means you have something left to do on earth. I truly believe that. If I had ended up taking my life, my daughter, Brionni, and the twins wouldn't be on this planet. I wouldn't have had the career I had. I wouldn't have touched people like I did—or the people I will touch moving forward. So, while that period was extremely difficult, it served to help me be better for others in the future.

◇◇◇

As I began to bring my life into clearer focus and to commit more to walking with the Lord, there was one major step I had to take to gain greater control:

I had to speak with my family.

It wasn't going to be easy, and very few people can understand why. Many people hear about professional athletes' contracts and think they have an endless supply of money to share with family and friends. It's not the case. I was a rookie, just starting my journey, and I realized that at any given second, I could blow my knee out, and that could be it. Perhaps I wouldn't come back and play at the same level. Maybe I wouldn't come back at all. Remember that in 1996, a torn ACL meant a 12-to-18-month rehab and a potential career-ending catastrophe. Medical techniques were not as advanced as they became in the 2010s, when Adrian Peterson could return from a shredded ligament in under a year and lead the league in rushing.

If that were to happen, I would probably get a settlement of a couple hundred thousand dollars, and that would be it. I would be twenty-three, with decades ahead of me. Others don't understand that short-term riches don't last forever. Yes, it is a lot of money, but after taxes and inflation and the cost of living, it can be gone quickly. When looked at over the course of a full life, it's not a lot of money.

There are different levels of NFL money. Rookies get good salaries, but they can't go spending like they are multimillionaires, especially if they are second-round picks. Now, if you get quarterback money, like what Kansas City's Patrick Mahomes got in 2020—ten years, $500 million. That's a different story.

But even $4 million, stretched over forty years, isn't a whole lot of money in the grand scheme, if not managed properly. That sounds weird to some people, but it's true. I wanted to be able to save what I earned, let it work for me and to grow and build wealth. Then I could help people. But I wasn't anywhere near that point my rookie year. I had heard about too many who had lost their money by spending it or giving it away. I was not about to do that.

My first priorities were Connie and little Brian. I still did for my family as I could. But it did put a strain on the relationship for many years. As my contracts improved, I was blessed to finally buy my parents a house that I promised myself I would. I will always do what I am led to do. They're my parents, and I love them. But it was tough going through that. My nucleus was my new family, and they deserved the bulk of my attention. Something Emmitt helped me understand. The word of God tells us to honor our parents, which I will always do. It also tells us to leave and cleave to your spouse. And I do and did both of these in Love.

But there was another "family" that needed me, and that was my new team. Despite everything that was happening off the field, we still had some football to play.

◊◊◊

When a college player is drafted into the NFL, he is excited and proud. Once he starts practicing, he can become confused and worried.

Most rookies don't get preferential treatment. They get yelled at by coaches—and, boy, did they scream at you during training camp with the Eagles. Few of the veterans have any time for rookies. And the football is so sophisticated and difficult that they rarely have any confidence in what they are doing.

In college, I made a lot of plays on instinct. I could sense what was happening, and I was able to react in a way that helped my team. I studied film and practiced hard, but I didn't really understand football the way players are supposed to in the NFL. The Eagles' playbook was a monster, and it wasn't easy to learn. Emmitt's defense had so many different nuances and checks that I spent a lot of time on the field thinking, rather than playing. When you're doing that, it's hard to be successful. When playing cards, we would say "You think long, you think wrong" when someone is taking long to play their turn. The scheme has to be automatic in your head, so that when a call is made, you don't even think about what you have to do. You just do it. You must be ahead of the play so that you can anticipate correctly what will happen.

It was complicated stuff, and I'll try to explain what made it so tough. Suppose the defensive call was an "Over 34." For the defensive backs, that meant there was a double call. If the offense came out in a pro formation, with receivers on each side, a tight end and two backs, you play a Cover Three. That means the free safety (me) covers one-third of the field—no matter who comes into the area— and the two cornerbacks have the other thirds. Underneath, four players—linebackers and the other safety—play the short zones.

That sounds pretty basic, until a receiver goes in motion from one side of the field to the other, putting two receivers on the same side. Then, you go to another call, in which the safeties and cornerbacks each cover a quarter of the field, with the linebackers underneath. If there is just a tight end on one side, then the safety can play Cover Two, and guard one half of field, with the cornerback underneath, because there aren't as many people to cover.

Now, if a back motions to the closed side...

See what I mean? You have to think ahead, and you don't have a lot of time to do it. Fortunately for me, the other safety for the Eagles at the time was Mike Zordich, who was basically a walking playbook. If somebody on the offense went in motion, I would look at Mike, and he would make the call, and I would echo what he said. Emmitt caught on to that, and he would sometimes take Mike off the field to see if I could handle making the check myself. He could see I was leaning too heavily on Mike to make the calls, and he wanted me to learn how to do it myself. It was stressful, but it showed he believed in me.

The first game of the 1996 season was at Washington, and I have to admit that I was happy I wasn't starting. I was excited, but I was extremely nervous because I wasn't completely confident with the playbook. I killed it on special teams because there isn't a whole lot of complex thinking on special teams as I saw it, as compared to what I had to learn on defense. You just run down the field, read the return, keep your head on a swivel and hit somebody. You better keep your eyes moving, though, to make sure somebody doesn't blindside you, but you just go make plays. That's what I did at Clemson as a freshman. I was the special teams demon. I did get some playing time at safety against Washington. They put me in some situations, and I did all right. One week later, at Green Bay, on Monday Night Football, I got the start.

Everybody had told me about the speed of the game and how it increased from the preseason to the regular season. It did—100 percent. It wasn't just the speed of the players. It was my anxiety and adrenalin. Not having dealt with that level of pressure before made everything feel like it was going at hyper-speed. I played on the outside on the punt team, and on every punt, I was in a death match trying to get down the field against two cats. The physicality didn't bother me at all. My mindset had been established a long time before about what I was going to do against anyone who got in my way.

I won't say it was the loudest game I ever played in, but it seemed that way at the time. Looking back, I will say it was pretty spectacular. Brett Favre was quarterbacking the Packers, and they kept coming out with more than two WRs on the field. And seeing as I could cover, I started as a Dime Corner. Simply put, they had a lot of extra receivers, and I was the extra defensive back. They had me playing cover corner. Even though I played safety for most of my career, I was a jack-of-all-trades kind of guy. I could cover. I could hit. So what do you know, that tweener chess piece is was a good thing all along.

After beating Washington, 17–14, in the opener, we got clobbered by Green Bay, 39–13. Favre threw for 261 yards and three touchdowns, and the Packers picked off Rodney Peete, our QB, three times. They got out on us, 23–0, in the second quarter, and that was it. But those first two games made me a lot more comfortable with the calls and with the speed of the game. I still made mental mistakes after that, but I didn't make as many. And after that, I was the starting free safety. Yet, still uncomfortable.

I tried to make sure I had as much down as I could of the game plan, but Emmitt had complex game plans, and Green Bay used a lot of personnel and shifted a lot. So, we were almost coming up with the game plan on the field, while the game was going on. I was not only trying to figure all that out; I was also going up against world-class athletes. The best thing you can do in any aspect of life is to have ownership of it. If you have to keep thinking and checking, you're not going to be as swift or smooth. It was a learning experience, but I was on my way.

My NFL journey was just beginning.

CHAPTER 7

Learning the Ropes

When people talk about the speed of the NFL, they often think it means simply how fast everybody moves on the field. Indeed, pro football players can move crazy fast, even the big cats. That leads to some big plays and violent collisions. Of which I'm often a huge fan.

It's hard to equate the game's pace with anything you face in life off the field. I would often loosely equate it to having a car crash where the airbag shoots out. How well you handle it has a lot to do with the mental awareness you have and the knowledge of the position you are playing. You must have the ability to anticipate. That's what slows things down. When you know what is coming, you're no longer anxious or surprised. When it happens, you are ready to deal with it. To get your body in position to either deliver or receive a blow. Your mindset is key as well. You can either be the hammer or the nail. The predator or the prey.

When you first start to play in the NFL, you don't know what's coming, so it's difficult to anticipate much. I didn't really know how to study film, so I couldn't effectively and consistently evaluate situations to see what was coming. I was basically reacting too much during the game. I couldn't make things happen, things were far too often happening to me and around me. During my rookie year, I was not just nervous, I was battling with fear, because I didn't want to make mistakes. So there were times when I would actually slow down, to make sure I didn't miss a tackle. Instead of playing the ball, I would just go to the man, to make sure he didn't get past me. I was being careful. If I went for the big play, and I failed, it would be a touchdown. It would be another year or so before I felt comfortable enough to go full speed and not worry about being wrong. The key is to take educated guesses, not just merely take chances.

We went 10–6 in 1996, and Ray became the first Eagles coach to lead his team to the playoffs in each of his first two seasons. Our defense was a good one. We had Troy Vincent on one corner and Bobby Taylor on the other. Emmitt did a good job matching things up. He had me covering some speedy guys out of the backfield, tight ends, as well slot WRs. Which I loved. We had a defense that would bend but not break. We gave up some yards, but we didn't give up a lot of points.

In the fifth game of the season, a 23–19 loss in Dallas, Rodney ruptured a tendon in his right knee and was out for the year. But Ty Detmer would come and do his thing in relief. We averaged 351.7 yards per game and had the best offense in the NFC. Ricky Watters was great running and catching the ball out of the backfield, and Irving Fryar had 88 receptions, which was a club record at that time.

Ricky was an interesting cat. He had a lot of talent, and he wanted to show it. But I had never seen a player get on the phone during the game and, let's just say, having strong words the offensive coordinator. I'm thinking, "Is this how we do it in the NFL?" He wanted the ball. Period. You love the competitive side of that, wanting the ball. And he was very confident. Rick would say, "Give me the ball. That's why we're losing." But he and offensive coordinator Jon Gruden had an interesting relationship at times, from my vantage point.

We were pretty good in '96, but we still needed to beat the Jets and Arizona in the last two weeks to get a playoff spot. We finished second in the NFC East and had to travel to San Francisco for the Wild Card game.

That game didn't go well at all. First of all, the weather was awful. A storm blew in from Hawaii—they call it "The Pineapple Express." And it rained so hard that they actually wouldn't let airplanes land at the San Francisco airport. They diverted them all to Las Vegas. The field was a mess. It was a real Mud Bowl. Still, we had plenty of chances to win the game. In the first half, the wind blew a 40-yard Gary Anderson field goal attempt wide. Later on in the half, we had a third-and-one from the Niner seven, and instead of giving the ball to Ricky, we called a pass. Ty was rushed hard by San Francisco linebacker Ken Norton and threw a pass under duress that was picked off by Marquez Pope in the end zone.

With just 37 seconds to go before halftime, we were down at the 49er five, when receiver Chris T. Jones collided with a ref while running a pattern. Ty had already thrown the ball, and what would have been a sure touchdown, was another interception. That was it. We didn't threaten again, and lost 14–0. The offense had been so good all year, but we came up short in this one. And we had a couple busted coverages that led to those 14 points.

My first year was extremely eventful, both on and off the field. It was notable for a lot of things, including my introduction to Veterans Stadium. As I already mentioned, the training facilities inside The Vet were well below the standard that I had enjoyed at Clemson. Things weren't much better outside. The practice fields had huge divots in them. Let's just say the grass field was an adventure. It was two fields slapped at the back of the Vet's parking lot. With a makeshift bubble close by. The bubble was dark, and the surface was worse than the Vet if you can believe it. Both fields were right next to an Italian restaurant that was like torture because you would smell those wonderful aromas coming from over there. Reminds me of a cartoon character when they smell something good, and they take a deep inhale and exhale through the nostrils. Then they proceed to picture the dish and immediately begin to float towards the heavenly aroma. What made it worse, is that the food that they served at the Vet was, let's say, edible. It was an adjustment, but it was our place, and we didn't want anybody else talking bad about it. And of course, I was blessed to be playing in the NFL, in Philly.

The playing surface inside the stadium was brutal. I can remember one time sliding on the turf and losing a good bit of skin on my arm. They said it was almost like a third-degree burn. The turf was dry, and if you looked, you could see the green of the turf, until it reached a dark skid line. That was the skin I left on the artificial surface. I saw it clearly when I went back and watched that on film. I would have to get that huge wound cleaned every day. It was torture. At night, the ooze and other things would stick to the huge wrap, which they would rip off every morning. I had a better understanding of what burn victims have to endure. And mine was on the milder side in comparison.

The turf was hard. It sometimes caught your cleats. But I approached it with something like a physical and mental, gladiator mentality. We knew how to prepare ourselves for it. Other players didn't. So, while they were thinking about the turf, we were making plays. It became an advantage against certain teams because they were so concerned about whether they were wearing the right shoes and what would happen when they hit the ground. They were thinking about other things besides football. It could be a real advantage at times. During my seven years playing there, we were 34–22. In 1998, when we were 3–13, all of our wins came at The Vet. It may not have been perfect, but it was ours. I didn't care about the bumps and the burns I received. It was worse for the other guys, and it all just made us tougher in my eyes.

◇◇◇

Even though I was new to the NFL, I was pretty clear from the minute I got to Philadelphia that I was going to be a physical player. A very, very physical player. From Pop Warner, through high school, Clemson, and then with the Eagles, I was always looking to deliver punishment. I couldn't really lay someone out every play, because I wasn't the biggest guy, and I didn't want to get hurt. That was another thing I would learn from Emmitt. My coaches at Clemson were worried I might do that, because I hit people so hard, so often. Emmitt taught me how to pump my brakes a little, to pick and choose when I was going to deliver the big shot. If I did it all the time, I wouldn't have survived, he went on to convince me.

Every time I tackled someone, I wanted him to feel it. But I had to be selective about the times I would just run through someone without gathering myself and protecting myself somewhat. That doesn't mean there weren't going to be some times when I really went after a receiver or running back or blocker for that matter. I wanted to be in opponents' heads. I wanted to inflict pain, but not injure them. I wanted them to think every time they went over the middle and the quarterback threw to them that if the ball was a little high, that I was coming for them. I wanted them to be thinking, where is that #20? I wanted them to have those gator arms, where they didn't want to reach out too far to catch the ball because I might blow them up. Or they would flat-out not even give the effort. Which could turn into a turnover or incompletion.

That was where the tipped balls happened, and the overthrows occurred—from receivers not wanting to go all out for the ball because they were thinking instead of playing. They wanted to protect their bodies. That was more important to them than catching the ball. Usually, that's because they saw a hit or were hit themselves, so hard that other opponents saw it on film. That's what I wanted to do: put crazy on film.

Crazy is me taking a receiver, dumping him or just running through him. Putting my forearm in his back. I wanted the rest of the league to see that on film, so that they were worried I might do it to them, too. That way, when they came across the middle, they were thinking, "That Dawkins dude is crazy." I didn't want to injure other players, because I didn't want to take money from their families. But if I could have you off the field for a series or two? If I could have you changing your game because you were worried about how hard I might hit you? That was just fine. I definitely wanted to inflict pain.

◇◇◇

Many people say that the biggest jump an NFL player makes comes between his first and second years. He understands the game better, both on and off the field. Everything isn't new anymore. He should have learned how to watch film more carefully. He should have a better understanding of how he must train and prepare—not only the importance of, but also having a plan to care of his body and deal with what goes on inside a locker room. In short, he is no longer a rookie.

All of that happened to me, but the biggest jump I made was in my faith. That's when the Second Letter of Paul to St. Timothy came in. One verse in particular spoke powerfully to me, and it helped me greatly with my ability to live as a man and thrive as a football player.

For the Lord has not given us a spirit of fear but one of power, love, and of a sound mind [or self-control]. – 2 Timothy 1:7

Thinking about that verse and meditating on it would help me overcome those anxious moments, even on the field. If a bad play happened, I might have had an instinct to play the next one more safely or carefully. I could have been afraid to give up another big play. Instead, I would repeat that message to myself, and I would believe it. And when the next play happened, I might step in front of a pass and take it the other way. Or I might make a big hit that changes the game's momentum. It made me more confident. I had a sound mind. I had self-discipline. I was not fearful of playing aggressive. I was operating in my full God-given power. And as long as I had been operating in fear, I wasn't giving all I had to give. Which was hurting my teammates more than me making an occasional mistake because I was taking educated guesses.

In that moment, the Lord did not give us fear. That is something we have brought on ourselves. The Lord gave us power and love and strong minds, and we have to accept those gifts and use them. The combination of my faith and belief in the good things the Lord gave me, along with understanding the game better, really knowing the playbook and being able to anticipate what would happen next, made me a better player. I believed I could run with those fastest wide receivers. I could tackle running backs that other defensive players struggled to deal with. Even take on the biggest of cats if need be. No, I didn't win every battle, but when that happened I was coming back harder next time.

I remember in 1998 tackling Hall of Famer Barry Sanders in the open field. Very few people could do that, because once Barry got past the line of scrimmage, he had so many moves he could make people look really bad. So, I was thinking, "Oh, I can play this game." It was a powerful feeling, because I believed in the gifts the Lord had given me, and I had the physical gifts and desire to put in the work. Talk about a great combination.

Meanwhile, I had Emmitt pushing me during practice and film study, showing me things I should have been doing. I was getting better, but there were more plays I could be making. He would show me how close I was to greatness. A lot of people see a safety make a tackle after a completed pass and think he has done his job. Emmitt wanted me to recognize what was happening early on and break up that pass or intercept it. Or hit the receiver in the right spot so that he fumbled. That's what we mean when we talk about making a play. It's not just doing your job. It's creating a situation that turns things in your team's favor and demoralizes the opponent at the same time.

When it came time for the 1997 season, my second, I had grown as a player through my understanding and applying Paul's message to Timothy, along with the other memorized verses I now knew. I stepped forward as a man, thanks to my faith. It was a great combination, and it allowed me to see the game strategically and with confidence and courage.

The only problem was that our team wouldn't be able to play with the same level of confidence and preparation, because injuries killed us in '97. We started forty-two different players that season, and we used three different quarterbacks. We opened the year 1–3 and lost our last three games, the last two by three points each, to finish 6–9–1. The defense was strong throughout most of the year, including in the second game of the year, when we shut down Green Bay, 10–9. The Packers were the defending Super Bowl champs, and they had scored a touchdown in 85 straight games. But we snapped that streak.

The thing that stood out in that game was the intensity of it. To fight tooth and nail with a team that was a perennial playoff team and that had won the Super Bowl, and to win, made it more of a statement. We could not just hang with the best. We could do what we needed to beat them. Looking back, games like that were foundation pieces that would help us grow in the years to come. We were building something together on the football field. Guys like myself, Troy, and Bobby, took that belief with us for years to come.

Our offense wasn't so sharp all year, and it scored fewer than 20 points in eight games in '97. There were some high points, like an overtime victory over the Cardinals when Chris Boniol hit a 24-yard field goal, and a 13–12 win over Dallas at home. Rodney hit Chad Lewis with an eight-yard TD pass with 45 seconds left.

But there were also some low points, and the lowest came in Dallas on a Monday night. We had just beaten Green Bay and were feeling pretty good, even though the Giants had knocked us around in the opener. The Cowboys had won the division in '96 and had reached the NFC championship game. It was always big to play Dallas, especially on Monday Night Football, and to lose to them the way we had was overwhelming. That still remains one of the toughest losses the Eagles and their fans have had to endure.

The Cowboys had taken a 21–20 lead with 0:51 to play when Troy Aikman connected with Anthony Miller on a 14-yard TD pass. Dallas went for two but didn't make it, and after the kickoff, we had the ball on our own 16. It didn't look good. But the offense started moving, and Ty Detmer hit Freddie Solomon with a 46-yard pass with four seconds left, to bring the ball to the Cowboys' five-yard line. Boniol, a former Cowboy who had made 46 straight field goals from inside 35 yards, came on for what was thought to be an automatic 21-yarder. It would be the perfect ending to a win over Dallas, in front of their fans and their crazy coach, Barry "How 'bout them Cowboys" Switzer.

But our holder, punter Tommy Hutton, bobbled the snap. Boniol never got the chance to kick the ball. The game was over. We had lost, 21–20. It was crushing.

But I have always tried my best to put myself in other people's shoes. I might not always be successful, but I try. I knew Tommy. He was a good dude. When he dropped the ball, I said, "Oh, man!" I hated that we lost, but I wanted to console him, to make sure he was okay. I guess part of me understood what it felt like to be alone. Going through that depression had taught me about loneliness. I didn't want him to feel that way, so I consoled him.

We had won two in a row when the Giants came to the Vet. Had we won the last three games of the season, we would have been a wild card team. Instead, we let Danny Kanell throw three touchdown passes, while Bobby Hoying threw three interceptions and was sacked four times. We lost, 31–21, and it didn't mean anything that we almost beat Atlanta and Washington because the season was over.

Worse, there was a feeling that Ray was in trouble. He wasn't fired after the season, but you could hear the little chirps. You saw some of the players they were bringing in to play, and you could see the bewilderment on Ray's face. On a Tuesday, a new player would show up, and Ray didn't have anything to do with picking him. The veterans were saying, "This doesn't look good for Ray." I was only a second-year guy, so I wasn't savvy to the business of football. But the veterans knew Ray was in trouble.

That year, I was named an alternate for the Pro Bowl, so I knew I truly belonged in the NFL. I knew more than other second-year players might have, because of Emmitt. He was pushing me to great things and wanted to see me look past good to great. So that was my mindset. I was going to work anyway because that's what I have always done, but Emmitt was giving me the mental part of the game. It's one thing to work hard. As the saying goes, Practice makes perfect. Or, If you work hard you will succeed. And while there is a ton of truth to that, it's not all good. If you work hard practicing the wrong thing, you will further cement a bad habit. So Emmitt helped me channel and focus myself. My spiritual life was increasing also, and my faith in the Lord was growing, so I was being challenged from every direction—physically, mentally, emotionally, and spiritually—to be a better version of myself. Thank you, Lord!

I began to understand that this was Ray's last year, and probably the last for the coaching staff. I grew up a lot because of this. I was soaking in all I could, while I could. And I knew I was auditioning for the next coach. Whoever that might be. There were battles from time to time, but I wanted to grow in terms of how I would handle different situations.

◇◇◇

Whenever media members come into a locker room, or TV cameras are allowed to be on, players are usually on their best behavior. Sometimes you see coaches after a game congratulating players or giving out a game ball, and everything looks perfectly normal. It's just a bunch of guys playing a game.

But a locker room can sometimes be a wild place. There is a lot of joking going on. You also have your pranksters. The number one rule is: Don't have a thin skin. If you do, your teammates will find out about it, and they will come at you nonstop. If you can't take a joke, you will be a constant target. It's sort of like the rules of the playground. If you get too angry about something someone says, you can bet others will keep saying it, just to annoy you.

There are also a lot of just fun times, when guys are busting on each other for things that happened in practices. If you let a player beat you deep, you're going to hear about it. Missed tackle? Get ready. Drop a pass? Here it comes. There's a lot of tearing each other down, in fun-loving fashion, but also plenty of building up. I think if you talked to a bunch of players, the majority would tell you that the thing they miss the most about the NFL is the locker room and the camaraderie with their teammates. Yes, they love the competition, because we are all highly competitive individuals.

But being able to see the guys every day is a great thing. You know you're going to be laughing, and you're going to have the opportunity to trip out with them, eat lunch together, talk about the crazy stuff that happens on the field and in the world and just release a little of the pressure that comes from our potentially high-stress lives. There is a lot that isn't easy about being a pro football player, and the average cat doesn't understand anything that we go through—the pain and sacrifice, not to mention the anxiety of having to perform at a high level every day or risk getting cut or traded. Like the time I broke my wrist. No surgery needed. So before every game for a couple of weeks, I had to get shot up. That would numb the area so it could be casted like a club, and I could play. I remember watching old Westerns and such, where they would bite on something to help deal with the pain. So that's what I did, bite on a towel. Fun times.

The locker room is not always the happiest place on earth. You're going to have a spat or two. You have some aggressive cats in there, and sometimes the fun and games go a little too far. That's when some conflicts can happen. Often, it's just words, but sometimes things get physical. It doesn't last too long. Five seconds, and it's over. Someone pulls the two cats off of each other, and we deal with the aftermath to make sure it isn't going to be an everyday type of thing. To the outside world, it looks awful. People can't believe teammates are fighting. They think it means the whole franchise is coming apart. But you have people from different backgrounds, with different beliefs and different ways of doing things. We're thrown together every day, and there are going to be times when a release valve has to be opened. It's no different than what happened in the neighborhood when you were growing up. Someone might push you too hard on the playground, and you get up real quick and throw a couple punches.

At least that's the way it happened when I was growing up. You handled your business quickly, and then five minutes later, you're riding bikes and messing around with the same dude you just fought with. It's usually very short-lived, and you cannot take that stuff to heart. I understood all of that.

◇◇◇

The 1998 season was forgettable for most Eagles fans, and going 3–13 wasn't too easy for the players, either. But before the year, Emmitt and Ray told me for the first time that I had a chance to be in the same category as Ronnie Lott. For those of you who don't know Ronnie, he was a Hall of Fame safety who was named to ten Pro Bowls and was an eight-time All-Pro selection for the 49ers (mostly), Raiders, Jets, and Chiefs. Ronnie was so good, he was named to both the NFL's 1980s and '90s all-decade teams. He could hit, cover, run and basically do anything on a field required of a defensive back—and do it all better than just about anybody else. And he was tough.

In 1985, Ronnie crushed his left pinky finger tackling Dallas fullback Timmy Newsome. Instead of undergoing bone graft surgery, which would have prevented him from playing at the beginning of the '86 season, Ronnie just had the tip amputated. That way, he wouldn't miss any time. He was tough, and like me he wasn't too big, just 6'0" and 203 pounds—which was still bigger than me. One of the things I loved most about Lott was his versatility. He could and did do it all. He filled up every stat column. He could cover, made the Pro Bowl at corner. Had range and could bring the heat, and made Pro Bowl and All Pro in both. He was a complete safety. Couldn't split him in half like some like to do, either strong safety or free. He was whatever you needed. A game-changer anywhere you put him. And the man who I mostly molded my freelance safety style from.

I hadn't seen myself as being like Ronnie Lott, but once they laid out that vision for me, I started believing that I had greatness inside of me from their perspective. I started to believe what they saw in me and what I was capable of doing. Ray had coached Ronnie in San Francisco, so he knew what Ronnie could do, and Ray saw similar potential in me. He also mentioned a couple of other great players he had coached that I reminded him of, and that gave me more confidence. He and Emmitt also began to trust me more with the defense, too. They let me call the signals and the changes. I was still "Baby Boy," but I was growing up, was more mature, at least on the football field. Off the field, I was growing as a man, too. But I could sense that I was becoming a better player, and the coaches could sense it, too.

That '98 season was brutal. We started off 0–5, and Seattle bombed us in the opener, 38–0. The linebackers coach for the Seahawks that day was Jim Johnson, who had them putting big pressure on our offense. That was his philosophy. He didn't want to sit back and let the other team dictate what was going to happen. He wanted his defense to take charge. That year, Seattle's did. The Seahawks scored ten touchdowns on defense, including eight on interceptions, the second-most in league history. He wasn't coordinating the defense, but you know he had plenty of influence.

The game was relatively close for a while. They led just 14–0 at halftime. But the way our offense was going, that was plenty. We managed just 222 total yards. Bobby Hoying completed only 9 of 23 passes for 60 yards and was sacked nine times. It was an awful way to start the season, but there was a funny story that came out of it.

Before the season, we signed Al Harris, a good, bump-and-run cover corner guy who had played for Tampa Bay in 1997, his rookie season. Al had to start against Seattle because Bobby Taylor was injured, and he was new to the system and still trying to pick it up when we played the first game. Emmitt had an audible that we made before the snap, called "Buster." If someone yelled "Buster," we automatically went to man-to-man coverage from zone. I would come down and match up against the guy in the slot, and everybody else would play one-on-one against the person in front of him. We struggled to get on the same page that game for sure.

Emmitt was so mad at him. It was hilarious. I know it wasn't hilarious to Al, and it wasn't quite so funny to the team or the coaches, because we got blown out, but in meetings the week after the game, Emmitt went so hard at Al. Al had thick skin, so he would just say, "Yeah, yeah, yeah." And what made it worse was that Al was very good at coming back at you if you said something to him. The other thing was, AL was a very good corner as well. So Emmitt would give it to him, and Al would go right back at him. We just sat there and shook our heads, and enjoyed the show. Oh, my goodness. I was loving this family spat.

Even though we were closer in our next three losses, it was clear the offense wasn't able to do much, and no matter how few points we gave up, it was always too many. We scored fewer than 20 points in fifteen out of sixteen games and had 10 or fewer nine times. Jon Gruden left as our offensive coordinator after the 1997 season to take over as head coach of the Raiders, and Ray brought in Dana Bible. That was a catastrophe, to say it kindly. I truly felt sorry for him. Coach was always a good man in my sight. But we struggled mightily on offense, so there was huge pressure on the defense. That D wasn't an outfit designed to dictate to the opponent. We were a "bend but don't break" kind of unit, so we would give up yards but not many points. That year, we let up 20 or fewer points ten times. But because the offense was so ineffective, we were on the field all the time. And that's not all on the offense, as there were times we failed to get off the field on third down. And things would get away from us in the fourth quarter. Once the other team had 13 or 14 points, we were in trouble, unless we could score on defense. But we didn't have the personnel to be that kind of domineering defense like we had when Jim Johnson came.

It was tough not to be frustrated with the offense, but I tried my best not to say anything detrimental to hurt team unity. I felt bad for Dana Bible. I felt bad for my offensive teammates. We just didn't have the explosive plays we needed. Rodney Peete was hurt again, and Bobby Hoying and Koy Detmer struggled. I could see the offense was fighting and trying, but they just couldn't get it done. Reminded me a lot of my time in Clemson, when we were searching for an identity and struggled for consistency. And the fans were really getting on them, booing. I tried to tell them the defense would pick them up, but there was only so much we could do. At the same time, I was a competitor, and I couldn't stand losing. We grew a lot as a defense during that time. That tough time allowed us to bond. We played for one another and really played to the last whistle.

We finished 3–13 that season, and it was pretty clear that Ray was in big trouble. There were whispers, and the media was talking about it. So, I just kept telling my teammates how important it was to keep playing hard, because when the head coach goes, everybody usually goes. At Clemson, when Ken Hatfield was replaced by Tommy West, only Rick Stockstill—the coach that recruited me—stayed on the staff, and that's because he and Tommy were good friends. We had some good coaches on that Eagles staff. Emmitt, of course, was one of them. But defensive line coach Mike Trgovac was a good dude. So was linebackers coach Joe Vitt. And the list goes on.

I was imploring guys to keep playing their butts off, but that's not easy to do. When a team starts losing, it's easy to start thinking about yourself and just think about making plays, rather than playing for the team. At the end of the season, I had a shoulder problem, and I could have sat out. Ray was probably going to be fired, so why should I risk getting seriously hurt? I felt that if my teammates were going to be out there, then I had better be out there, playing as hard as if we were trying to make the playoffs. That's what I chose to do. I can't say all of my teammates approached things that way, or that what I did was the smartest thing to do, when I was risking further injury. But I could not stay off the field if my teammates were there. I knew cats like Troy Vincent had something going on in terms of an injury, but he was out there. I had to play, too.

But losing was so tough. When you are losing game after game, it can be difficult to keep working hard, especially when you're a young player. You can develop the "here we go again" syndrome, as I called it. Instead of continuing to be aggressive and attacking, as soon as something bad happens, you think the loss is inevitable, and if you are not on top of your game mentally, it can shut down that part of your mind that tells you to make plays and to play winning football. You can go from trying to win, to simply surviving. I was aware of that, as I had witnessed that kind of thing back in Clemson with a few of my teammates. And because I was conscious of it, I was on the lookout. Looking into the eyes of my teammates. And offering encouragement where I could. And of course, trying my best to lead by example.

That year, I didn't even want to leave the house. I felt so embarrassed going to the store. I didn't want to get recognized. That's how I felt. I felt we had let the fans down, and I don't like to disappoint people. And I hate to lose. I. Hate. To. Lose. I was fighting that natural urge to shut it down early and just go home. Or to think of myself only. I was going to keep putting in extra work on the field and in the weight room. I kept watching more film. I was going to hold up my end. No slacking. That was the mentality I fought to keep. Finish what you start, fighting the entire way.

With two weeks left in the season, Ray told the press he was going to be fired and asked that the Eagles do it as quickly as possible. The day after our last game, a 20–10 loss to the Giants at home, owner Jeffrey Lurie fired Ray. Ray Bob was a class act to the end. At the press conference announcing the move, he said that when a coach doesn't win, he doesn't get to stick around. Ray didn't win, and he didn't get to stick around. But he won my respect in many, many ways. From how direct and up-front he was, to chewing me out when he saw me not living up to my potential. But this one took the cake. We had a bunch of African Americans on our staff, but especially interns. That's not the same at other teams around the league, where the majority of coaches and interns were my white brothers.

Left: Connie and me at the Junior Prom. Check out that haircut and bowtie.
Right: Connie and me at the Senior Prom. I was the luckiest guy there.

Photos courtesy of Brian Dawkins

Graduation Day at William M. Raines High School, 1992. We made it!

Photo courtesy of Brian Dawkins

Top and Bottom: Here I am zeroing in on enemy ballcarriers while at Clemson.

I could play some big-time defense, but I was dangerous with the ball in my hands, too.

Connie and I at Clemson. She was my backbone and number one fan.

Left: Here's a family portrait of Connie, me and our first born, Brian Jr.
Right: I'm one proud father to be holding my eldest daugher, Brionni.

Photos courtesy of Brian Dawkins

Here is the whole family at Super Bowl LII after the Eagles finally won it all!

Photo courtesy of Brian Dawkins

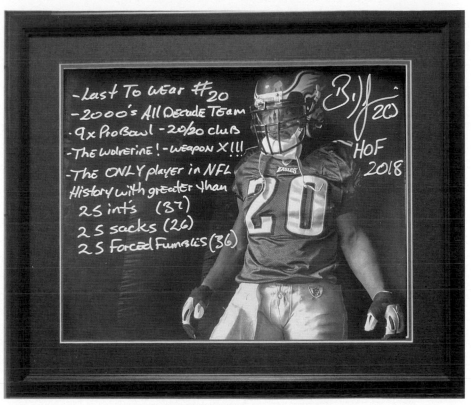

My favorite piece of memorabilia.

My footballs!

I'm often compared to The Wolverine due to
our similar characteristics: resiliency and power!

Courtesy of BrianDawkins.com

When I got to Canton for the Hall of Fame induction ceremony,
I couldn't contain my happiness or gratitude.

Courtesy of Philadelphia Eagles/Kiel Leggere

What a moment it was when my great friend, Troy Vincent,
put the Hall of Fame jacket on me.

Courtesy of Philadelphia Eagles/Kiel Leggere

I was so proud to see the bust that will be displayed in Canton.
It's the perfect culmination of my career.

Courtesy of Philadelphia Eagles/Kiel Leggere

Waving to the fans during the Hall of Fame parade was so exciting and a great moment.

Courtesy of Philadelphia Eagles/Kiel Leggere

Ray said, "Baby boy, you see how many I have on the staff as interns that look like you?" I said, "Yes, it reminds me of back in Jacksonville."

"They might not be able to get it done," he said then, "but I have to give them a chance. Because if I don't, who will?" My respect level for Ray was already high, but after that exchange, it skyrocketed. I respected the man he is even more than the Coach. I went and looked for myself to see just how bad it was across the league. And the sad thing is, in many ways, it's still the same. Be my guest if you are so inclined—look for yourself. And of course, this may or may not bother you, and I understand that. Yet I can promise you, it bothers those who continue to get passed over time and time again, with no sign of change in sight. Especially with head coaches, offensive coordinators, GM's, and of course, ownership.

After such a bad season, it was clear a change was coming. A Big Red change.

We didn't know it yet, but the Eagles would be soaring soon.

CHAPTER 8

Stepping Up

Even though I had spent three seasons proving myself to Ray and Emmitt and the other coaches, it was time to do it all over again. A new staff was coming in, and although I had put good work on film for them to evaluate, I felt as if I had to audition for my role all over again. I was actually in familiar territory, as I had done that same thing at Clemson prior to this.

Losing Emmitt was particularly hard, because of all the faith he had shown in me and all of the conversations we had, especially during that difficult first season. By the time he left, I understood more of what he saw in me and what he expected of me. I remember that after Ray was fired, Emmitt said to me, "If you learn your stuff [except he didn't say stuff] with the next coordinator, the things you will be able to do are limitless." When he got me, I was a young emotional cat who didn't know what he could really do. When he left, he had fully awakened the beast within.

Also, it was tough, because people don't think about coaches' families and what they have to go through when they are released. You get to know the staff and their wives and children as people, not just as coaches. It was like a team of uncles getting fired and having to find somewhere else to go. And in comes the new group, and we have to prove ourselves all over again. I never minded doing that, because I always tried to play one way.

That was another thing I had to explain to the guys as the 1998 season ended. We were auditioning for the next job opportunity. I wasn't expecting anything to be given to me, so I wanted to make sure that whoever the next coach would be, he could put tape on of

Brian Dawkins and see what kind of player I was. No matter what the score was or how well the season was going, I was going to go one speed—all out. That was constantly on my mind, playing until the clock had zeroes on it. That's the way I approached every new season, too. I had to make the team. It didn't matter whether I had been All-Pro the season before, I had to prove myself once again.

My heart was hurting for Ray and Emmitt, but playing pro football is tough. We love the game. We have to, because of all the pain and sacrifice we go through. We make connections with players and coaches—and even with fans. In the end, though, it isn't just a sport. It isn't just a game. It's a business. Players get cut. Coaches get fired. And someone new comes in.

◇◇◇

If Jim Haslett hadn't told people publicly and privately that Philadelphia wasn't his first choice as a head-coaching destination, Eagles fans may have never heard of Andy Reid. Haslett had been the Steelers' defensive coordinator, and he was the first person Jeffery Lurie, director of football operations Tom Modrak and executive VP Joe Banner interviewed, because Pittsburgh didn't make the playoffs in '98. But Haslett wanted the Seattle job, and he wasn't too quiet about his desire.

That didn't sit too well in Philly. One of the many things I have learned about this town is that people aren't going to beg you to be part of it. If you don't want it, it doesn't want you! Andy had coached in Green Bay for seven seasons, and in '98, he was quarterbacks coach and assistant head coach. Because the Packers played in the wild-card game (and lost to San Francisco) that year, the Eagles had to wait to interview Andy. Once they connected, it was a quick courtship. Four days after Jeffrey, Tom and Joe met with Andy, they announced his hiring. There were other candidates besides Haslett, like former Packers coach Mike Holmgren. But the Eagles loved Andy's knowledge of the game and passion. It didn't matter that at forty years old, Andy would be the second-youngest coach at the time in the NFL, behind Jon Gruden. They wanted him.

When Andy came in, he brought Jim Johnson with him, and the main thing I remembered about Jim was that defense Seattle had when they beat us 38–0 in the 1998 opener. The Seahawks blitzed a lot. A whole lot. They got a lot of interceptions and returned a lot of them for touchdowns. I knew it was an aggressive defense, and I loved that fact. I just didn't know how he was going to use me.

The one thing that was immediately clear about Coach Johnson was that he was demanding. The whole coaching staff was. That's often what happens when a new regime takes over a team that hasn't been successful. Andy's first camp was brutal. It was actually worse than Ray's, although it was shorter because of new NFL rules. I believe Andy was making it as tough as possible to weed out those who didn't belong or weren't willing to make the commitment to win. Where had I seen this before?

The first thing we had to do was a conditioning test that consisted of 14 half-gassers. That meant you had to run across the field and back in a certain amount of time, depending upon your position. Linemen didn't have to run as fast as defensive backs. A field is 53 1/3 yards wide, so we were running 14 106-yard sprints in the heat. Timed. That was the first day, and it was no joke. What made it worse was that he chose the field with the greatest crown in the middle—meaning that as you head to the middle of the field from the sideline, you're going uphill.

The next day, we came back and did two-a-days in full pads, with full contact. Our legs were already dead from the conditioning test, and we were tackling to the ground—except for the quarterbacks. Anything we were allowed to do in terms of contact, we did. That first year was the worst of Andy's camps. Some guys couldn't handle it. They hadn't put up with what I did when I played for Coach Humphrey, and there was nothing the coaches could do that wouldn't make me want to come back, as it pertains to contact or running. I wasn't going to break, because I had been through practices that were worse, in my mind. No chance.

Some guys quit or were released, not necessarily because of the work, but because of their attitudes and the um, choice words they used to describe the practices. I figured that showed the coaches they wouldn't make it. Believe me, many who stayed said those same or similar words about the practices, but they kept working.

Pain is part of football. A big part. And if you can't handle it physically or mentally, you won't make it. It comes in a lot of different varieties. The training camp variety is more fatigue and just getting used to the pain that comes from contact again. But there are far worse things that we endure. Obviously, the pain from broken bones, torn ligaments and tendons and dislocations is overwhelming. That's the kind of stuff that keeps a player out for a season or more. But some of the "less serious" injuries sure seem pretty bad, too, even though many times we fight through.

I can remember one time I played through a hyperextension of the back and whiplash. I was completely bent backwards. Sometimes, you can get by with numbing injections, as I did with my wrist. Other times, you just have to fight and hope the adrenalin kicks in to the point where you can keep playing. But some injuries made me alter the way I tackled.

Still, you play anyway. It's not the smartest move to play hurt, but I thought we were a better team with me on the field. I knew that my teammates counted on me doing certain things. Even if I was a decoy in certain situations, that still helped them make plays. And I didn't like to miss time. I didn't want other people playing in my position. Nothing is guaranteed in the NFL, and there are plenty of stories of injured players—stars—losing their jobs when they got hurt.

There were certain things I couldn't play through, like ankle injuries. I had one that was so severe that I couldn't push off of my foot. Then, I was a liability, and I didn't want to be a liability. A lot of it comes down to a player's pain threshold. In pro football, hockey and rugby, because of how physical the sports are, it's amazing the level of pain you can convince your body doesn't exist, just so you can keep playing. Some guys can't do it. Some can't.

Some of the treatments they give you to help you get back on the field are brutal. There was one, called an ARPwave, which puts a jolt of electricity into the area next to an injury or along the trail of it, in an attempt to speed up the healing process. It's so intense, and the power can be turned up as high as a person can tolerate it. The pain can be excruciating. And that's just to get you back onto the field—so that you can get banged up all over again.

Come game day, there wasn't a lot you could do for an injury besides tape and pads—and Toradol. Toradol is the brand name of a drug called ketorolac that is a non-steroidal anti-inflammatory many players began taking on game day in the late 1990s. You can either get a shot in your rear end or swallow a pill, but it's fast-acting, and it serves to tone down the pain you are feeling. And make no mistake, just because a player is out on the field, that doesn't mean he isn't feeling pain. He's hurting. Count on it. Some of my teammates would call this the vitamin T shot, while others would call it the suit of armor.

Although no one has an idea of Toradol's long-term effects, some doctors are convinced it can cause some problems down the road. I don't remember when I started taking it, but once I did, I took it every game. But getting your liver checked was a must.

It surely was a suit of armor. And football players felt we needed all the armor we could get.

◇◇◇

With a new head coach, a new coordinator a whole bunch of new players—there were fourteen rookies on the roster—and an offense that struggled, the 1999 season felt like my second year in the league, not my fourth. It had nothing to do with my lack of familiarity with the league or NFL football. When I was a rookie, because Rodney Peete was playing quarterback, we had the potential to score some points. That second year, we really weren't able to do much, and 1999 was like that '97 season when we didn't score much at all.

In '99, the defense once again felt like it couldn't give up any points. Because we were all learning a new defense, things weren't going to be perfect. There were going to be busted coverages and missed assignments. Jim Johnson was going to dictate to the other team. He wasn't going to let us sit back and bend. He wanted to make the offense as uncomfortable as he could. Jim was going to blitz. When a team blitzes and everybody still doesn't know what they are doing, there are going to be some gaping holes. But what I loved about Jim's defense was that he was going to let me blitz. In Emmitt's scheme, I was more of a cover guy. When Jim saw that I could blitz and that I could disguise what I was doing for long periods of time because of my timing and range, he started asking me, "Can you do this?" or "What about that?"

Because I could move, and I studied the game, Jim had confidence in putting me in different situations, and he put me all over the place. I was still covering guys. That was always part of the job, but now it wasn't as much as it was before. And as the years went on, he came up with even more ways to use me.

It didn't take long for it all to pay off. In fact, that first year, we led the NFL with 46 takeaways, including 28 interceptions. We even returned five for touchdowns, which tied a team record. Troy Vincent had seven picks, which was tied for first in the NFL. The last Eagles player to be first in interceptions before that was Bill Bradley, way back in 1972.

Troy is one of the most demanding dudes I know. He is extremely direct in the way he communicates at times. He's very straightforward. One of the things he has a gift for is asking people open-ended questions. He wants to know about you, and he doesn't try to lead you in one direction. He wants you to go down a path and to try to find answers for yourself. Which is a gift.

The other thing that drew me to Troy was that he was meticulous in his preparation and how he lived his life. He paid a lot of attention to detail. As a player, he was extremely careful in how he warmed up and in his footwork and his technique. I gravitated toward him, because I hadn't focused as much on technique. I was going to make the tackle, make the play. I was going to cover someone because I could run. It wasn't about technique for me. It was about effort and desire and my talent. So, I mirrored him as much as I could. I have talked about chasing "rabbits." As I've mentioned earlier, he is one of them, to this day.

It's funny. When I went back to the Eagles as an executive, one of the video staff members put together some of my old tape so that

I could show players how I did things and what I saw. I could show them why I took this step or moved that way. I could show them where the ball was and how I attacked it. I could have explained it, but it was better for me to show them. They were already gifted players, but if they improved their thought process, they could be even better. I wasn't telling them to play exactly how I did, but I wanted to show them the things I did.

The funny thing is that when you look at Troy and look at me earlier in my career, you almost couldn't tell who was who, except for our numbers. I watched myself run off the field, and I looked just like him. I was mimicking his movements, and how he did things in press coverage because he was so sound. He had come into the league four years before me, so he had been around. We both arrived in Philadelphia in 1996 (Troy had played with the Dolphins from 1992–95), and he was teaching me NFL stuff. More than that, he was showing me how important it was to have great technique.

Learning that from Troy, and then having Jim feel comfortable using me a lot of different ways, allowed me to become a lot more active as a player. Instead of staying back as the last line of defense, I was getting after people at the line of scrimmage. It got to the point where other teams started to slide the line to me to make sure I couldn't get to the quarterback. Sliding the line means having a guard and center put more emphasis on blocking one side than the other. Disguising things became huge. Jim wanted me to be as aggressive as possible when I was going to blitz, or when I was faking a blitz. Yet, he didn't want me to move. He didn't want me show them where I was coming from. And I would push the envelope in practice to see just how far I could go with all types of disguises.

I don't want to give away too many secrets, but here's one specific example:

Before a certain play when the opposing offense was going to pass, I might have stood right across from the left "A" gap, between the center and the guard. So, it looked like I was going to be blitzing right up the middle. And I would hold that and hold that, even though in reality, I was supposed to play the other half of the field in coverage. I wanted them to slide the line to the side of the field where I was standing, because we were going to blitz the nickel cornerback from the other side.

Here's where it became even more important that we had good communication. If I had to get back and cover the deep area of half the field, the cornerback on that side might play a little softer at first, just to make sure I had time to get back there so that nobody beat us deep, in those rare times a team would quick snap on third and medium to long. He didn't have to do it for too much time, just long enough for me to get in position. Then, he could come up hard and jump the hot route they were going to throw when the pressure came from the opposite side. Because of my ability to run, I could get to where I had to be. And I was no longer fearful because I knew my assignments so well. I could be aggressive. I could take educated guesses in order to make plays. And I was blessed with speed. Jim saw that and the tenacity with which I played, and he knew I would do whatever it took to make one of his blitzes work. It's important to know that a blitz doesn't work unless the defense gets to the quarterback. If the blitzer doesn't get there, the defense is exposed, because it has one or two (and sometimes more) fewer people in coverage.

Because I was going to be blitzing a lot, I started working on pass rush techniques. I would be in drills with the defensive linemen. I would go on to learn different techniques from (three-time Pro Bowl) defensive end Hugh Douglas and from the line coaches. I was even learning when I got to Denver later in my career, from Elvis Dumervil. I would go mimic them. I had a spin move, the double-swipe, the arm over, the dip and rip. I could bull rush you. So, I was not just blitzing to add pressure. I was rushing the passer. Creating pressure, hurries, sacks, and most of all, making someone think about me, rather than their job. It didn't make any sense for me just to run in there and get blocked.

When possible, most folk would come up with a plan of attack before they take on an opponent, and I was no different. I began to study the QBs I would play against, study their desired launch point and their escape tendencies, to name a few. I had to get home. My brothers at that time Bobby, Al and Troy at that time, were out there

on the expressway. So, I did a lot of stuff that really didn't have anything to do with the "safety" position. I learned corner techniques
from Emmitt and Troy. I learned very early on about leverage, keeping your feet behind you being the key to you getting your body
in a position with leverage to strike, from all the way back in Pop
Warner being a small dude at center. Now I could pass rush. In my
mind, I was almost a glorified defensive end as well, because I blitz
so much. I also worked to perfect the art of causing fumbles and
wound up becoming very good at it.

That gives you an idea of how a defense must work together
in order to be successful. I had to do my job. The blitzer from the
other side had to disguise that he was coming. The cornerback had
to protect us from deep throws for a couple seconds before I could
get back into place, after holding my disguises. And that doesn't
even begin to describe what the other eight players had to do. Even
though we went 5–11 that year, our defense was really good, and
with Jim running the show, it was only going to get better. Besides,
he had inherited a defense that was battle-tested, and had bonded
during a very dark time in Eagles history. All we needed now was
directions on how these dogs could hunt in this new defense.

Not that it was always easy to work for Jim. Put it this way:
There's a reason Jim was never mic'd up by NFL Films or anybody.
Every other word would have been, "Bleep, bleep, bleep, bleep,
bleep." Even in practice, he was like that. He was so impatient when
it came to his blitzes. When he put a new one in during practice, and
you messed it up—even during walk-throughs—he would lose it.
That was Jim. But the other side of it was, especially after you spent
a few years with him and he began to believe in you, he would design
things especially for you. Once he knew what you could do, he would
put you in a position to succeed. So, he would design something
around you. If you didn't get it right, then you were messing with his
baby, and he would lose his mind. Later I would come to understand
that he would go on to design the defense around me. Especially in
crunch time. He actually designed the defense around a safety. That's
unheard of. But because of Jim, I was no longer just a safety that
could hit and cover. I had indeed become a weapon. Weapon X!

◇◇◇

From the time Andy took over as our head coach, it was clear that he was never going to rip a player to the public, or let people know what was happening in the locker room. It frustrated the heck out of the media and the fans, but as a player, you have to love that. I know I did. Whatever conversations he and the other coaches had with us stayed with us. He wasn't going to speak to us through the media. I can't always say that about the front office. They did that at times, and I didn't like that. But Andy? No way. Jim? No. They took the responsibility themselves and then had conversations with players. If something needed to be fixed, they handled it inside. We all appreciated that, even if people on the outside didn't.

When Andy first came in, he was full of fire and brimstone. He was that way for the first couple of years. He was quite strict on things. He told us exactly how he wanted things done, even if we didn't understand why he wanted them that way. For instance, when we were over at the Vet, there was a way you could enter the meeting rooms from the locker rooms. You just walked across the hall, and you entered the back way. He didn't want that. He wanted us to walk around to the front and enter there. It was the same way when we left. We all wondered why we had to walk all the way around, and to this day, I still don't know why. If you didn't do it, he disciplined you. I never got disciplined, but still, it didn't make any sense to us.

There were other things, like making sure your jersey was always tucked in. You couldn't wear fancy cleats. He was really regimented on what he wanted us to do, and he didn't hesitate to call you out on it to make sure you got it right. If someone wasn't dressed right, Andy would send him off the field until he fixed it. Ray tried to treat us like men, and we all appreciated that, but some of the guys took that and ran with it. They began to act more like adolescents than men. That's just my opinion. When Andy came in, the culture had to change. We had to be more disciplined. I for one was more than fine with it. Even though I still don't know why we couldn't just cross the hall and come right into the meeting room area.

That didn't always show itself during the first season. We went 5–11, and started the year 2–7. The defense was really good. Of course, Troy was there, and Bobby Taylor played the other corner.

Jeremiah Trotter was in his second year in the league, and he was showing what a force he was going to be at middle linebacker. With his downhill play and his patented celebratory Axe Chop. Willie T was in his last year with the team and he was still playing well, and Hollis Thomas was a monster in the middle of the defensive line, with Big Hugh among others bringing that heat from the outside. Troy picked off seven passes, and Bobby, Al Harris and I all had four interceptions.

That was the season I made my first Pro Bowl. I had been an alternate the year before, but this was huge. It meant I finally got past LeRoy Butler and Darren Woodson in the NFC safety pecking order. Darren was someone I always looked up to, and since LeRoy was from Jacksonville, I was always shooting for him. I finally beat them out. It was huge for me, because I saw what I could be. And obviously, the NFL did too.

The Pro Bowl was different back then because the guys still played the game hard and very physical. And going to Hawaii and being around the best players in the league and seeing how hard they were practicing was great for me. Nobody was just jogging around. The receivers were running their routes hard during work-outs. I had arrived at the place that Ray and Emmitt saw for me. I had the Pro Bowl as a goal, and there isn't a player who doesn't have it in mind. But the question always is whether it is realistic. I didn't know 100%, but because I kept listening to Ray and Emmitt, and they kept working to convince me that I had something special inside of me, I made it.

When I got there, it was great. I played safety and some corner-back during the game because one of the corners got injured. The rules don't let defensive backs get right up on receivers in the Pro Bowl, so I was a little nervous, but I knew I could run, so I would be okay. I was better than okay. I had two interceptions.

Connie didn't have such a good time. They put her up in the nosebleed section of the stadium with Brionni, all by herself, so by the time she and Brionni got in their seats she had missed a lot of the action. I didn't know that until after the game. How could they do something like that? So, she didn't have a good day at the game, which I was none too happy about. Everything else was good. The hotel and the parties and everything were outstanding, but putting her in bad seats was just wrong. We got that fixed quick, fast, and in a hurry the next time, Jack.

And the key was getting there the next time. And the time after that. I forget who told me that it's tough to get to the Pro Bowl, and harder to stay. It's extremely difficult to be voted back year after year after year. Now that I had a taste of it, my mindset was that I was supposed to be there. And not only that, but I was going to be All-Pro. It was one thing to be in the Pro Bowl. That meant you were the best in your conference. All-Pro players were the best in the whole NFL. I was voted second-team All-Pro in '99, but I wanted more. I looked at the guys who were on the first team, Tampa Bay's John Lynch and New England's Lawyer Milloy, and that's who I was gunning for. They were the rabbits I would be chasing.

It's one thing to have the individual success, but what I really wanted was to be having success that was helping my team have consistent success as well. But the season wasn't great for the team. However, in most folks' minds, we weren't expected to be good. Andy was trying to create a new culture, and it was going to take some time, especially on offense. We really struggled there. Andy brought in Doug Pederson, who had been a backup in Green Bay, to start at quarterback. A lot of fans didn't like that, because Doug was clearly just holding the spot for Donovan McNabb. But Doug knew the offense, and Andy didn't want to start a rookie from game one. First, it was very tough for a quarterback to do that, due to the difference between the college and pro games. Second, we didn't have a lot of playmakers—beyond Duce Staley. As a matter of fact, Duce *was* the offense. So Donovan would have had a hard time succeeding. The offense finished thirtieth out of thirty-one teams in total yards and twenty-fifth in scoring. Andy was a West Coast Offense disciple, and it was going to take some time for the team to adjust to his system, and for him to get the players he needed to be successful.

So, Doug started the first nine games of the year, and we went 2–7. It certainly wasn't all his fault. Remember that he had played in the NFL for ten years, and had been with Andy for three years in

Green Bay before they came to Philadelphia. So, he knew his stuff, particularly about Andy's offense.

Donovan got the start in the tenth game against Washington, and we won, 35–28. The fans were excited about Donovan playing. We managed only 258 total yards, and 198 of those came on the ground. Donovan completed 8 of 21 passes for 60 yards and no TDs. We needed four Norm Johnson field goals and an 89-yard kickoff return for a touchdown by Allan Rossum to win. The biggest thing was, Donovan did not turn the ball over. And it was Donovan's first of many wins to come.

One of the big issues surrounding the Eagles' decision to draft Donovan was the style of offense he ran at Syracuse, which was very little like an NFL attack. 'Cuse ran a veer hybrid that had a solid passing component—McNabb averaged 21 passes a game as a senior, but was also asked to run often and to handle option responsibilities. The attack had some serious pop when it got rolling. In a 38–28 win at Michigan, Syracuse piled up 433 yards in total offense, with an almost equal run-pass balance. But converting a player who had operated an offense like that in college to an NFL starter—even if he did connect on 62.5% of his throws as a senior—was going to take some time. That's a big reason why Andy brought in Doug. He wanted to make sure Donovan was reasonably comfortable when he started playing.

The win over Washington didn't exactly lead to a late-season run that put us in playoff contention. We lost our next four games and didn't score more than 17 points in any of them. But we did rally at the end to beat New England and St. Louis. Donovan missed the Patriots game with a sprained left knee, but he was back against the Rams and threw three touchdown passes. Granted, St. Louis had already locked up the best record in the conference before that game, and wasn't playing its best people, but it was a strong way to close the season.

Those final seven games (Donovan played in six of them) gave us glimpses of what the offense was going to be like with him at quarterback. You could see his ability to get away from the rush and to extend plays with his leg. He was slippery, even in the pocket.

He could escape. I knew he had the juice, and I knew we were eventually going to score points. I was already very impressed with his escape ability from watching him on films years before as Clemson prepared to play Syracuse in the Gator Bowl in 1995. So I was telling teammates when we drafted him, We got us a keeper. To combine that with Jim's attacking style, I knew that added up to something that would give us the opportunity to start winning games again at an impressive clip. He was a rookie, and it was going to take some time to grow. Still, it was exciting to think about what Donovan could become, and I certainly wasn't going to doubt him, after what I saw him do to Clemson in that Gator Bowl game my senior year.

The NFL had learned a little about Donovan in 1999. The next season, the league would learn a whole lot more about him.

And about the Eagles.

CHAPTER 9

Taking a Big Step

Even though I was in the NFL, I still watched a lot of college football, and I knew how good Texas running back Ricky Williams was. He had won the Heisman Trophy in 1998 and rushed for 2,124 yards and 27 touchdowns. He looked unstoppable when he had the rock, and it's understandable why fans in Philadelphia wanted the Eagles to take him. He looked like a sure thing. Ricky was such a good athlete that he played minor-league baseball in the summer while he was in college.

The Eagles had the second overall pick, and it was clear that Cleveland, which was picking first, was going to take Kentucky quarterback Tim Couch. Couch, by the way, didn't play in a pro-style offense, just like Donovan. He was in Hal Mumme's "basketball on grass" spread attack, so he wasn't exactly ready for the NFL, and his career numbers in the league proved that.

Eagles fans wanted Ricky Williams, and Angelo Cataldi took a bunch of WIP listeners—the infamous "Dirty 30"—up to New York for the Draft. They knew the team was going to take Donovan or Edgerrin James, a running back from Miami, and they were going to let the world know how angry they were that Ricky wasn't coming to Philadelphia. When commissioner Paul Tagliabue announced the Eagles had selected Donovan, Angelo and his listeners went nuts. They booed and screamed and carried on for a long time. In some ways, they never stopped.

I think that introduction to some in the city never left Donovan. The city and the fans never lived it down, and Donovan carried it with him. I understood why they were upset because I knew Ricky was the dude. But we didn't pick him. We picked Donovan. I was thrilled with the choice. Thrilled. I had seen Donovan play up close. The fans had not. Especially back then. They weren't able to be as savvy as fans are now, because there wasn't as much information or as many games on every week. No videos flooding the airways like they are today. They listened to who the media said was the best player, and for Angelo and a lot of the media—not to mention former Philadelphia mayor Ed Rendell—Ricky was that cat.

When the fans booed Donovan, I don't think he ever let that go. It's one thing to use something like that as a chip on the shoulder, and he did use it as a chip, but sometimes I thought it hurt his and the fans' ability to get close to each other and get into each other's hearts. Because of that, Donovan became guarded. He presented a certain image, a certain way in front of the camera. But he was different away from it. The fans never saw that side of Donovan. They saw what he wanted them to see. I understand that, because we all kind of did that to a point. But I never got to the point where I was so guarded the fans didn't see any of the real me. So that booing really hurt his relationship with the fans.

Donovan is a fun-loving cat. He's a prankster and a jokester. You could see that during the 2018 Hall of Fame Enshrinement Ceremony. One of the highlights of Chicago linebacker Brian Urlacher's career that was shown on the video board was of Urlacher sacking Donovan. It was a pretty ordinary shot, but from the first few rows of seats on the field, people could hear someone booing. It was Donovan, and he had a big smile on his face while he was doing it.

Donovan learned over the years when it is time to work and time to have fun and kid around. Sometimes, when he first came into the league, he didn't know when it was time to put away the silliness. Which is understood when you have a guy with his quick-witted ability, and gift of gab. He would horse around in the locker room and on the practice field sometimes. There are certain instances when you have to be able to dial in completely and not have any distractions. Sometimes he was not always able to separate the two things early on.

Another thing about Donovan that I have noticed over the years from being around him is that the more nervous he gets, the sillier he gets. He would do quirky things from time to time when he got nervous. Some people tap their fingers. Some people mess with pencils or pens. They do nervous things to get their energy out. Sometimes, Donovan would do things to eliminate his nervous energy, like playing air guitar in the tunnel in Dallas before a playoff game. Fans and media didn't understand what he was doing, and they didn't like it.

But the biggest trouble he had with the fans was the strict way he presented himself to them. It was just "Yes" or "No," almost military in nature. He was probably upset with the media and upset with the fans about how they booed him, so the way he approached them soured a lot of people on him, which is a shame.

On the team, though, Donovan grew into a leader. When you are the quarterback of a football team, you have the position to lead the team down the field, but it doesn't mean you are going to be a leader. It's not given to you, though front office executives, as well as coaches, have doomed a lot of talented men by trying to make them the leader they want to see. You have to earn it on the field and off the field. Once you produce, the other players will look to you, and what you do with it is up to you. He didn't have to do a lot of talking, because we had many guys on the team who would step up to have conversations with other players and to say tough things that had to be said. So, Donovan didn't have to give many speeches. We had leadership on offense already, with Duce being the lead. We just needed him to play. I would always tell him, "We're going to go as far as you will take us."

That was the truth. The way the offense was set up, Donovan had the ball in his hands a lot. He had to make a lot of decisions. He also had the athletic ability that allowed him to get out of bad situations. I loved that. We had lost all those games before he became the starter, so to see him taking the team down the field and putting points on the board was, was, doggonit, it brought tears to my eyes I was so happy. If we could hold onto the ball and get it into the end zone, I knew we were going to win some games.

Donovan was a phenomenal athlete. He could move in the pocket, but I played basketball with him, and he could move like a point guard. And he had some hops as well. A lot of people don't realize how strong Donovan was. He could really put up some weight, especially when he was bench-pressing. He was stronger than me, to be honest with you. I think that strength was one of the reasons he would fire the ball into the ground sometimes. He was so jacked up, and when he would get that adrenaline going, he would lose his touch. It's like when you play golf, right after you've been lifting weights, and you want to go out and rip a drive. The ball could be sprayed anywhere, because you don't have that touch.

But that was only a small part of who Donovan was as a quarterback. And during the 2001 season, the rest of the NFL began to see what we already knew.

◇◇◇

We started the 2000 season with a 41–14 win over Dallas that featured an onside kick to open the game and 201 yards from Duce. But all anybody wanted to talk about was pickle juice.

The temperature at game time was 109 degrees, made worse by the fact that old Texas Stadium was covered in artificial turf, which reflected the heat up and made it about 130 degrees on the field. Before the game, at a request from Duce, trainer Rick Burkholder had some of us drinking pickle juice to help prevent cramping. When people found out that we did that, they went crazy. Pickle juice? That's wild.

The fact is, if you were from the south, you knew about pickle juice all along. That's one of the things we would drink to prevent cramping. It has a lot of sodium in it and some potassium. It gets into your system quickly and can help stop and ward off cramping. When you're young, you hear all about how drinking water is the right thing to do when you're sweating. But when you see some of the more pigmented brothers and sisters sweating, you can see the white residue on their bodies. That's the potassium, not just the fluids. When you drink water during exercise, you only replenish the liquid. You don't replace the minerals and electrolytes you use.

Pickle juice helps prevent cramping when you are sweating, and when it's 130 degrees, you're going to sweat.

There was a study done that proved the point. They jolted people's tibial nerves with some electricity to stimulate toe cramps and then gave some of them water, and some pickle juice. Many of those who drank pickle juice enjoyed almost immediate relief. The water drinkers still suffered.

You shouldn't drink too much pickle juice, though, because it can be a diuretic, and then you become dehydrated. But a little of it helps. It wasn't that hot here in Philly when we left for Dallas, but it was bad down there, and we knew we were going to use pickle juice. The guys from up north and out west knew nothing about it, but for the folks from down south, like Duce, it wasn't such a big thing. You drank pickle juice to stop cramping.

The onside kick was all Andy. He said after the game that he'd seen something on tape a month before the game about the front of Dallas' kick return team, and decided to go with it. It shocked the Cowboys when Dameane Douglas caught David Akers' popped up kick on our 42-yard line. Andy didn't stand in front of the team and announce we were going to onside kick. I'm sure the special teams people knew it, but the rest of us really didn't find out until the game was going to start. And when you hear about that, you get a look in your eye, and you say, "Yeah! Let's do it."

From there, it was almost all Duce. He gained 45 of the next 58 yards. Donovan hit Jeff Thomason with a one-yard TD pass, and we were off. We jumped out to a 24–6 halftime lead, sacked their quarterbacks five times, gave Troy Aikman his ninth concussion, and allowed only 167 total yards—34 fewer than Duce had by himself. It was a great start to the season.

◇◇◇

Our defense was pretty good in 1999, especially when it came to creating turnovers, but we were a lot better in '00 because we were in the second year of Jim's system. The first year in a defense, you just do what the coach tells you to do. The second year, you understand his philosophy. Some players may have still been trying to get comfortable, but I wasn't thinking anymore about what Jim wanted. I was just doing it.

What I'm trying to say is that I took ownership of the position. When Jim gave us the game plan, the template for that week, he was telling us how we could be successful. His experience was telling us what would work, but I knew that with my skill set, I could add to what Jim was trying to accomplish. That's what I mean by taking ownership of the position. I wasn't trying to do my own thing. A defense can't be successful when that happens, on the regular. If everybody is using his talents to complete their responsibilities, then the defense is a well-oiled machine. I didn't want to do somebody else's job. I wanted to do my job. And the great thing about Jim is that if I had a better way to do things, he was open to it. You still had to stay within the scheme, but you could add your own touches to it, to make it better for you, which made it better for the team.

That year, we had some games that didn't go so well defensively—we lost to the Giants twice, making it eight in a row to them, and gave up 57 points in the two games—but we held eleven teams to 17 points or fewer. And only four teams scored more than 20 against us. We were fourth in the league in scoring defense and tenth in yards allowed.

Offensively, Andy was going to run his offense and stick with it. We weren't going to have a "number one" receiver. There were going to be a whole bunch of number one receivers, and we were going to have running back by committee. That's the way he was going to do it, no matter what fans and media said. He wanted to have a bunch of pieces he could move around, like Duce and running back Brian Mitchell. People weren't excited about Charles Johnson and Torrance Small as our main wideouts, but it worked.

You saw something similar to that in the 2017 Eagles. There were a lot of people who could do the job. Three running backs split up the carries, and three different receivers caught more than 50 passes. I'm not saying Andy was the first guy to do that, because others used that approach before him. But there are many coaches who began running Andy's version of the West Coast offense. Now, people will start running Doug Pederson's version.

Andy wasn't a vertical shot guy early on. He was a get-the-ball-out-quickly guy. That's the classic West Coast system: get the ball out quickly. Get it into the playmakers' hands and let them make people miss and run after the catch. When we got Todd Pinkston and especially Terrell Owens, we went vertical more, because those guys could bust the top off of the defense.

Even though we began the 2000 season with that big win over the Cowboys, we lost the next two, 33–18 to the Giants and 6–3 to Green Bay. In early October, we were 3–3, after a loss to Washington. But here's what I came to understand about Andy. Because our training camps were so tough and physical, the first part of the season was up in the air. It was like we didn't have our legs back yet. Those camps were so physical that they drained us. We naturally might not be at our best in the first game. But because we were hitting and going so much in camp, right up until the end, we were tired and sore. I noticed over time, we didn't come out early in the season ready to bust up opponents all the time.

Once we caught our second wind, we were tough. So, while those training camps were a bit of a problem early in the season, they helped build us mentally and physically for the entire sixteen games. In the last half of the season, we seemed to be playing at a higher level than our opponents. We were playing better and faster than a majority of teams, and we were healthier because we were used to physical play. It's like chopping wood. You might bleed a little early on. But when you build those calluses, you're going to be able to chop longer and chop harder later on. That's what we did. We didn't always start off well, but nobody (in the locker room) would panic. We would pay a little more attention to detail, work a little harder in our areas, and we would win those late games.

If you look at us from 2000–04, we went 6–2 in the final eight games of each season, except for 2003, when we went 7–1. In 2000, we closed on a 6–1 tear and clinched home field for the wild card—the Giants won the division—with a 16–7 win over Cincinnati. We were back in the playoffs.

◇◇◇

Tampa Bay had lost twenty straight games in temperatures 40 degrees or colder when they came to visit us on New Year's Eve for the wild card playoff game. That day, it was 34 degrees, with a wind chill of 11, thanks to some serious gusts that reached 31 mph. I don't put a lot of stock in that cold-weather jinx, but the frigid temperatures didn't bother us.

Donovan played well that game, but the defense was really stout. We held Warrick Dunn, who had rushed for 1,133 yards that year and earned a Pro Bowl berth, to one yard and the team to a total of 199. Donovan threw for two touchdowns and ran for one more in a 21–3 win. It was our first playoff win since the rout of Detroit in 1995, and it was another step forward for the team.

Unfortunately, waiting for us, in the Meadowlands, were the Giants, who had beaten us eight straight times. New York wasn't consistently dominant from 1997–2000, although it made the Super Bowl in '00. But we couldn't beat the Giants. We lost close ones— 16–15 and 23–17 in overtime in 1999—and got whipped pretty good a couple times—20–0 in '98 and 33–18 in '00 —so when we met them in the playoffs, we wanted to get them.

In my mind, the Giants were the hurdle we had to get over in order to be considered a good team. It wasn't Dallas, and it wasn't Washington. The Giants had our number, and we needed to beat them.

Unfortunately, it wasn't going to happen in that playoff game. The Giants' Ron Dixon returned the opening kickoff 97 yards for a TD, and that set the tone. New York's defense did the rest. The Giants blitzed Donovan almost every play it seemed, sending so many rushers that he couldn't find any room to move around. He completed only 20 of 41 passes, but it was hardly all his fault. The Giants stuffed us, and even though our defense held them to just a pair of field goals (New York's only other touchdown came on Jason Sehorn's interception return after a remarkable catch), we weren't yet ready offensively to hang with the better teams. That's no crack at Andy or Donovan. It just wasn't our time. And so, we lost to the Giants—again—20–10.

We knew we were heading in the right direction. We could see that and sense that. Back in the day, every team that was on the rise had a team it couldn't beat. At one point, Michael Jordan's Bulls couldn't beat the Pistons. For us, it was the Giants. We didn't get them that time, but once we finally did beat them, we felt like there was nothing we couldn't do.

When we began the 2001 season 2–2 and headed up the Turnpike again to face New York, it didn't look like we were ready to beat the Giants. But remember what I told you about starting the season slowly? We only lost to the Cardinals two weeks before (we played the Giants after an early bye) because Jake Plummer hit MarTay Jenkins with a 35-yard Hail Mary pass with nine seconds left. So, we should have won that game. All right, woulda, shoulda, coulda. And we lost our first game, the opener, to Seattle in overtime. So, it's not like we were limping into the Meadowlands for that Monday Night game. We were 2–2, but those were two games we should have won, and we knew that. But we had lost to the Giants nine times in a row, and some of the guys on the team had never beaten them. We had to break the "here we go again" syndrome.

That one was a real slugfest. Neither team had 250 yards of total offense, and the Giants didn't score a touchdown. But they still led, 9–0, deep into the third quarter. After giving up three field goals before halftime, we didn't let them have anything in the second half, just 59 total yards and three first downs.

David Akers kicked a 25-yard field goal late in the third to make it 9–3, but we were still down with 5:52 left when we got the ball on their 40 after a poor punt. We drove to their 18-yard line at the two-minute warning, and that's where Donovan did what he does. This is what drives me crazy about people with short memories. People don't remember how elusive Donovan was. The pocket broke down, and he sprinted right. He froze Michael Strahan with a slight dead leg/pause fake and found James Thrash in the back corner of the end zone for a touchdown. It took them two full minutes to review the catch, but it stood, and after Akers kicked the extra point, we had a 10–9 win.

In my opinion, that was the game that gave us tremendous confidence. We kept fighting, and we overcame that "here we go again" feeling against the Giants. We were fine against everybody else, but that Giants defense was so tough, and we couldn't score against it. All they would do is run, run, run against us to waste the clock, and we couldn't move the ball on them. They would just grind us, grind us. It would be so frustrating.

So, when we beat them that Monday night, we really celebrated. Big smiles all around. And to make it even better, we beat them at their house. Once we beat them, once we got that thorn out of our side, we wouldn't worry about anybody else. No, we weren't scared of the Giants. I can only speak for myself on this one, I have a heck of a lot of respect for that organization and team. We hadn't beaten them in what seemed like forever. Once we did that, we knew it was on in the NFC East. Had we lost that game, I don't know if we would have had the mindset we needed to win the division, and have as much success as we did that year. It was just one regular-season win, but it felt like a lot more.

I can tell you there was a huge celebration in the locker room after that game. We finally got over that hump. It was a mental and physical hurdle. Once you find what you need to do to get past that hurdle, the sky is the limit to what you can accomplish.

That was the year we really established our identity. We finished 11–5, just like we did the year before, but we won the division, went a franchise-best 7–1 on the road, and allowed only 64 points in those games. We were beating people playing our game, which was to keep the score down on defense and get a lead so that Jim could blitz the heck out of you. We wanted to force you to make mistakes after we had the lead, and then build it up so much that we could just run it out late. That's the way the Giants did it. When we beat them at *their* game, we knew we could beat everybody else at *our* game.

Beating the Giants early in the season gave us the confidence that we could win the East. But it wasn't until we took care of them at the end of the season at the Vet that we knew we were the best in the division.

It wasn't an easy one—again. And it started early when a few of our players got into an altercation with some Giants during the pre-game warmups. As you might imagine, the Eagles fans loved that. Things only got wilder from there. The score was only 7–0 at the half, we led, but the Giants took control of the game in the second half, and with 2:43 left, held a 21–14 lead.

That's when Donovan went to work. He led a 67-yard scoring drive that ended in a seven-yard TD pass to Chad Lewis. We stuffed them on their next possession, Donovan led the offense 54 yards to the Giants' 11, and David Akers kicked a 35-yard field goal with seven seconds left to give us a 24–21 lead. Game over, right?

Wrong.

Akers sent the ensuing kickoff through the end zone, and the Giants took over at the 20. Kerry Collins threw a pass down the middle to Tiki Barber, who ran to the New York 37. There, he lateraled to speedster Ron Dixon, a backup wideout, who turned the corner and headed up the sideline. The clock was filled with zeroes, but Dixon was still going. We had enjoyed a "Miracle at the Meadow-lands." Was this to be "Vindication at the Vet" for the Giants?

No. Damon Moore, my safety partner, tracked down Dixon and tackled him at our six. There was no time left. We won, 24–21, and had our first division title since 1988. After losing nine straight to the Giants, we had beaten them two in a row. We were headed back to the playoffs. And Tampa Bay was coming back to Philadelphia.

◇◇◇

A big part of our winning the division—beyond dumping the Giants twice—was that the offense had become much more reliable than it had been in previous years. A lot of that was Donovan's maturity. He was in his third season and had become pretty comfortable and productive under center. Another big reason was Andy. He was great at scripting the first fifteen plays of the game based on what he had seen on tape from the other team. Sometimes, he was trying to figure out how opponents would respond to certain formations. Other times, he was exploiting weaknesses. But the results were usually the same: the offense was getting better.

You saw that against the Bucs. Donovan threw two touchdown passes, and we whipped them, 31–9. And just so everybody doesn't think it was only the offense responsible for the big win, know that we picked off four passes, held them to 63 yards rushing, didn't allow a point in the second half and scored the final touchdown on Damon Moore's 59-yard interception return. The Bucs were gone, and we moved on to face Chicago, which had gone 13–3 during the regular season.

It was homecoming for Donovan, who had grown up in Chicago, and he sure seemed at home against the Bears. The game was close for the first three quarters, and we held a 20–17 lead early in the fourth. But three big defensive plays—a fumble recovery by Quinton Caver and an interception by Rashard Cook—set up a pair of late scores that iced a 33–19 victory. And the block Hugh Douglas made on Chicago's starting QB, Jim Miller, which knocked him out of the game. No, it was not a dirty hit. Hugh told me he told him not to move. And he moved. So Hugh blocked him, hard. It was a great team effort, but Donovan was particularly good. He threw two TD passes and ran for another. After the game, Chicago defensive tackle Blake Brockermeyer said that Donovan "just killed us," because he kept escaping tackles and keeping plays alive. We knew we were coming to town with talent and that we could do whatever was needed to win.

The Rams had the best record in the NFL in 2001, 14–2, and they were averaging 31.4 PPG. "The Greatest Show on Turf" was back in full force after slipping a bit in '00. And while we were on the move as a team and a franchise, most people considered them the best team in the NFL. Not that they had been all that overwhelming in the first week of the season when they beat us, 20–17, in a game we could have—and probably should have—won. We sacked Kurt Warner five times and forced a couple turnovers. Their touchdown "drives" were only 12 and 30 yards, and they came after recovering our fumbles.

And then there was the killer. In the fourth quarter, after we tied the game at 17, Aveion Cason, a St. Louis rookie, fumbled the kickoff inside the five, and three of our players had a chance to fall on it. Instead, Quinton Caver tried to scoop the ball up and run with it, and St. Louis recovered to avoid disaster. They won in overtime on a field goal. But we had our chances. Donovan had more passing yards than Warner (312–308), ran for 48 yards and led a great, eighteen-play, 98-yard TD drive in the fourth quarter to narrow St. Louis' lead to 17–10.

Because we came so close at the beginning of the season, we weren't afraid of the Rams. Everybody else thought it was going to be easy for them, and that we were playing with house money. They were congratulating us on a great season, but they didn't think we had much of a chance against the Rams. But we did, and we almost beat them. And almost is a good thing, even if it's just a moral victory. But when you cut the champ and you see that he can bleed... we knew we were closer than ever.

When the Eagles brought me to Philadelphia, one of the first things Emmitt said to me was that they liked me because of the different things I could do. I could cover and blitz and intimidate. That would all help us against a team like St. Louis, which was so good offensively.

Early in the second quarter, the Rams were leading, 10–3, and I was thinking that I had to do something. They had gotten into a little groove and had taken the ball from their 12 out to our 33. On second and five, Jim called a blitz, and I was able to time disguise and time the blitz perfectly. I dumped Marshall Faulk for a two-yard loss. On the very next play, third down, Warner threw to Az Hakim, and I rocked him. The ball came out for an incompletion, and they had to try a 53-yard field goal that was no good. After Jeff Wilkins missed the kick, I ran down to where the ball rested, patted it and said, "Good job." I got excited by the play on Hakim. The sideline got excited. I was flexing, because I was blessed to help change the momentum. I had help in some of the energy I was feeling from the fans that made the trip and my teammates on the sideline. I had said to myself, "Dawk, you gotta do something. Go do it."

After they missed the field goal, we went right down the field in four plays and scored a touchdown. We scored again right before halftime and were up, 17–13, so we had momentum. And we felt good because we weren't supposed to be leading them. But in the second half, they really used Faulk a lot. This was a team that had thrown the ball all year, and while Marshall was a great back, we were surprised they ran the ball so much. Faulk finished with 159 yards, and that's how they beat us. They didn't score a lot on us, and we forced them to punt it a few times in the second half.

I remember before the last drive for our offense, I found myself screaming on the sideline "You've got to believe!" No, really, I was walking up and down the sidelines looking for someone that had weak eyes or posture, and screaming "You gotta believe!" I'm talking teammates, coaches, doctors, trainers, equipment cats. It didn't much matter. But hopes were dashed when Aeneas Williams picked off a Donovan pass on our last drive, and we lost, 29–24. It was so close. And we were right there. We had the champs on the ropes, but we couldn't knock them out. They went on to lose to the Patriots in the Super Bowl, but they were still the NFC champs. I'm not one for moral victories, and we all wanted to go to the Super Bowl. We were very confident we could get to the NFC Championship Game.

What made things even worse after the loss was that I had a full-body cramp after the game. The worst I have ever had. And I've had my share of them. I had never felt pain like that. Everything I moved cramped up. The whole team had to wait to leave the stadium because I had to get IVs to stop the cramping, ice bags to cool me down. It hurt so much. All I could do was sit as still as I could so as to not cause anything else to cramp, and cry. I'm talking snot bubble cry. The worst thing was, they had to massage the area that was cramping with ice, which made it hurt worse. So, not only did we lose a tough game; everybody had to wait for me to leave. It was brutal.

But it also showed us that we were growing as a team. And the distance between us and the Champions had gotten even tighter. And I was going to do all I could and do my part to close the distance completely during that coming off-season.

CHAPTER 10

Working Harder and Harder

My off-season workout regimen depended on how long the season lasted. If we went deep into the playoffs, I might take off two or two-and-a-half weeks before getting started. If we didn't get into the post-season, I probably had a month off, but it was active rest. That means I was riding a stationary bike or hitting the elliptical machine almost every day. I wouldn't do anything crazy, like sprints, but just some kind of workout to keep moving. Maybe even some kickboxing. The goal was to build a foundation.

Then, once I got started for real, I would go into almost body-builders mode, because I wanted to get stronger. I was pushing some real weight. So it was build the foundation, and then make it stronger. Along the way, I would still be getting massages and doing a lot of stretching, because I didn't want to get bulky and not be able to move. But I would start to move the strength soon after. Doing movement drills designed for me to stay low, as I tended to raise up, especially when I put on mass or when I got tired. I did not want stationary strength. I wanted to be power in motion.

In July, I would head out to Arizona to train in the heat. I would bring the family for a vacation, but I was going to the Fischer Institute in Phoenix to work with Brett Fischer and his crew. I was turned on to him, and in Arizona, because of Donovan, as he had invited myself and others out to train. I would still be pushing weight, but there was a lot of movement involved, too. We would be done with mini-camps and other team workouts, and it was time to do some "touch-ups" in the heat. I would also spend time in Chandler, a Phoenix suburb, with Ann Frederick at Stretch to Win, and use a different level of stretching that was unique. When I could not make it to Arizona, I thought I would enlighten one of the best masseuses I've ever had, and see if she was open to learning the special techniques from Ann and her team. She obliged and added that to her repertoire. Which became a deadly combo. Mrs. Kate Decker, CSCS, USATF and USAW Coach, FSS Level 3-Medical, ART Provider, or Coach Decker, as she is also called, is gifted in the art healing with her knowledge, hands, and faith.

It wasn't just stretching the muscles. It also involved stretching the fascia, which is a thin layer of tissue surrounding the muscle. I would focus on that with the hamstring, where I would always get tight. Ann taught me different stretches I could do for certain areas to keep the muscles firing. Another area of concern was the left quadriceps, that teardrop muscle just above the knee. If that wasn't fully flexible and firing, it could activate the tendonitis in my left knee. Because I broke my leg in ninth grade, that knee hyperextends farther than the other. So, I was always working on that teardrop so that I could activate it, and so the tendon wouldn't hurt.

Sometimes, we might also go down to Tucson, to Canyon Ranch, a holistic resort and spa. Everything there is natural, and you have the ability to create your own schedule—yoga, boot camps, cooking classes. You can put together what you want to do. I did some hot yoga and other things there, but the one thing that was always non-negotiable was stretching. I had to make sure my flexibility was where it needed to be. I had to make sure my body was balanced on every level. So that meant that I would also get blood drawn so that my levels could be tested. I'm not talking about your average test either. It's what I did at least twice a year, to see what I was low in, or if there were any areas of concern.

From that test, Dr. Brian Popiel, a great naturopath in Arizona, would then discuss any concerns with me. He would then put me on a regimen that was tailor-made to me. I still do this same thing to this day. I take anywhere from 15 to 20 vitamins and the like per day. I also would get my IV's and B12 from him. This is something I would tell everyone to do. To find someone that is able to do something similar. Someone that will send you down a natural path to developing the best you that you can become.

Because of the way I threw my body around, I had to have someone that could help get me back every week when it came to my
neck, back, hips, feet, etc. One of the best is Dr. Andrew Kirschner,
my osteopathic specialist and friend, who helped me during the season and after if need be. He was truly a godsend. Dr. Kirshner developed a technique from working on more elderly and potentially
fragile patients. A way that he could still manipulate different places
that need adjustment, without adding more pain or trauma to the
person. Guess what I had a lot of after every game, and after a tough
week of practice preparing for our next opponent? You guessed it,
areas that were out of whack, as well as different levels of trauma.
He would sometimes spend 45 minutes to an hour quieting down
my noisy body, before setting things back in place. He helped me get
back to peak performance and then some with the "magic table," as
I dubbed it.

I watched film of myself and tried to notice areas where I needed to improve. If I had struggles with certain things, I tried to attack
those areas in off-season training, so I could be better and more
efficient.

The Eagles didn't drive this. Back then, most of what players
were doing during off-season training was the same old stuff, like
power cleans and squats. So, some of what I was doing was ahead of
its time. Simply because I understood that you cannot put a ceiling
on how to improve. I was constantly looking for ways to get better.
For things I could add to my own repertoire. It was just a desire
for me not to get stagnant in my workouts. I believed that muscles
could get used to the same things and not continue to develop, as
could my brain if I didn't constantly challenge them. So I would try
to figure out ways to shock my body, shock my system. I wanted to
come up with things that worked areas I hadn't been hitting in my
usual regimen.

I discovered a lot of things that I can teach other guys to utilize
now. And it all came from thinking outside the box and trying to
come up with things that would give me an edge, and keep me on
the cutting edge. It was like I was my own guinea pig. I would find
something that helped, and it gave me a little pop. So, I added it.

Sometimes I would do kickboxing. But the one that I gained the most from was MMA. Before it got as grand as it is today, with all of its rules and such. (Sarcasm.) It was "no holds barred" ultimate fighting. During one off-season, I was blessed to see this big dude in the gym when I was blessed to buy a home in Jacksonville during the off season. I watched him and a few other cats he trained with, and the sick intensity they went at it with, and I thought to myself "I gotta get in on that right deh!" I saw these dudes on a couple of occasions as they were working out, pushing weight at a breakneck pace, stopping to throw up because of the pace, only to be ready to go for their next set. Like nothing had happened. I FREAKIN' LOVED IT. So I waited till the next day and asked Tim Catalfo ("Obake") to get me started.

I also tried to eat right, which didn't really happen consistently until I was in the NFL, because before that, I was always trying to gain weight. Anything I put on, I would burn right off. In college, I paid attention to nutrition somewhat, but it wasn't until year three of my NFL career that I started to watch what I was eating. It was a simple concept. Look at a luxury car. You're not going to put bad fuel into it. If you do, you'll tear up the engine. It just made sense. The better the stuff I put into my "engine," the more capacity I had to perform, and the more I would get out of it. That same philosophy works when it comes to your mind: What you meditate on or read, watch, listen to, will fill your brain with either good stuff, or junk. And your actions will be the byproduct.

Because I pushed myself so hard in training, I could tell when the energy I expended wasn't quality energy. So, I ate right. Chicken, fish, vegetables, fruits, and a steak every once in a while. So I'm eating right, blood tested so I have my vitamins on point, stretching, getting my back, neck, hips, and feet aligned continuously, on a never-ending search for better ways to improve my workouts, to bring more and more out of me. I even got amino acids designed for me later on in my career, when I, dig this, was diagnosed with "Overtraining Syndrome." As I wasn't recovering like I once was, and I knew it wasn't just an age thing. And I even was told that I was not eating enough calories.

So I actually had to start eating more of the right foods for me. All the way to what I should eat immediately after a hard workout. Simple sugars was one. I chose Skittles. So as you can plainly see, I was spending a grip taking over my corporation. No, I'm not talking about another company. I'm talking about me. This body. This vessel. This temple. If I was to be one of the greatest, if not the greatest to play at my position, if I was going to play consistent football for an entire career, if I was going to help redefine a safety position, I had to live outside of conventional thinking. From hyperbaric chambers, vibrating plate, to microcurrent machines. I got 'em all!

The goal was to put in the right fuel, work out the best way and do whatever I could to prepare my body for consistent success. Practice is important, but what you do before the season and in between team workouts is even more vital. And let's not forget recovery. Add it all up, and you get sixteen years of consistently physical and play-making football in the NFL.

CHAPTER 11

So Close... Again

One of the most important things about a team is that everybody has to know their role. There can't be twenty-two stars among the starters, so there have to be players who just do their jobs. One of the great qualities about the Eagles when I played for them was that we had guys who knew who they were and what they were supposed to do. We had our share of guys who could be considered superstars, but we also had a lot of guys who knew their roles perfectly. That's why we felt comfortable as a team.

We were very accountable to one another. We weren't going to let people slide when they didn't do the work or messed up assignments. And that included me. If I made a mistake, I expected someone to tell me about it. We were like an engine with all the parts moving in sync for a good portion of time, especially in the second half of the seasons. Andy and Jim didn't have to say a lot to motivate or correct us. We knew what had to be done.

When Donovan went down with a broken right ankle in the win over the Cardinals during the tenth game of the 2002 season—he still threw four touchdown passes in the game while hurt—we didn't panic. He was such a big part of our team, but we had so much more. We just altered things a bit. We said to backup QB A.J. Feeley, "A.J., we got you, bro. Just don't turn the ball over." All he had to do was to play his game and do what he did best. The defense wasn't going to put him in situations where he had to come back from big deficits. We ran the ball more. The defense picked it up and played even better than we had been playing.

After Donovan went down, we were 7–3. With A.J. at quarterback, we won our next five games. We were also fueled by the overwhelming majority of the football world saying our season was over. We should start looking to get the best draft picks and the like. We gave up only 64 points during that stretch, and A.J. actually had some strong performances. He threw for two touchdowns in a 27–20 victory at Seattle. He threw for 220 yards and two TDs in the 34–21 win over Washington, which was the last regular-season game at The Vet. We clinched our second straight NFC East title that day. Donovan came back for the playoffs, but A.J. did a great job while he was out. A.J. had a lot of help, though. We were a true team, and everybody stepped up.

◇◇◇

It didn't matter who was playing quarterback for the other team; we felt we could rattle him. I'm not taking anything away from the passers we faced, but in Jim's meetings, he didn't care whether you were mobile or a statue, we were going to hit you. You had better get rid of the football because if you didn't, we were going to hit you… hard… and often. Jim was adamant that we attack upfield, rather than getting caught inside. That's who we were, and I loved it. Ever since I was a little kid, playing center and angry that I had to do it, I wanted to hit people. Not just hit them, punish them. That's how my father—"Hit Stick"—was, too.

So, when we played Atlanta in the 2002 playoffs, the big challenge was keeping the Falcons' QB, Michael Vick, from being able to move around. Even though Atlanta went just 9–6–1 during the regular season, the Falcons had whipped 12–4 Green Bay, 27–7, on the road in the first round of the playoffs. Vick passed for 117 yards and ran for 64 and gave the Packers a lot of trouble with his ability to move.

Even though the Falcons had won in Green Bay in their first playoff game, we felt good having them coming out of that dome where they played their home games, with all of the comforts of that facility. They were coming to the frigid air of Philadelphia and our awesomely crazy fans. I know coming from Florida that it took me a minute to get comfortable playing in cold weather. It didn't happen right away. I could only imagine what those cats felt playing against us. But no matter how cold it was, we had to stop Vick.

Vick was most dangerous when he got outside the pocket, because he could run like a tailback, and when things broke down, and he was rolling out, it was harder to cover guys. So, Jim was preaching to us all week, "Stay outside!" That meant our ends had to contain him by not trying to move inside. If they did that, Vick could get around them and make big plays. We wanted him to have to step up in the pocket, where we could get to him more easily.

One of the problems with that was that Hugh Douglas was always going to step inside. So, Jim had to create a stunt for him in certain situations to try and keep us from giving up a big play. That goes to understanding your personnel. So, if I was blitzing on Hugh's side, I was going to see what he was doing, and I was going to make things right. So, if he went inside, I went outside. That allowed him to be free, to play without thinking too much. Jim created some stuff to let Hugh be Hugh. I loved that.

Hugh had a huge personality. I remember when we first brought him in here on a trade (from the Jets in 1998), watching him and listening to him. Hugh never shuts up. I love that about him. What that does during grueling training camps and practices, is it makes you forget the fatigue. He keeps your mind off the pain. He and (defensive tackle) Hollis Thomas connected quickly. Hollis is a prankster himself. He's a funny, quick-witted cat. The two of them would get together during warmups and just pick at people. "Look at what he's got on." Things like that.

Hugh didn't care when or where he talked. He just talked. We loved the movie "Friday" that starred Ice Cube and Chris Tucker. One time, we were in a meeting, and Hugh was talking too much as Coach Brasher was trying to talk. And Tommy Brasher, who was a grizzled, tough, old-fashioned defensive line coach, said, "Hugh, shut the H--- up!" It was quiet for a second, but then Hugh said, "I'll be quiet, but when we leave? I be talking again." We fell out, because that's what Smokey, Chris Tucker's character in the movie Friday, said to Deebo (played by Tiny Lister Jr.) when Deebo stole the bike. We were laughing so hard in the meeting, because that's just Hugh. He and Hollis would say funny stuff to mess with people, but that's what kept meetings light. It kept fun in the game, because they were always going to find something about people to laugh at or pick at.

I also knew this about Hugh: he was going to give you every-thing he had. He was going to work hard. And in those big moments, he was probably the one who was going to get pressure on the quar-terback for you. He might have been silent for a long time, but he was the one who was going to get there at the right time. You knew that about him.

Jim wanted us to stay outside against Vick, but he also wanted us to hit him as hard and as often as we could. We hit him through-out that game, and I may have had the most vicious hit I ever had in my life when I hit him that game. He had scrambled up the middle in the third quarter and was heading toward the goal line, and I came across the field and drilled him at about the one-yard line. He made it into the end zone (the play was called back because of a holding call), but he didn't get up for a while. I was thinking two things as I approached him, maybe three. One, this joker is looking outside at Bobby and doesn't even see me coming. Two, I can hit him and cause a fumble. And three? Take this with you. You see, my philosophy when it came to cats scoring or getting out of bounds and the like, was, You may get it, but take this knot with you. Take this bruise with you. Take this painful shot, that could possibly tight-en up in the fourth quarter to have you be just a tad bit less effective later on.

I had been running for about 15 or 20 yards, full speed, and he had been running about 30 yards full speed. I didn't break down and gather myself before I hit him. I knocked myself out, too. I shouldn't have played the rest of the game. I wasn't the same after that hit. I don't think I made another tackle in the game. I wasn't all the way there. I was seeing things that were happening on the field, but I couldn't react in the right way to do anything about it. In my dumb mind at the time, I knew we were better off with me on the field, so I fought through it. But I don't think I made another tackle. However, I did have an interception in the fourth quarter.

Donovan played for the first time since his injury that game. Thanks to the bye we earned by winning the division, he had eight weeks off. On the second play of the game, he took off on a 19-yard run that erased any doubt about whether he would be able to move.

He threw for 247 yards and a touchdown in a 20–6 win. We sacked Vick three times and picked him off twice. Bobby Taylor returned one of the interceptions 39 yards for a touchdown. Vick only ran for 30 yards, and their offense couldn't do anything against us.

Even though I was foggy during the Atlanta game, my head was clear a week later when we played Tampa Bay in the NFC championship game. It would be the last game ever at the Vet, and we were heavily favored. The Bucs had never won a playoff game on the road, and we had beaten them four straight times, including during the 2000 and '01 playoffs. Then there was the cold weather thing. It was 26 degrees at kickoff, so everybody thought they would just crumble.

Only that didn't happen. That was one of the most frustrating games ever. I really thought we were heading to the Super Bowl. We had so many guys playing at such high levels at that time. I thought this time we would win it all. I really, really, really did. But we didn't, and that was extremely painful.

Tampa Bay coach Jon Gruden did a great job of putting his offense in running formations and then passing the ball. Jim would counter with players who were better against the run, taking Hugh and other pass rushers off the field. Gruden would then send a receiver in motion that would put him in coverages against some of our run-stoppers, and the receiver would have an advantage.

We took a 7–0 lead quickly. Brian Mitchell returned the opening kickoff to their 26, and two plays later, Duce scored from 20 yards out. Only 52 seconds were gone, and it looked like we were going to do it. After they hit a field goal to make it 7–3, the play everybody remembers happened. Tampa had the ball, third and two on its own 24, and Brad Johnson threw a quick pass to wide receiver Joe Jurevicius that was designed to get a few yards and a first down. Jurevicius was running a crossing pattern from right to left and had one of our linebackers on him, instead of a defensive back. He caught the pass and headed to the left sideline. Safety Blaine Bishop, who had torn his groin muscle off the bone but was playing anyway, fighting through the injury like we all do, let him get up the sideline, 71 yards to our five.

On that play, I had an angle on Jurevicius, but there were so many of our guys around him that I thought, "They got it." All of a sudden Jurevicius broke loose, and I turned on the burners and caught him, and knocked him out of bounds on the five-yard line. That just sucked the air out of the place, and we could never get our bearings again and get back on top of things. We were running the ball well early, and they couldn't stop us. And I was just screaming at Andy, "Run the ball! Just run it! We got you!" I meant that if he kept grinding against them, the defense wouldn't let up any more points. Not that he heard me.

That play happened, and the whole momentum swung. Their defense picked up, and our offense couldn't get into a rhythm. On defense, we couldn't do anything to change field position. We weren't giving up points, but we weren't getting turnovers to change field position and give our offense a shorter field to work with.

We had a chance to come back, when Donovan led a drive that reached Tampa Bay's 10-yard line with under four minutes left and the score 20–10, Tampa Bay. But Donovan tried to hit Antonio Freeman with a pass, and Ronde Barber intercepted it and ran 92 yards for a touchdown. That was it.

I felt like we had the better team. That's just the way I felt. They had star players, and their star players played well, but there were a couple of plays here and a couple of plays there, just like it happens in most playoff games. We just didn't do it. Defensively, we could have done a better job of changing the field position, of doing something to get the ball out of their hands. We should have made them more uncomfortable and forced a turnover. We did intercept Johnson once, but it wasn't enough.

Our defense wasn't supposed to be about three-and-outs. Three-and-outs allow them to punt the ball deep, and our offense would have to drive the length of the field in order to score. We would punt it back, and we couldn't get a turnover. That's how the whole game went. We weren't able to do anything significant, like a sack that causes a fumble or anything like that. We had dictated to other teams all season. We couldn't do it against Tampa Bay.

What makes it even more frustrating is the Bucs blew out the Raiders in the Super Bowl, and we felt we would have done the same thing, the exact same thing. We should have won the Super Bowl. But we didn't. And an unfortunate theme would start to follow us.

◇◇◇

The loss to Tampa Bay closed the season, but it also ended the Eagles' run at the Vet. As I said earlier, the place was rough, from the rats in the corridors to the hard, unforgiving turf on the field. But the fans there were the best. And it was like the Vet belonged to all of us.

I loved the energy, the enthusiasm and the almost theatrical and almost animalistic way people acted in the stands. Opponents knew when they came in there that you would be playing against the Eagles and a group of loud, passionate fans. I know Seattle describes its fans as "the 12th Man," and they have earned the right to call themselves that. But the noise from our fan base when we were playing like we did at the Vet meant that other teams had to be mentally tough when they came there to play. They were going to be verbally assaulted by the fans, and they were going to be dealt with physically on the football field, too.

Obviously, there are some things I didn't agree with, like the verbiage some fans used and the fights, and things like that. I don't necessarily agree with some of that. The atmosphere was a very intense one for opposing teams, and what made it even tougher was that they had to play against a good team. The two of us together—the team and the fans—were a lot for teams to deal with when they came to the Vet.

◇◇◇

After the 2002 season, I remember telling the guys that I was going to come back with my arms looking like my legs. That's how much I was going to work out during the off-season. I was going to be ready to go that year, and I was prepared. And they were too. We opened up the '03 season against Tampa Bay and lost to them, 17–0. I had a Lisfranc injury during the game, and I missed the next six weeks. I was lucky that I didn't suffer a fracture, but it was brutal to be off the field. We had come off that epic battle against Tampa

Bay in the NFC Championship game, and I entered the 2003 season expecting big things. Then, I went down with an injury. I remember Bobby Taylor went out that game, too, with plantar fasciitis.

That was the first time in my career that I missed a lot of games in a row, and I didn't know how to deal with that. Seriously, I was one miserable cat. I was an angry dude, and Connie kept telling me to get out of the house and just go do something. Go to physical therapy. Go get treatment. I couldn't travel with the team, so I would just be home. On game days, I would close myself in the room and watch the game. Of course, my competitive juices were still going, like I was about to get ready to play. I would sit there, screaming at the TV.

After a couple weeks of that, I said, "I have to figure out how to do a better job with this." So, I began to work out. And when I say, "work out," I mean push weight. Push a lot of weight. And I actually got too big. I was all swelled up. I couldn't work out my legs yet, so I focused on my upper body—I got really big—and on my wind, by using the arm turning machine.

But here's the other thing I did: I helped the guy behind me on the depth chart, Clinton Hart. Clinton was a rookie who had played two years in the Arena Football 2 League. He had a look in his eye that was very familiar for me. I remembered it from back in the day when I had it. He wasn't scared, but he was nervous. It was all so intimidating for him. He was a very good special teams player, but now he was thrust into a starting role. Not just any role, he would be playing safety. I had told the young cats in one of the first meetings after they got there, that the position of safety may be just another position everywhere else. But for the Eagles, it's a game changer's position. That was tough enough, but because I had played the safety position in a certain way over the past several years, there were certain things expected out of that position. They expected the safety position to be played differently in Philadelphia because of the way I played it, even going back to Wes Hopkins and Andre Waters.

When I couldn't get onto the field, I poured myself into helping him. I would watch film with him, and I would let him see different things that I had brought up earlier. I wanted to show him as much as I saw, and let him see how much he would then own and digest. I would say, "Look at this. Look at that. Attack that. See how the back is carrying the ball. Here's how to attack him." I was giving him as much as I could of myself, of how I saw the game, to help him slow it down as much as possible. For a couple of the games I sat out, I was playing vicariously through him.

I was watching him to see what he would do. Clinton probably had some of the best ball skills I had ever seen. He's not the best, but he's up there with the best in terms of catching the ball. That was never the problem. The trouble he had was sometimes mental, being new and sometimes physical, being young. He had trouble with positioning himself properly to make plays. I was trying to help him with that. But he balled out so much during the games when I was out that I started to think, "I had better get my butt back onto the field." Clinton was intercepting passes, making plays, blitzing, just balling. I could see in his eyes that he was getting more confident. This is one of the first times I noticed how pouring myself into a teammate could help him achieve great things. I don't know if he thought he was capable of doing that for himself at the time. But I know now that, I can only help bring out what the Lord has already put into a person, that may be laying dormant. Waiting on a word.

Clinton only stayed with the Eagles for two seasons, but he was able to get himself a good contract with San Diego (four years, $12.25 million). I'm thankful I was blessed to be used to help wake something up in him that was already there, that maybe he didn't recognize he had. All of a sudden, he started to play confidently. Even when I came back, they were using him in some packages with me, because he was playing so well, and Jim wanted to get him on the field, especially with those ball skills. As well as being more productive on Special Teams. So newfound confidence and growth in one area, will increasingly affect many other areas? Got it!

That might have been the turning point for me in terms of sharing my knowledge and experience with my teammates, to the max. I saw that look in Clinton's eyes; it changed from wide-eyed to a squint. That squint is saying, "How can I go make a play? What am I going to do to make a play here?" When I saw his confidence growing, I wanted to see how many other teammates I could help. I began to pray about finding ways to help my teammates. I would take them to the side and speak with them, take time out of my day to see if I could help them out.

This was a bit selfish, too. I knew the more confident they were, the better they were going to play. The better everybody played, the more games we would win, the more opportunities we would have to win that Lombardi Trophy. When that happens, players can make more money with new contracts, and they are able to bless themselves and their families. So, by helping out my teammates, I could help change the team's dynamic. A light bulb had gone off in my head. Instead of sulking about my injury and not being able to play, I reached out and tried my best to bless Clint and others even more than I already was.

◇◇◇

We finished the 2003 season on a 10–1 run to win the division for the third straight year. Our only loss during that stretch was in overtime to San Francisco. We were really rolling. We had the bye, because we went 12–4, and we hosted Green Bay in the divisional playoff game. It wasn't going to be easy. In the last regular-season game, against Washington, running back Brian Westbrook tore a tendon in his arm and was done for the rest of the year. That was a big loss because he scored seven TDs that year and was beginning to emerge as a real weapon as a receiver and a runner.

Before this game, Donovan and I flew Ann Frederick in for a prime pregame stretch earlier in the day. I felt like my knees were touching my chin, and my heels were hitting me in the back of the head when I ran. It was so free-moving and effortless and I didn't get tired as quickly. Oftentimes I would get gassed early on purpose, so I could get to my second wind. Not this game, though. It was like some sports cars. Most of them have other gears, so the higher they are pushed, the faster they go. For instance, there's a gear that kicks in when you push a sports car past 120. This is how I felt. So this is when I came up with the thought, How can I get this kind of stretch on a week-to-week basis, without asking Ann to do all that flying.

Green Bay was ready. Brett Favre threw two touchdown passes to Robert Ferguson, and we fell behind, 14–0. Meanwhile, the offense couldn't get anything going. It was three-and-out, three-and-out. Midway through the second quarter, Donovan hit Duce with a seven-yard TD pass, and early in the fourth, he found Todd Pinkston from 12 yards out to make it 14–14. Green Bay sacked Donovan eight times, but he set a QB playoff record with 107 yards rushing. A turning point was when we stopped with a goal-line stand before the half. They went for it on fourth down twice on that drive. The first was around the 50-yard line, when Ahmad Green burst through on the right side of the line. I took an angle to go get him and prevent a TD. All I was thinking was, Get him down, to give us a chance. We had had plenty of enemy offenses that got into the red zone. But we took pride in not letting folk score. We were stout, to say the least. I could often be heard saying, "It don't matter! It doesn't matter how they got down here. Our jobs are the same. They don't score a TD, and a field goal ain't a definite!" And so we stopped them with the ball on the 1-yard line. Four times! I remember the crowd going crazy, just like we were going crazy on the field. I remember folk sprinting into the locker room as if the faster we got into the locker room, the sooner we could get back out there. I was blessed to have 8 tackles, 1 pass broken up, and 1 interception to help our cause.

Still, after a Green Bay field goal with 10:21 left in regulation, we were down, 17–14, and couldn't get anything going. We had one more chance from our own 20, with 2:21 remaining. Duce ran for 22 yards, but Donovan threw two incomplete passes and was sacked for a 16-yard loss. It was fourth-and-26 from the 26. It didn't look good.

Every Eagles fan knows what came next. A play that seemed to have happened in slow motion. Donovan hit Freddie Mitchell with a 28-yard pass with 1:12 left to get the first down and keep our hopes alive. The Packers had seemingly jammed the WRs at the line of scrimmage all game. But for whatever reason, they gave Freddie clear room to run. And Donovan hit him with a laser. They had to measure, which was like slow motion, and it was just enough to keep hope alive. We drove to their 14, and David Akers hit a 37-yard field goal with five seconds left to force overtime.

In the overtime, GB had the ball first. And on the first play of the drive, Jim called an overload zone blitz, off of Green Bay's right side. A blitz that sent our outside LB Ike Reese and strong safety Michael Lewis. Ike did a great move on the tight end to beat him to the inside (where he was supposed to go anyway) which left Mike untouched heading to Favre. Pre-snap, I showed like I was going to be going to the other side, by aligning about 3 to 4 yards outside the hash mark. At the snap the pressure happened quick, so he could notice that I was actually rotating to the side of the blitz, where Lito Sheppard was playing hard corner. Meaning he has no deep responsibility and could jump any short throws.

We had noticed on film that in a blitz situation where Brett saw a one-on-one, he often threw a tight post route or favored a one-on-one matchup with Javon Walker. So this was Jim giving the perfect call, offering the perfect look, and it worked out as planned. Pressure, forced throw, turnover. Things don't always go as planned. This time it did. David would hit a 31-yarder in OT to give us a 20–17 win. Afterward, Freddie Mitchell said they should put a statue of him next to the Rocky statue on Pattison Avenue and he'd thanked his hands. Typical Freddie.

Freddie had been a surprise to me. Many were very surprised when he was taken in the first round in 2001. The thing Freddie could do was catch the ball. I will say that. Freddie could catch the rock, in tight coverages. He has very good hands. But he had trouble getting separation from defensive backs. With his being on the outside, that was a problem. His strength was working in the slot, catching tough passes. That fourth-and-26? That's him. He made gritty catches.

Freddie also had a very healthy idea of himself, which is cool. He was very confident in what he could do. Sometimes, that came back to bite him. When he left here, he made some comments that weren't too cool with some folk in the know. You have to learn in this life that once you say some things, you can't take them back. So what you say initially should be something that you can look back on weeks or years from now, and be okay with. Away from the emotion of the moment, I have always tried to be someone who wants to build as many bridges as I can. I don't want to burn any if possible, especially in the National Football League. That coaching fraternity is a tight group of individuals who converse a lot. When you start talking really heavily about one group of individuals, and they eat lunch together and play golf together and vacation together, that can cause problems. You have to be careful with how you speak about people.

◇◇◇

We were back in the NFC championship game, for the third straight year. But as we started to prepare, that voice started to come back into my head, the one that was so loud when we were losing early in my career: "Here we go again." I had to fight through those "here we go again" moments. I had learned a lot about how to pick up my teammates during tough times, and they had learned from me. We were winning, but there was a feeling around Philadelphia that the regular season didn't matter. Not even the first part of the playoffs mattered. It was all about what we were going to do when we got to the NFC Championship game. Basically, the fans were saying, "Wake us up when you get to the championship game. We'll come and watch that game." Obviously they didn't do that, they were there every game to torment the other team, which I loved.

Carolina had finished the season 11–5 and had beaten St. Louis the week before in double overtime. But we were at home, and people expected us to get to the Super Bowl. Instead, we lost, 14–3. Donovan threw four interceptions, but he suffered torn rib cartilage in the second quarter when Greg Favors hit him late. The only play I remember is the touchdown Muhsin Muhammad caught in the second quarter. That play still haunts me, to this day.

Carolina lined up in a formation that had me covering the tight end, but the tight end stayed in and blocked. That meant it was a one-receiver pass route, and I was freed up to give Bobby some help. I ran back deep, and the quarterback (Jake Delhomme) never saw me. But I misjudged his pass and made a centerfield turn to run after it. All I had to do was run up to the ball and pick it. Instead, I turned and lost it. When I did that, Muhammad came back and caught the pass for a touchdown. That one hurt. People said it was Donovan's fault, and it was the receivers' fault. In my mind, I gave up seven points. Yes, we lost, 14-3, but seven of those points belonged to me. That's the way I looked at it. They belonged specifically to me!

After losing that game, I started thinking about that great team up in Buffalo that had a lot of success in the regular season but could never win the last game. For us, that last game had been a little earlier, because Buffalo lost four straight Super Bowls from 1991–94, but it was the same thought process. What was it going to take to get over this? To Andy and Joe Banner's credit, they finally looked outside their norm and went out and got two high-priced individuals, who were also ballers. One was the freak defensive end Jevon Kearse.

The other was some cat with the initials T.O.

It was about to get wild in Philadelphia.

CHAPTER 12

Climbing the Mountain

We had lost three straight NFC championship games, and I started thinking about the plays we could have made. The Muhammad catch against Carolina. On the other Panthers touchdown, DeShaun Foster broke three tackles to score. If we had stopped him there, maybe things would have been different. So, I started to rationalize things in my mind about how close we were.

Donovan got hurt on a late hit. If that doesn't happen, maybe he doesn't throw the interceptions. In our minds, we were in those NFC Championship games, except for a few plays, here and there. With all that we had on the team, all we needed was to finish the doggone thing. Do the small things, and the big thing will take care of itself. That's how we thought, but Andy thought differently after the loss to Carolina.

He went completely away from the way he felt about offense. Andy had been sticking to the idea that his offense would spread the ball around, and we didn't need a big-time number-one receiver. Now, I'm not saying that I agree with that, because I thought we should have been running the ball more. That's because I'm more of a physical-minded player, I guess. I believe that my curveball works better when my fastball is potent, so to speak. So, the fastball is the running game. If I can physically pound you and punch you in the mouth, over and over again, and I know I can, then everything else is going to work even better.

When Andy brought in T.O., he went completely away from what he had been thinking. He was a West Coast Offense true believer.

Why run the ball, when you can complete a short pass for five yards? Once T.O. came in, it was like lightning from the jump.

◇◇◇

The thing about the 2004 season wasn't whether we were going to beat you. It was by how much we would beat you and how quickly the starters were going to be resting on the bench. That's the way it was. Select starters were going to sit in the fourth quarter, and we knew that, because we were going to beat you that bad.

That year provided another challenge for the defense, because we had to learn how to play with big leads. If you look at our stats, we didn't look great. Granted, we were second in points allowed, but we were only tenth in yards allowed. Part of that was Andy took the starters out. Another part is that it's different playing when you're ahead by a lot of points.

It's tough to keep your foot on the gas, go full tilt for four quarters, when you're up by 30. It's tough to stay dialed in when you have a big lead because you aren't thinking that every yard you give up is precious, like you do in close games. In your mind's eye, the game's already over, and you don't want to give up any more points. The yardage isn't at a premium anymore. The clock is what you are playing against, and you want that thing moving as quickly as possible. That's what you are fighting against.

We were all loving it. We knew that this was the year we were going to the Super Bowl. And we believed we were going to win the Super Bowl. One of the knocks against us going into the NFC Championship game against Carolina the year before was that our receivers were soft. Their cornerback, Ricky Manning Jr., said the Panthers were "going to jam them up." And they did it. When we brought in T.O., that knock against our offense not being physical went away. It wasn't just because of one person, but his work ethic and his run-after-the-catch mentality, his ability to break tackles and bust games open made us a better offense. Now, who do you game plan for? Do you game plan for T.O.? Do you game plan for Westbrook? Do you game plan for Donovan? Who are you going to roll your coverage toward?

You couldn't leave guys like Todd Pinkston open, because he was no slouch in terms of getting deep on you. He could run. T.O. opened up so many aspects of the game and the field, thanks to his gifted athleticism, and his mentality. A mentality that rubbed off on the other WRs. So, with our offense so much better, we knew we were going to the Super Bowl. This year was going to be a lot different.

T.O. was a huge part of that team and a big reason why we were able to reach the Super Bowl, but Brian Westbrook was great that year too. It was his first season as the team's featured back, and he had 1,515 total yards—rushing and receiving—and nine touchdowns. Brian had an ability to change gears at full speed like very few could do. He could pause, speed up, pause, speed up, stop, pause, skip to the left four yards, speed up again. But the whole time he's doing it, he's moving quickly.

B-West's ability to make you miss was phenomenal, and I saw that right away when he first got here. It was hard to get a true hit on him because he would always shift at the last second. He could make people miss him without turning his shoulders. He could attack defenders straight on by running them over or by getting past them without turning his shoulders, and that's a scary thing for opponents. He was able to go side-to-side in a heartbeat. That's what separated him. And he was a very, very smart guy. The other thing that people didn't recognize about him was that he was an excellent blitz pick-up guy. The thing he's probably supposed to be the worst at as a running back, picking up blitzes, he was one of the best at, especially at his size (5'8", 200 pounds).

We could flex B-West out into the slot and let him go one-on-one with linebackers and safeties. He was a mismatch and a nightmare. Brian was especially dangerous in the screen game because he could disguise the screen so well. Then, he'd get out in the open field and make you miss, then he'd pause, start again and run past you. It was phenomenal, bro. For several years, he was the best all-purpose back in the game. That's not just my opinion. He could run, catch, return, everything. You put blocking in there, too. He was the best for several years.

But that doesn't mean I took it easy on him in practice. He still says the hardest hit he ever took was from me during a training camp practice when he was a rookie. We were going first defense against second offense. Another back or receiver had broken down the sideline, and Brian was running with him. He leaned toward me to give me a half-hearted block, and I lowered my shoulder and rocked him. He couldn't believe I did that, but I had to set a tone. The thing about it was that I didn't even hit him as hard as I could have. Had to welcome him to the NFL, bro.

◇◇◇

That 2004 season was amazing. We started 13–1, losing only to Pittsburgh after winning our first seven games. Four teams all year scored more than 20 points against our defense. And the offense was top ten in points, yards, passing yards and a bunch of other stats. We were rolling along and were so good that we clinched home-field advantage throughout the playoffs in the 14th game of the season, by beating Dallas, 12–7. We also lost something big that day, too.

On the second play of the third quarter, T.O. caught a pass and was dragged down from behind by Roy Williams after gaining 20 yards. He grabbed the back of his right leg immediately, and the eventual diagnosis was a fractured fibula and a high ankle sprain. He needed surgery to install a screw that would stabilize the joint and allow for quicker healing. T.O. was definitely going to be out for the rest of the regular season and the playoffs. There was an outside shot he could play in the Super Bowl, when we got that far.

We lost our last two games of the season, but we only played the starters one series, in a Monday Night game against St. Louis. In the final game against Cincinnati, none of the starters played. We were outscored, 58–17, in the two games, but it didn't matter, because we had already clinched a bye and home field advantage. Some of us thought Andy should have played everybody in those last two games so that we would be sharp going into the playoffs.

One would think that without T.O., we were basically the same team as the year before, except that we also had Jevon Kearse, who had 7.5 sacks and made our defense even more dangerous. But our mentality had been added to on offense, not just T.O.'s playmaking ability. We felt we were going to win the conference. Everybody was going to do his job, and that was going to get us there. It had nothing to do with the other team. It was all about us. If we played the way we were supposed to play, especially on defense, we were going to be fine. We felt no one was going to score on our defense. No matter what was going on offensively—and we still did have a good offense, because of Donovan and the other pieces—we were going to be okay. But of course, we were going to hold it down for him. I knew our first opponent had our attention for sure, with Randy Moss on the field. That was Minnesota.

Donovan said it best after the game when he told reporters that he guessed we "weren't too rusty." As many thought it was the kiss of death that we rested the starters and broke up our winning streak at the time. We were up on them, 14–0, before the second quarter was even a minute old. Donovan threw for 286 yards and two touchdowns. Brian rushed for 70 yards and caught a TD pass. Freddie had a big game, catching five passes for 65 yards. We beat Minnesota, 27–14, and earned a fourth straight NFC championship matchup, this time with Atlanta.

The Falcons had blasted St. Louis, 47–17, in the divisional playoff game, with Michael Vick rushing for 119 yards, a playoff record for a quarterback. Atlanta also had Warrick Dunn. And so even though they were a dome team, and even though it had snowed and was extremely cold (17 degrees, 35-mph winds), people still thought they had an advantage because they were a running team, and we were sixteenth in the NFL in rushing defense. Again, I told you about stats. Stats don't always tell you the truth.

But they were talking about their running game and their defense, and how we were going to struggle in the snow because we were a passing team. I was thinking, "They are coming into our house, and we are the number one seed, because we earned that seed, and you're going to tell me that we should be underdogs? In our own house? Against a team that's coming from indoors to outdoors? And they're going to beat us?" Okay. Okay.

Somebody had to pay for that.

That just happened to be Alge Crumpler. And it wasn't just me. If you look back on that game, Hollis hit Vick early. He just rocked him. Defensive end Derrick Burgess did a great job switching to Vick's throwing side and then containing him and sacking him. We were hitting him, hitting him, hitting him. There was a feeling on the team that we had been disrespected that week as a defense, and we were going to let everybody know we didn't appreciate that.

And it was cold out there, so cold that the heated benches didn't help. They weren't heating up the way they usually did. That's how cold it was. It was freezing. But I was still wearing short sleeves. It's a mental thing. They have this stuff that helps cover up your pores. It's a cream, and you put it on, so the wind won't be so bad. But if you're not used to the cold, if you just moved up here from Florida, it's going to take some time for you to adjust, like I was way back in the day. Some people never get used to it. Your body has to get acclimated to it. Once it does, it's a mind thing after that. Mind over matter. If you don't mind, it don't matter. I may have been cold, but I knew how I was going to play.

When we went out for the coin toss, that's when I had an idea the game was over, to be honest with you. Atlanta defensive end Patrick Kerney had no sleeves on, but I could see his hand shaking. Warrick Dunn had a jacket on, and he was shivering. I thought, "Uh-oh." They were thinking about the cold so much, and it was affecting them then, before the game even started. When it's really cold, you don't want to get touched. It hurts more to be hit. When you're used to it, it's no big deal.

The hit on Crumpler was me trying to let them know just what our defense could do. He was a Falcons tight end, and he weighed about 60 pounds more than me. But when he caught a pass from Vick at our 13 with just under three minutes left in the first half, I got him good. I heard him gasp, and I freakin' loved it. And since I'm being honest here, that junk hurt me too, Jack. That's a big dude. If you go back and look at the hit you can see me getting my feet in position to deliver a hit, yes, but to brace myself as well. You will also see me wobble a bit right after impact. So he was not the only one that felt that impact.

I wanted to deliver as many of those as possible. You know, constantly put crazy on film. Not so gentle reminders.

We had the upper hand for most of the game and won, 27–10. The media and a few of their players had talked before the game about their running game, and we held them to just 99 rushing yards. They were the best ground team in the NFL. The Falcons only had 202 yards. There was too much talk about them coming into our house, making noise about how we were the underdogs, and they did little that day against us. In a last-second move, Jim moved Derrick Burgess to Vick's strong side to contain him. It was a surprise to us all. But he was a beast. DB is that cat you want to take to fight with you for sure, Jack. Derrick Burgess had two sacks. Trott had eight tackles. I picked off a pass. Even when we led just 17–10, we were still in control. Atlanta struggled to do anything consistently anything against us.

The fans loved that. They were great the whole game. The run to the 2018 Super Bowl championship finally gave fans a feeling of what the Linc was supposed to be like. I'm not saying it wasn't loud at other times, but when the Eagles were winning on the way to the Super Bowl in '18, it reminded me of the championship game against Atlanta during the 2004 season. The electricity that day was *crazy*. It's what the Linc should be like. But the players have to bring it to the fans, and they will give it back to you. That's what I think the Super Bowl championship team realized, and they did a good job bringing the energy, first.

That's what we did back then. We brought the energy to the fans, and it reverberated. They sent it right back to us. That victory over Atlanta is the one I will remember more than any other victory. We finally won. People don't understand the significance of it. It wasn't just another win. It wasn't just the opportunity to play in the Super Bowl. It was us finally winning a freaking NFC championship game, after failing those other three times.

◇◇◇

When it came to the Super Bowl, we really believed we were going to win. It wasn't going to be easy. We knew it would be tough, but we were going to win that game. I had that feeling all the way up until the end. I believed in our ability to make one more play than they did. That's what we needed.

But we didn't get that one more play.

We lost to New England, 24–21. All Eagles fans who were around when that game was played know what happened. The score was tied, 7–7, at halftime, and again at 14 entering the fourth quarter. That's the first time the Super Bowl was ever tied heading into the final 15 minutes.

But New England scored 10 straight points, on a two-yard run by Corey Dillon and a 22-yard field goal by Adam Vinatieri, to take a 24–14 lead. But there was still 8:43 left after Vinatieri's kick. The teams exchanged punts, and we took over on our 21-yard line, with 5:40 left. We scored, on a 30-yard pass from Donovan to Greg Lewis, but the drive took too long. We needed thirteen plays and 3:46 to score at a time when a touchdown alone wouldn't do it for us. To this day, people still talk about that, and they should. It was a brutal way to lose such an important game.

When I peel away all of the layers, I look at the bare necessities of a championship team. To me, one of the biggest is how it handles the details at the end of the game. We just did not detail ourselves. We did not do a good job of getting off the field on defense.

We allowed a long drive in the fourth quarter that ate a lot of time off the clock (3:46), that made it 24–14. On offense, we did not do a good job of time management. We got the ball with 5:40 left, down 24–14, and needed 3:53 to score a touchdown. That left just 1:47 on the clock. When you don't manage time well or get off the field when you have to—you see it time and time again—you don't win. That's why situational football is talked about so much more often today than it ever was. It's so important. You learn how many games are won and lost because teams do or don't take care of those details.

There are a lot of plays in a game, but when you boil it down, a lot of times it comes down to the last four minutes or even the final two minutes. Look at the 2017 Eagles. They didn't allow a point in the last two minutes of any game all season, including the Super

Bowl. Seven of the team's wins in the regular season were one-possession games at the end. You have to be able to play well at the end of games. How do teams use their timeouts? How do they get off the field on defense?

You have to detail your work. You have to understand how to save as much time as possible. You have to get your offense good field position. It's all of those things. And we didn't do a good job of it. We did not do a good job in the last four minutes. That's just my opinion. We gave up that drive that let them kick the field goal. Some people celebrated because they only scored three points, but we did not do a good job of understanding that we didn't have a lot of time to work with. We had to do a better job with all of it.

As great as it was getting to the Super Bowl and finally winning the NFC Championship game after three failures, losing to the Patriots was far worse than those other losses. You can be a Hall of Famer, an All-Pro or a Pro Bowler, but "Super Bowl Champion" stays with you as a team forever. That hurts. It hurts a lot. This is going to sound crazy, because I was blessed to be part of the organization when the Eagles won the Super Bowl for the first time, but that hurt. Getting the rings was a joyous occasion, even though I couldn't help imagining what that would have been like back then.

I am so happy and excited for the fan base and for the good folk on the team, the coaching staff and in the organization. And it will forever be inside of me. I'm going to own the Super Bowl ring I received as an Eagles executive with pride. I am. Yet I still can only imagine: Donovan, Westbrook, Trotter, Hugh, all of us, celebrating a championship that we won.

◇◇◇

I have said at times that the best way to know somebody is to spend time with him. To really learn about him. If a person is only able to know somebody from the comments they make to the media or from the relationships and interactions they have had with other people, it limits their ability to truly know the person. We have all formulated opinions about others that way, but in those unique situations when you get to learn about or really get to know somebody, you benefit. That's what I chose to do when it came to T.O.

I learned that T.O. does have a big heart. He's a different cat when he's talking about family. I saw a different dude then. When he gets in front of a camera, he becomes somebody else. There were times when I would hear him talk on camera and just shake my head and ask, "Why would you say that?" But then we would talk, and it would be a different conversation between me and him.

T.O. was a very perplexing player for me personality-wise, because I'm someone who tries his best to read people's body language. I'm not going to bother you if you don't feel it. I try to be respectful of guys, and sometimes, T.O. would come in and you could tell that everything was cool. Other days, he would come in, and I would think, "Oh, yeah, I'm not going to mess with him. He's feeling some sort of way." But I was like that with all my teammates. Yet I noticed it more with him at times.

On the field, T.O. changed the way some of our receivers attacked things. Their preparation improved. Their willingness to try to earn respect from people grew. His work ethic was tremendous. T.O. would work really hard in practice. And he taught me some things about the off-season. He's the reason I bought a hyperbaric chamber. I respected the way he took care of himself, and I asked him some of the things he did during the off-season, and he mentioned the hyperbaric chamber. I bought one, and it helped me tremendously. So, there are certain aspects of what he added that helped our football team. Then, there are some other aspects that began to divide, and when you start having those divisions, it's a recipe for disaster.

I don't think that happened a lot the first year he was with us, 2004. What happened was that in one game, he and Donovan got into something that they never worked out between themselves. It's not for me to provide the details, so I won't. All of T.O.'s antics seemed to be about his contract. He thought he should be making more money and he was going to do whatever he could to get more. It was a business move for him, in my opinion.

We sat and watched him doing the sit-ups through his interview after having a verbal spat with Andy, and I said, "Look at this joker doing sit-ups in the driveway. Is he serious?" We were laughing at it, to be honest with you. And when Donovan and T.O. continued to have problems getting along, that caused a rift. Some guys began to take sides, and that caused a bigger rift. And then when T.O. and Hugh got into that fistfight, I wished it had been two other guys. So it would have been like most locker room fights. It lasted about five to ten seconds, and people separated them. Kinda like my neighborhood fights back in the day. Usually, people talk things out after it, then laugh at the details. But now that I think about it, with all that was going on between them and their unwillingness to talk it out, that probably would not have been the outcome. I know, I know, wishful thinking.

◇◇◇

After playing in the Super Bowl against New England, I was convinced we were going to be back in that game in 2005. In my comments after the game, I said we had the talent to get back and sit at that table again, to put our hat in that ring and go at it. But it didn't happen, and that's frustrating, because I saw the potential for T.O. and Donovan to just rewrite the record books in Philadelphia. They would have just smashed records in the NFL, too. Had they been able to get along and resolve their differences, they would have been un-freakin-believable together. They were already good. Being able to work out problems during a season at all levels is one of the keys to teams winning Super Bowls. From the problem that comes when player after player goes down, to how you handle a few-game slide, to how you handle things with your fellow teammates. We failed that test.

It was frustrating that those two individuals couldn't see past the anger at the time, whatever else was going on, and to get together so that we could do something magical. To help us win a Super Bowl.

There were definitely two sides, because any time you have something going on like that, players are going to line up behind one guy or the other. That's why it's best to have only one agenda, and that's winning a championship. That should be the number one agenda. When you start having guys having opinions on how things are being done and not agreeing with the coaches and their teammates, then you don't have a team anymore. Some guys were interested in what T.O. was saying. Other guys were interested in what Donovan was saying. You have guys on different ends of the spectrum, playing the game of football. We're playing as a team, but we're not really a team. And when you are no longer a team with one goal, you become individuals with many goals.

Andy did what he had to do in that situation when he suspended T.O. Andy couldn't have anyone disrupting the team. No matter how valid your opinion may be, if you can't then get back in the meeting room with your coach and with Donovan and hash things out, then we have to separate. We have to go in different directions.

In my humble opinion, emotion, not logic, ruled the day. All I want to know is what we can do to fix a problem. That's the type of cat I try to be. So, even if I wasn't responsible for starting a disagreement, sometimes you just have to hold your hand out a little further to end it.

◇◇◇

We opened the 2005 season with a 14–10 loss to Atlanta. We had to play that game without Trott. Because that no good so-and-so Ike Reese, who had signed on to play for the Falcons that offseason, started a fight that got Trott ejected pregame. He knew what he was doing. He better be glad I still love him. But we won our next three games and were in pretty good shape. But because of all the things that were going on, and because of the injuries we suffered, we really were in trouble. Things may have looked good at 3–1, but they weren't.

Donovan suffered a torn core muscle, and he had to have surgery that knocked him out for the season. Tra Thomas, Brian Westbrook, Todd Pinkston, (center) Hank Fraley and (defensive lineman) Jerome McDougal were all lost for the season at some point during the year. Mike McMahon had to play quarterback for us, and even though he worked hard, he wasn't Donovan. The low point was the Monday Night game when the team retired Reggie White's number. It was a snowy December evening, and Seattle clobbered us, 42–0.

If you go back and watch that game, I was taken out with something like four minutes left in the game. I made the tackle on the play before I was taken out. I was still busting my behind, running all over the place, because I didn't want anybody looking at the film and seeing me taking a play off, especially my teammates. If I'm on the field, I'm going to give you everything I've got. I don't care what the score is, and in that game, it was extremely embarrassing. I didn't always have to be so-called in front to lead, but my job in the moment was to lead from the front. I'm not going to lead by telling you what you should do. I'm telling you what you need to do by my example. During that time, my thought process whenever I got in front of the team was to encourage, and to do my job like my life depended on it. I won't say demand, but I would urge the guys, and hold them accountable. Then I could ask them to do what I was already doing with ease.

Go back and watch any game that year and try to show me where I loafed, where I didn't go all out, where I took a play off. If you can show me that, then we have an argument. If you can't show me that—and you couldn't—then you have to bring your own game up. If we want to win, that's what everybody has to do. The only way we were going to get back into the playoffs and back into the championship conversation was to keep working as a team and holding each other accountable. That's what we did, even during that tough time. One of the things I have been blessed with is to have an understanding that leading isn't telling people what to do. It's showing them. It's having the party first. And having a good time doing it. And then, inviting them to my party.

With a championship team there has to be an extremely delicate balance. And that's why you hear coaches talking about not being a distraction. They want to get rid of all the things that separate you from doing your job as best as you can. When small conversations start in a locker room where people are not happy or not willing to do what it takes to win, there's no longer a shared spirit. There's no longer a camaraderie, where players say, "I have your back." It's more like, "Yeah, I got your back, but only if it suits me." You can't have that, and if you find that on a team, and that person isn't willing to change, he's got to go.

So, not only did we have guys hurt, but we had dysfunction if I can use that word, in the locker room. One of the things you hear coaches say, and not just coaches, because this is pretty significant for life, I would think, is that if everybody is not pulling in the same direction, it's not going to work. It might work, in rare cases, but you're not going to beat a team that has everybody working together. I saw it in my life, that when I started thinking about things outside of what I was supposed to be focused on, I was spending effort and energy on things that wouldn't help me win. And I was really not giving 100 percent of what I could truly give. It's like when people have trouble at home, with a spouse, or if you have other things to deal with outside the game or your teammates, it's going to be tough to give everything you actually have to give.

Most coaches understand that, and they look for ways to make sure everybody is working toward the common goal. And when there is a bad apple, and those pocket conversations start, people start to second-guess what's going on. Guys begin to start coming late to meetings. They start to park where they're not supposed to park at the training complex. They start to cut corners. Not cleaning up their areas. All those little things show up big in the fourth quarter, in the last four minutes.

And that can ruin a team. And a season. Like it did in 2005.

CHAPTER 13

One Last Season in Green

One of the toughest things for a professional athlete is being able to talk about his problems. It's getting better, because more guys are focusing on it. Like I said before, growing up, you are told not to discuss what's bothering you. We were taught to bottle up our feelings and not discuss them. Many times in homes, domestic violence, whether that be physical, verbal, or emotional, happens far too often. Along with other traumatic things. These terrible situations should not be bottled up. Especially by a child, or a teenager. These traumas are a tremendous challenge for most adults to overcome, let alone youngsters. They need consoling and help. So to tell young men to "not say a word to anyone," can leave them in a place of constant pain. With the events running over and over on their heads. Which often leads to problems in school and in many cases, problems in adulthood.

As you get older, you start to understand that's not the way to do things all of the time. There are some things that, yes, you can suck it up, you can deal with it. But it's not the way you should do every situation. There aren't any cookie-cutter cures for everything that happens in this life. You might need somebody to talk to about them. One of the things I am blessed with is a group of "accountability partners," my "Blessed Pack," or people that I can trust in my life to talk problems through with me.

If I have things going on in my life that are tough to handle, and this goes back to the time when I was dealing with depression and suicidal thoughts, I now have people that I can talk to. I can call them and say something like, "Send up some prayers for me."

That person might say, "Got you. Is there anything specific going on?" Boom. We're off. Or I can simply text the same things to them instead. That's how we do it some of the time. Other times, I'll text "hit me ASAP." Those are the times when I tell them what's going on with me. They listen, comfort, give me words of wisdom, and then we pray together. Now I know I have outlets. I know I'm not by myself. I know that those conversations can help me deal with something I might not have been able to handle by myself. When you are young, and you have not been taught those things, you're going to go through life pretending a lot. Putting on a mask. Just pretending and pretending.

At times when I was struggling with a problem, I would focus on that, rather than football. If I had a quiet moment, I would just start thinking about the problem. Even on the practice field in certain situations. Oftentimes I'd be making mental mistake after mental mistake. What am I going to do about it? How's it going to work out? Who's going to be calling? How are things going to be when I get home? Instead of thinking about that week's opponent or its offense, and how I was going to operate in a new defense that was just put in, my mind was occupied with the other things.

Once I understood it was okay to get some help in those areas, I was able to put ALL of my focus and attention on the game of football. This same formula works in my life today. I have always said and believed that if you coach the person first and the player second, you will have more success with that player. The "person" is who we have been talking about now. He has problems at home, issues with his parents, issues with his girlfriend or issues with his children. If you help that person figure things out when he has stuff going on, then you'll get a better player, because he's a whole player, not a fragmented one. He isn't sectioned off with the other things he has to deal with, with things to which he doesn't have answers, which causes stress, anxiety that could lead to anger or even depression and all its ups and downs.

One of the worst feelings I had in school was when there was a test, and I knew I hadn't studied—and it wasn't multiple choice. Oh, my goodness. It was the same thing when I was playing pro football.

If I didn't have an answer to a problem off the field that was causing me so much pain, and I didn't know who to talk to about it, I was going to have problems. And there's another part of it. When I kept things bottled up for so long, and I was not creating a release, all it took was one thing to trigger me, and I would explode and release all that anger on somebody else in an unrelated situation. It might not have been a big deal to start with, but because I kept all that inside and had all that anger and frustration, all that bitterness, it became bigger.

My faith has helped me deal with things better than I used to. I have been able to get answers and not fill myself with bad things that affect my relationships with others, for the most part. I have become more aware of my emotions, not hiding them or ignoring them, so when the heat is turned up, being led by them.

Andy Reid did a good job coaching the person. But the culture of football has been—and in many ways still is—about coming to work and doing your job. Players are supposed to forget about all that other stuff, off the field, and get to work. That's why it's good when players come out and talk about their problems to the right people. Eagles guard Brandon Brooks did it in 2016. After he sought out help, he talked about the anxiety that was affecting him. It's not as taboo as it used to be. In the past, if someone did that, people would say, "He's just not tough enough." It has nothing to do with toughness. I hope more and more players come to understand they can now have more conversations about their problems, to the people they choose to share them with, because more people are becoming more understanding.

I have an understanding of it, because of what I went through. When I saw a guy like Brandon going through what he was going through, I could have a conversation with him and talk about what happened to me. Hopefully, I could help him out so he could figure some things out. I talked to a lot of players, because it became known that I had some experience with these kinds of problems, and I wasn't going to judge them. I could potentially help them and understand them. I was them, to a certain extent.

◇◇◇

When Donovan got hurt in 2003, we told A.J. Feeley not to worry. The defense would pick him up. Just don't turn the ball over, and we'll be okay. And we were.

In 2005, when Donovan had his core muscle tear and ended his season in Week 10, against Dallas, the defense felt tremendous pressure. The thing about pressure is that when you apply it to yourself, you make mistakes. That's what happened with us. The offense was struggling, and we tried to do too much and made mental mistakes, one here and one there. We gave up plays we shouldn't have, and when that happened, we would be down 14 points with an offense that sometimes had difficulty scoring consistently. So, we tried to make more plays, and then we made more mistakes. It's a compound thing.

During those times, mental toughness has to come in. I guess that's what I mean about some guys not being able to tell that other voice to shut up. That's the mental toughness you have to have. To tell your emotions and that other voice to shut up.

I made the Pro Bowl again that year, and that was tough for me. We were losing, but I was performing at a high level. Part of me says, "Well, yeah, the team is losing, but I have to get mine, right?" I had a family to support. But I had to tell that part of me to shut up. That was a conversation I was glad to have with the selfish part of me. When people don't think I have thoughts like that, they are sadly mistaken. Yeah, I had those thoughts.

I would say, "If my ankle is hurting, and I have a chance to play in the Pro Bowl, why would I play in the last, meaningless game of the 2005 season?" If I looked at it that way, I wouldn't have played in that game. But it wasn't a meaningless game. It meant a lot. That game would tell my coaches and teammates what I was about going into that next season. I was telling them that I was a leader. Even though we were out of the playoff picture, it was not a meaningless game. The media could use the fact that we had no chance at the post-season as an excuse for why players shouldn't give their best efforts. The fans could use it. Even some players could use it. As a leader, I could never use it. And because who I choose to be, that would NEVER happen.

There's no such thing as a meaningless game. There are millions of fans that would love to do what I was doing. I was blessed to be in the freakin NFL. I'm going all out.

We finished the season 6–10. We lost eight of our last ten. Injuries played a role. So did the rift between Donovan and T.O. As I headed into my 11th season, I was ready to get back to the top. To do that, I would have to change my training routine a little bit, to stay at the top of my game. To keep my muscles and my system guessing.

◇◇◇

The average career in the NFL is three-and-a-half years, and no matter what we do in life, it's impossible to stop the process of getting older. Our bodies change, and so heading into 2006, I decided to train a little differently. I did some mixed martial arts work. When you say MMA, people think about kicking and punching, but this was more about exercises focused on stabilizing my muscles. It wasn't just about my core. It was about a lot of new things that athletes are doing now, like explosion. I was doing side jumps, bands, and stability ball stuff because I noticed my reaction time wasn't the same. My ability to change direction wasn't quite the same. It was part of my body getting older. So I dug deeper into my hips and their stability and flexibility. It was about, what could I do?

I began to do some research and add different things to my repertoire. To help me have that explosion. I was doing twists, diving, landing, tumbling. I was stretching even more aggressively than I ever did before. That's what helped me continue to play at a high level as long as I did. I was always adding new exercises and ideas to my workout regimen. A stability movement here. A core exercise there. Different techniques. I was always looking for something to keep my body at its peak, even if time was fighting me.

Our bodies are smart things. The Lord made them that way. Our muscles have memory, and they get used to new things quickly. I was always trying to keep my muscles guessing in my workouts. I was always doing new things, so my muscles wouldn't get complacent and used to doing the same things again and again. That's how you stagnate. I wanted my mind to experience new things, too, just like my muscles were. I was never going to relax and get comfortable. That's another big reason for my long career.

◇◇◇

The 2006 season was another tough one. We were coming off a 6–10 year that had all sorts of drama, from the T.O. thing to lots and lots of key injuries.

After five games, it looked like we were heading in a great direction. We were 4–1, and it didn't look like we had any training camp hangover. Donovan was healthy and playing well, and the defense was playing well. The fifth game of that stretch, a 38–24 win over Dallas at the Linc, was particularly interesting, and not so much because of what happened on the field.

T.O. had signed with the Cowboys after leaving Philly, and there was a whole lot of interest in the game leading up to it. Everybody wanted to know what it was going to be like for us to play against him, and really, it just went back to when he was on the 49ers, before he became an Eagle. He was just a cat in the wrong jersey. When you become a guy in the wrong jersey, that means it's equal opportunity for me to hit you if I can. T.O. is a phenomenal athlete, a great player and a Hall of Famer. We had to game plan for him, obviously. We had to know where he was and make sure we'd run hard to the ball when it was thrown to him, because he breaks tackles so well when he's running.

I didn't personally hate T.O., but we already didn't like Dallas, and he was a Cowboy. We wanted to beat them badly, but there was nothing personal against him. I didn't like some of the things T.O. did when he was here. When he went to Dallas, he was just a dude in the other jersey, and if I got a chance to hit him, I would. Once you leave here, and you are going to play against me, I'm an equal-opportunity cat. When it comes to play, I don't care if you are my best friend, that week I'm not talking to you. We getting after it.

The thing I was most mad about when it came to T.O. playing for the Cowboys, was that we had to play on Christmas. As soon as he went to Dallas, I knew they would make us play Dallas on Christmas, doggonit.

It did make it a little more intense because he was with Dallas. The media and the fans drive it home constantly: "We hate Dallas." You know that. So, I went back and began to look at why Eagles fans hated Dallas so much. I didn't just listen to people saying it; I looked at the close games back in the day. I looked at how the Cowboys won so much back in the day. And I understood. But here's a funny thing about it, and people aren't going to like this.

I was a huge Dallas fan back in the day.

Yes. Growing up in Jacksonville in the '80s and early '90s, when I was in high school, we didn't have an NFL team. Whatever team was on TV the most, that's the one we picked. You had the Steelers and the 49ers. Buffalo. And the Cowboys. Remember that I wanted to be a Florida Gator. I loved the Gators. Loved them. And (Dallas running back) Emmitt Smith was a Gator. Loved Darren Woodson. So, I was a Cowboys fan. The funny thing about it was that his brother, Emory, was my roommate at Clemson for a year. So I had ties to the team.

But when I got to Philadelphia, I was told, "We hate Dallas." So, I thought, "I guess I have to start hating Dallas." So the reprogramming began quickly. It was easy, as I didn't really have roots in the team from Texas like I would have if the Jags had been around and won championships. The Philly faithful always say, "Dawk, we love you!" Well, the feeling is mutual. And that feeling began early for me. There are some dark sides to me, and I have talked about them. There are things that I came through in my life that were dark. That's why the Marvel superhero Wolverine was so big for me. As the true Comic-Con geek knows, there are a whole lot of dark sides to that joker.

Philly fans have some dark sides to them, too. I can contain mine. A lot of times I can hold mine back. Some of the fans in Philadelphia can't always do that. They're going to let you know exactly how they're feeling. I'm cool with that. I'm cool. Where I grew up, in Jacksonville, I was used to hearing some verbiage from coaches that wasn't so nice. Junior high. Even Pop Warner. They got after you. I learned to filter out the good stuff from the bad.

So, I came to understand the Eagles fans. They are very passionate about the game of football. When I got there, they were tired of losing. They're not very patient, either. I read stuff about them and watched old tapes of the Eagles. They don't like people who complain about things, because they work hard for what they have. And they're not afraid to show their emotions. I identified with that right away, because that's how I am on the football field. I'm not afraid to show my emotions. I'm going to have a good time. And I'm going to give you everything I've got.

I said this a long time ago, but I do really, really believe this: If a Philadelphia Eagles fan woke up in the morning and had a chance to play in one game, all of a sudden something had happened, and they were moved out of their bed and into the team hotel, and they were able to eat the pre-game meal and know the game plan and had the athletic ability, the leaping ability and everything they needed to play the game, they would play the game the way I played it. I believe they would go out there and have a good time. They would laugh. They'd be dancing. They would be angry. They would show their emotions, and they wouldn't hold back.

That's why I think the fans and I hit it off when I came to Philadelphia. They knew how I was. They knew from me coming out during player introductions that the way I did was an every-game thing for me. They knew it wasn't a show. They knew I was trying to put on a show all right, a physical show. It was who I was. They knew I was going to give my 100 percent all the time, and my teammates' missed assignments and blown plays were going to be my fault, even when they weren't. I was going to take responsibility. I was never going to pass the buck to anybody, and never to one of my teammates. I never threw any of my teammates under the bus. They hopefully also saw that I passed the buck only on one occasion, after we won.

◊◊◊

After that fast start in 2006, we went 1–5. The only win came after a bye, and Andy just about always won after a bye. There was a chance we could have snuck into that "here we go again" mindset, especially after Donovan tore his ACL in our tenth game, against Tennessee. We had to find a way to break out of that. The thing that most teams do is break up the season into quarters—four games each.

The math isn't perfect on this, but after those six games when we went 1–5 were over, we moved on. We had a fresh slate to work with. And that started with the next game, against Carolina. When you look at things like that, instead of all sixteen games at once, it's more manageable and less likely to make you feel overwhelmed.

The journey of a thousand miles begins with a single step.

– Lao Tzu

Everybody has heard it. You hear it in high school. You hear it in college. We looked at those losses and figured out why we lost. What can we learn from the losses, in order to be stronger for the next time? I don't want to make the same mistake. It's a learning process. No repeat offenders. Everybody could and would be held accountable.

And it does sound like a cliché, but it's true. A lot of fans get the schedule when it comes out and says, "Oh, we can win that game. We got that game. We're going to win that game." Players probably do that, too. But when you play the games, they are all different. Every opponent has different strengths and weaknesses and players to be concerned about. One of the reasons the Patriots are so good is that they are able to forget about the last game and move on to the next one, the quickest of anybody. They learn from it, get what they need from it and then move on.

The best teams don't look past games. That's why people always talk about "trap games." A team will look past one opponent to get to the next. That team may not go out and give its most focused effort. The players really want to face that next opponent, so their minds aren't on the job in front of them and how they can give their best in that moment. I might think I'm giving my all, but because my mind is on something else, I would be giving what I have left. But that's a bunch of crap. Our jobs are to give maximum respect and effort, no matter the opponent.

So, fans can look past teams. Players can't.

We won our final five games that year, including three straight on the road against NFC East rivals, to win the division. I remember that people were doubting us toward the end of the season, because we had all of those road games, and because Jeff Garcia had taken over at quarterback, after Donovan's injury. But we won them all, including against the Giants, who beat us in overtime earlier in the season. We faced them again in the Wild Card round, and everything looked good when we had a 20–10 lead.

But Jay Feely kicked a field goal early in the fourth quarter to make it 20–13, and Eli Manning hit Plaxico Burress for an 11-yard touchdown with 5:08 left to tie the score. Eli won two Super Bowls, and he's a good quarterback, but he would often have bad body language, at times. As a defender you loved that, because that meant we were in his head. His shoulders would slump, and he would move his head from side-to-side. If you are a defensive player, it's great to see that.

We got the ball back after the TD pass to Burress, and this time, we wanted to burn the clock, unlike in the Super Bowl. We used it all, and on the last play of the game, David Akers kicked a 38-yard field goal to give us the win and to send us to New Orleans for the Divisional Round. It was especially great that we beat the Giants to get there because that meant we beat them twice in less than a month.

The thing I remember most about the Saints game was how sick I was. I hated that. I was throwing up. I had to get IVs before the game to put some fluids in me. It was bad. And then, we were trailing, 27–24, at the two-minute warning, when Andy went for it on fourth-and-10 on our 44. Garcia completed a pass to Hank Baskett that would have given us a first down, but a false-start penalty brought it back. So, with 1:56 left, Andy punted it and put his faith in the defense to get the ball back. But New Orleans ran the ball and got a first down, me and my defensive mates did not hold up our end of the bargain, and that was the game. We lost, 27–24.

It was tough, because we didn't do our job. You know how that little joke goes, "You had one job!" We had one job, and that was to get the ball back for our offense, and we didn't do it. It was frustrating. We couldn't do it. It goes back to those days early in my career when we couldn't beat the Giants. We couldn't get off the field against them in those critical moments. They would just run the ball at us, and we couldn't stop them. We would practice those two and four-minute situations, but we couldn't do it against the Giants. And we didn't do it against the Saints, either. We couldn't give the offense a last chance.

◇◇◇

Andy didn't wait until the 2007 season started to create some drama. He did it four months earlier, on draft day, when he chose Kevin Kolb with our first pick (36th overall). It was surprising that we took Kolb, especially that early. Maybe you draft a QB later on when you already have a proven starter. Teams do it all the time now. They always draft a quarterback for the future and see how he works out. Maybe they can trade him or something like that later on, once he has developed and been seen in action. Or, maybe he becomes the guy. For it to happen here was different. It goes back to Donovan's relationship with the fans.

There was always a segment of fans that didn't care for Donovan. Whenever he struggled, or whenever there was an opportunity for them to get on him about something, they would jump. So, this was a great opportunity for them. If he struggled in a game, they would yell, "We want Kolb!" A few years earlier, they were actually screaming, "We want A.J.!" I was like, "Are you serious?" Nothing against A.J.—come on, man. So this was just another thing for Donovan to deal with.

It's football. Teams bring in players to replace other players. But you don't usually see it with the quarterback position. The business of football is that teams sometimes bring in other players who are less expensive because of the salary cap. And if the Eagles had drafted someone to take my place, I would have helped him, but then I would have done everything I could to make sure he didn't take my spot. That's my mentality, but it's not everybody's mentality. I may feel a certain way about a move a team makes, but the only thing I can control is my work that I put in. To get better and to keep playing at a high level.

We went 8–8 that year, but we won our last three games, and people thought that we had built some momentum for the next season. That might work in the NFL unless you lose ten or fifteen guys and bring in a bunch of new players. If you still have the core nucleus and add some young guys, then it can work.

There's a feeling you get when you start stringing things together. That's how you build momentum. There's a rhythm to it, like when you go into practice and meetings and get the game plan every week. There's a flow to the thing. If the practices were good, and you get into a game and there is some adversity, you can fall back on the good practices to pull the game out. You like the way that feels, so you do it again the next week. You feel a certain way heading into the game. That's why some coaches wanted to have "perfect" Friday practices. You want to be in that groove. It's a feeling. Those last few games of 2007 were what we wanted to reiterate when we started 2008. That's what the coaches want to emphasize.

When we started training camp in 2008, we started looking at highlights from the last season. Usually, coaches will have a reel they'll show to help the players get that feeling back. Now, you want to pick up where you left off. You want everybody to feel positive. You want to get the energy you need so you can see yourself having success in the games that are coming up.

Even though 2008 was the last year of my contract, I wasn't worried at all about getting a new deal. I was sure we were going to get something done. Yes, It was my thirteenth season, and I turned 35 that October, but I felt the team saw me the same way I saw myself. I had proven it to them. I had separated myself from most safeties, in the way I played the game, the way I took care of my body, the way that I led. I was different. I was going back to the Eagles after '08 with a new contract.

We were a good team in 2008, but we weren't as good as our team that reached the Super Bowl. We went 9–6–1, and we really caught fire at the end of the year, just as we had before. Those tough training camps always had us in better shape than our opponents, though Andy began to tone them down a whole lot because we kept going so deep into the playoffs year after year. But still, it was a weird regular season. We tied Cincinnati, 13–13. And we went into the final game of the season needing a lot of help to get into the playoffs.

We got it. Chicago and Tampa Bay both lost, meaning if we beat Dallas at the Linc, we would reach the post-season. We did. We killed them, 44–6. It was 3–3 after one quarter, but we scored 41 straight points. Six of them came when Chris Clemons picked up a Tony Romo fumble that I was blessed to cause when I sacked him. And Joselio Hanson also joined in on the TD parade when he scooped up the rock and took it 90 yards for a TD. After I was blessed to again force a fumble. This time on Marion Barber. The regular season wasn't pretty, and we were the sixth seed, but we were in the playoffs. We were a solid team with a great defense. We were third in fewest yards allowed, fourth in rushing defense, third against the pass and third in points allowed. During the last five games of the season, when we went 4–1, we allowed just 12 points a game. For the year, we only let up 18.1 a game. We got into a groove again. Everybody had a role, and everybody played it to a T.

I was able to dial into my role even more that year. I was playing more strong safety, and we when met Minnesota in the wild-card game, my role was to be a hammer. The Vikings had Adrian Peterson, and that year he gained 1,785 yards. I was going to hit him every opportunity I got. Nothing new, right? I wanted to deliver extreme blows. Anything I could to slow that cat down a bit.

We beat them, 26–14, and even though Adrian got loose on a 40-yard TD run, he didn't do much after that, carrying the ball 19 times for 43 yards. He couldn't get loose. And we were on to New York to play the Giants. They were the defending Super Bowl champions, and even though they beat us early in the season, we got them later and were confident heading to the Meadowlands. It was justified confidence. We beat them, 23–11. The game went back and forth for the first three quarters, but we scored 10 straight in the fourth and never allowed a touchdown. Afterward, I told reporters that we had "one collective heartbeat," which is "a powerful thing," and I meant it. We had come together at the end of the season, and we were on a roll heading to Arizona for the NFC Championship game.

The Giants agreed. Their running back, Brandon Jacobs, said that we were a hot team and that he was "on [our] bandwagon" for the Super Bowl. It felt good to hear that from cats you've gone to war against time and time again, but we still had to beat the Cardinals. Kurt Warner had taken over as their quarterback, and they had the league's fourth-best offense and second-best passing attack. As we prepared, we kind of out-thought ourselves. We put in a bunch of new defensive sets, and I remember the last couple practices going into that game, I was a little uncomfortable with how we were executing. We weren't 100 percent. And once the game started we weren't good on defense, to say the least.

We had beaten Arizona badly on Thanksgiving that season, 48–20. They came into a bad place that night. We had lost to Baltimore the week before, and Andy had pulled Donovan for Kevin Kolb. He didn't even name Donovan as his starting quarterback for the Cardinals until the Monday before the game, and this was a short week. We had to have the game, and if you go back and look at that game, my mentality was to be a jackhammer and punish everybody I could. We played well. Donovan threw four touchdown passes. Brian Westbrook ran for 110 yards and scored twice. I'm sure the Cardinals were thinking about that when we went out to play them.

During the first half, it seemed like we were thinking about something other than the game. You know that rhythm I have talked about? I always wanted to come out of Friday practice and the Saturday walk-through and go into the weekend feeling great. That week, I didn't. I tried to convince myself that we would be fine, but lo and behold, we made the same mistakes during the game that we made in practice. Our calls and checks weren't right, and those were the same problems we had early in the week.

Give Arizona credit, because they made the plays in the first half, when they went out to a 24–6 lead. But we certainly helped them. We had one half of the field playing one defense and the other half playing a different scheme. The line was blitzing, and the secondary was doing something else. We gave up too many big plays and weren't holding up our end. We made too many mistakes. And Larry Fitzgerald was having a big game. He finished with nine catches for 152 yards and scored three TDs.

Larry was like a man possessed that post-season. He was catching everything. Well, even more than usual, as he had hands like glue anyway. He had some of the strongest hands that I have ever seen. I would venture to say that he's in the top five all-time in terms of fewest drops. Through 2017, he averaged one drop per 41.7 catches, second among active players. That's amazing. And he's a phenomenal dude. He has phenomenal character. He's one of those guys I have to stay away from on the field because he's talking to you all the time. I would always think he was trying to get me out of my game. So, I would walk away, and he would say, "Oh, are you going to be like that? Like that, Dawk?" He's a hard-working guy, and I respect the heck out of him.

In the second half, we stopped using the new stuff and went back to our old defense, and we got back in the game. In fact, we had the lead, 25–24, in the fourth quarter, but they scored late and beat us, 32–25.

I had a feeling that would be my last game as an Eagle. I actually felt that earlier in the year. When we played Dallas at the Linc in the final regular-season game, I was blowing kisses to the fans, just in case this was my last time playing at home for the Eagles. And it was a big game. We needed a lot of help to get to the playoffs, including a win over Dallas. It was a 4:15 p.m. kickoff, and we needed Oakland to defeat the Bucs, and the Texans had to beat Chicago for our game to matter. Before a game, you try to block everything out, but you can't help but catch wind of what's happening. All the dominoes fell the way we needed them, and we just had to do what we needed to do.

I was playing with a double ear infection, and I wasn't 100 percent. I didn't practice a lot that week, but I knew I was going to play in that game. I was blessed in that game to do what I had prepared to do. I had been watching film, and knew what to anticipate on the field. My dream of a perfect play involves me as do what I do, and I hit someone and cause a fumble that my teammate would then pick up and run in for a touchdown. I was blessed to do it twice, first for Chris Clemons and then for Joselio Hanson. It was a great game and a great way to end my time in Philadelphia.

Even if I didn't want it to be the end.

CHAPTER 14

Leaving Home

I wanted to stay in Philadelphia. My plan was to play two more seasons with the Eagles, to bring the total to fifteen years, and then I would have retired. I was going to stay around Philadelphia, keep a home here. I would live in Florida full-time, but I would have a presence here.

The team didn't want to do anything with my contract during the 2008 season, and that was cool. But when they came to me with an offer after '08 was over, it was low. For them, the situation was more about my age. The team told me it was a good contract for a player my age. But if you looked at my numbers, I was still killing it in many regards. I was blessed to make the Pro Bowl. But even more importantly, I was Defensive Player of the Month for December.

I wasn't asking for the money that (Pittsburgh's) Troy Polamalu and (Baltimore's) Ed Reed made, because they were younger than me. I understood that. But I thought that I had proven I was different by that time. I was thirty-five years old, and I was still playing at a high level at that point. I wasn't hurt, and I thought I had proven myself.

By then I was playing strong safety. I can remember going to (then defensive coordinator) Sean McDermott and telling him that I thought Quintin Mikell was better at covering than I was. I knew I could still have success playing free safety, but Q could cover better than I could. Now, you had him and me back there, and we both could cover, and we both could blitz, so you had no idea where the blitz was coming from.

Sean used the analogy of Michael Jordan's career. No, I'm not saying I'm Mike. But Sean said that later in his career, Mike wasn't doing the high-flying stuff he did when he was younger. He was playing with his back to the basket more. So, he said that allowing Q to handle the covering more from the safety spot would be a tremendous thing. I wasn't changing direction like I once was. I could see it. I'm not blind. I could see certain things on tape. I wasn't doing things quite as well as I used to. I was still at a high level, making Pro Bowls and being named All-Pro, but a young cat, with that quick twitch, he could do it a little better, and that made sense to me. And I also dug the fact that he used MJ as an example, as I was a HUGE MJ fan growing up. So I knew exactly what he was referring to.

So, even though I made the position change, I was still playing quite well and felt Philadelphia should have recognized that. But the offer was lower than what I felt I deserved, and I had to look elsewhere. If the team was scared about injury, I get that, but if you look at 2009, my first year in Denver, I was All-Pro and in the Pro Bowl. So, injury clearly wasn't a problem. But they just said, "This is where we think you should be." There was no wiggle room. As many times as my agent, Jim Steiner, and I went back, and that was not something we would usually do, they wouldn't change. I kept saying, "Go back. Go back. Ask them this. Ask them that."

But Denver came with an offer that blew the Eagles out of the water. And still, I was hesitant. I asked Jim, "Do you think we can go back and get a counteroffer?" He said we shouldn't. The Eagles had let us know where they thought we should be with salary. And that there was no need to come back with any offer. Denver basically bid against itself. I wasn't trying to play hardball; I was hoping the Eagles would come to their senses, but it was crystal clear. The Broncos really wanted me. And the Eagles made it clear they weren't going to change.

It was awful. At the time, I said it was "a pain in my heart," and I meant it. I really mourned. It was like somebody died in my life. It was painful. I was crying. I called Troy Vincent, and he was in a hotel in Indianapolis when we talked. He told me that this was "a reset." He told me that Jerry Rice, the greatest receiver of all time, didn't finish his career in San Francisco. Joe Montana didn't finish his career in San Francisco. He asked me why I thought I was different. Even Emmitt Smith went to Arizona, and nobody could have imagined that he would wear a jersey other than the one with the star on it. Troy was trying to tell me that it wasn't personal. It was business in the NFL. He also told me something that hit home. "It's better to be appreciated, then tolerated."

Still, after it was over, I was wondering what my Eagles teammates were doing at certain times. I was wondering whether I made the right decision. It was something I had to work through myself. I didn't need a lot of people to talk to.

I had to figure it out on my own. The other thing I had to figure out, was who was going to help get my body back and aligned every day. I believe the Lord put people right where you need them. Especially when you ask. And that's where I met Dr. Nelson Vetanze (Doctor of Chiropractic, Bachelor of Science, certified Chiropractic Extremity Practitioner, Certified Chiropractic Animal Practitioner) in Aurora, Colorado. I don't know what all that means, but he is a *bad* man. I would virtually stay over at his house, it seems. From my feet to the top of my head, this man with his mind and gadgets would help me get the most out of my body and mind, right into my late thirties. And Dr. Shawn Caldwell, DC, a Chiropractor who took my advice to go learn from Ann Frederick at Stretch To Win, so I could get the freshest, loosest legs as possible. And Dr. P. Michael Leahy (developer of ART Active Release Techniques) and Steve Hamilton, Massage Guru. These gentlemen were essential in my late-career success. And I would go on to learn a lot more about the body from them working on me.

◇◇◇

If Denver had been a bad team, I wouldn't have considered going there. But the Broncos had finished 8–8 in 2008, and I felt they were on the cusp. I didn't want to start over with a team that had won only two or three games. What they had been doing was starting fast and then fading late. They just kept doing it. They had Champ Bailey at cornerback there, and they had Brandon Marshall at wide receiver. The defense was pretty solid. I thought, "You know what? I can go there, to a team that can win, and I hope I can add to it and hopefully be a part of changing that trouble at the end of the season." I wanted us to be on a team that finished well, because that's what we did in Philadelphia. I wanted to earn the right to have some conversations with my new teammates so we could understand how to end the season strong. I had to earn respect first, and then hopefully, I could help.

I was also going to bring my Wolverine personality to Denver. I've always had that extra energy, but it was not always used in the right ways. I grew into it, and it developed as I became more confident and more of a playmaker, in Philly. Once you show your teammates they can count on you during practices, meetings, and games, you can be whatever you want, so long as you aren't disrupting the team.

When the Eagles were in the playoffs during the 2000 season, a newspaper reporter came into the locker room and saw all of the Wolverine action figures in my locker, and wrote a story about it. He asked me why I liked Wolverine, and I told him. That's when it blew up. TV stations put it on the air, and then Marvel got involved. They reached out to me, and they did a mockup of me as Wolverine in Eagles gear, and I was like, "Wow! That's Marvel Comics, bro. Marvel Comics!" The cat who actually draws Wolverine drew me as Wolverine hybrid, Jorge Molina. That was sooooo dope. I Still can't believe it.

"I'm the best there is at what I do. But what I do isn't very nice." – Wolverine

The thing that makes me identify with Wolverine is that he is a hand-to-hand combat dude. He is up in your face. Here's how we're going to get down, down and dirty. He has a checkered past, and there are some dark edges to him. He doesn't back down from fights, even when he should. He's always there to back up his team. But the thing I loved about him is that when he fights someone, there's just a different level of darkness about him. It's almost like an animal instinct. That translates well to the football field, that animal instinct to anticipate and then go pounce on fools.

The backstory on Wolverine is that his original name was Logan. A government agency kidnapped him, and put a super-hard metal called "Adamantium" into his body and then washed his brain clean. That made him Weapon X. The government wanted him to be a killing machine. They would have him kill and then erase that memory from his brain. He was a weapon. He eventually escaped and moved to Canada, where he became Wolverine, a superhero. He was able to remember some of the awful things he had done in his past, and that's where the darkness in his life comes from. I could relate to that.

I called myself Weapon X because Jim Johnson used me in so many different ways. I was a weapon. And I was blessed with the gifts to do them all. I was a blitzer. I could cover. I could tackle in the open field. I could rush the quarterback and bat down passes. I even caught a TD pass. Jim could use me however he wanted to use me. That's why I was Weapon X. There were some significant numbers in every category. I truly wanted to have the ability to affect the game in every category for my teammates.

Some guys, they could do one thing, maybe two very well, but Jim could use me in all areas. Weapon X was the perfect name. The perfect alter ego. When I sign autographs, fans often ask me to write "Weapon X."

I started the bear crawling onto the field at The Vet. It wasn't a Wolverine thing. That's what I felt like doing at the time before the game. When we got to the Linc, the story got bigger. It was a serious thing because football is a business. But it's the entertainment business. It's a show, and I was having a good time. There aren't too many occupations in the world that you can bear crawl into work. We were entertaining people. I'm a football fan, and I want to be entertained by the game. So in a way, I was entertaining myself as well.

People always say that if they had a chance to score a touchdown, they would just hand the ball to the ref afterward. No, they wouldn't. They would celebrate. So, I felt like I was going to have a good time while I was on the field. But I have learned to contain that part of me, to keep it under wraps so to speak. I only use that part of me when it's relevant. I'll talk about Weapon X and Wolverine in the third person, but sometimes, when I work out, I can let Weapon X out. It's time to work out, so let's get it. I start competing. I can't be as physical as I once was, but mentally I can attack you. That's when you're going to get the whole me. The energy I use to compete and go at people when the time is right is the same energy I want to use to help and care about people. In my opinion, energy can be transferred, and I consciously do it often.

There is an abundance of energy in my body. I get hyped easily. I get real excited when I talk. That's inside of me, and I can use it in different ways. Checking in on people. Helping them. Singing when I want to. Dancing when I want to. I can bring that energy at any given time. But I am careful when I show it, because I hate being embarrassed. Nobody likes it, but I hate it. Sometimes, I would purposely not do things so nobody would laugh at me, unless I was trying to make them laugh. I have become a very observant person. Connie and I will go somewhere, and she'll engage people, and I will just sit there and listen. Take it in.

Before a game, I wasn't worried about being embarrassed. I wanted to see who was going to come with me into battle, who wanted to join my party. I would often walk around the locker room and ask every one of my teammates "Let me look into your eyes to see if you ready for this." I wanted to know if he was willing to sacrifice his body for the win, because two teams were about to enter the stadium, and they were going to lock the gates and see which one was going to come out. I also did it to loosen things up. All week long, I would give 100 percent in practice. I would push the envelope on my disguises. I would run full speed to the ball when I was on the field. I would take notes in meetings. I would work out in the weight room, but you didn't hear anything much from me. The closer I got to kickoff, the closer that controlled fury got to the surface. I was like a ticking time bomb, and I wanted all of the other 44 players dressed for that day's game to come with me. We weren't going to hold anything back, and we were going to give fans a show.

◇◇◇

The 2009 season was the Broncos' first without Mike Shanahan, who was fired after '08 after fourteen years and two Super Bowl championships with Denver. The other big change was at quarterback. Jay Cutler wasn't happy being part of the team, and he was traded to Chicago for Kyle Orton and two first-round picks. I didn't know they had gotten rid of Jay. I said, "Okay, who did we get?" Not only did we get rid of Jay, we got rid of the team chaplain.

When I got to Denver, I was doing Bible study with the guys, and counseling. These weren't things that necessarily fell on me. I was blessed to be able to do them. But it was more than I thought I was going to be doing, the Bible studies and the counseling. I was even blessed to counseling some coaches on things. My number was called to serve, and I accepted.

Losing Jay was surprising. I thought he was a reason the team was up and coming. We started 6–0 in 2009, and we even beat the Patriots in overtime. Then came the bye week. And the dreaded week off. To which I screamed "NO!" when new coach Josh McDaniels announced it. I thought at the time we were too young of a team. Not so much in age, but in behavior. We had a rhythm and a level of focus that reminded me of my time in Philly. I didn't think we could handle that week off. After that, we lost four in a row and eight of ten to finish 8–8. It was a strange season because even though we went into the last game, against Kansas City, 8–7, we still had a chance to get into the playoffs. But we lost, 44–24, at home, and that was it.

The toughest part of the season was playing against the Eagles. That was brutal. I knew we were going to play the Eagles that year because Denver was playing the whole NFC East. The game was in Philly, and it was the only time in my professional career that I did not come out for warmups. I could not do it. I was crying. I was a mess. I was so anxious to play the game and just get it over with. I wanted to win to see if we could get into the playoffs, but I didn't want to see any of the guys on the Eagles. It was too tough. I felt a lot of pain because I had left there.

It wasn't that it was difficult mentally to play against the guys. I had practiced against Donovan for so long, that I was able to anticipate some of the things he would do. I also expected them to flex Brian Westbrook out to put me one-on-one with him. I was able to make some plays to prevent anything big, but the whole experience was tough.

The thing about that season was how I took everything that had happened, the pain and frustration and anger, and I focused it into having one of my best seasons in the NFL, even at the age of 36. I wanted what had happened to motivate me. I was dialed in more than ever, and I took all of my energy and put it toward being as successful as possible.

I was 100 percent conscious that I was doing more. First, I had to earn the respect of my new teammates. But I also needed to make sure my body was ready to go full speed every game, even at age 36. I didn't miss one day of being in the training room. I was obsessed with it. And I didn't take any time off in practice, either. I was grinding my body. I already had a lot of mileage on my body, but I kept going full speed. Sometimes, coaches would tell me to take a couple reps and then sit out. But I didn't do that. I wanted to play every snap that first year in Denver. After that, I would have to.

It was great that we were playing the NFC East, because I hadn't built up a dislike for the Broncos' traditional rivals, like the Raiders and the Chiefs yet. But I already had that for the teams in the East. Unfortunately, we lost to the Eagles, 30-27, in the next-to-last game of the season. It was tough because all players want to beat the team that let them go, and I was no exception. And I hate to lose, period. It always leaves a nasty taste.

Don't get me wrong; I wanted to win. We had lost two in a row, and I wanted to get back on the winning side. That season taught me that not everybody wins and loses the same way. In Philadelphia, there was a level of accountability at all times. We had a mentality where everybody did his job. And that was there win, lose or draw. That was not there when I went to Denver. Cats kind of behaved the same no matter what the outcome of the game was. I wasn't digging that. It wasn't everybody, but the vibe was looser. It happened during the week, too. Some cats were way too loose too late into the week for my liking. And some guys would be just as loud after a loss as they were after a win. I couldn't dig that. I never got used to that. I tried to have some conversations with guys about it, but I didn't always get through to them.

There was also some trouble between the head coach, Josh McDaniels, and defensive coordinator Mike Nolan. That's why we fell off in the second half of the season. They didn't get along. Nolan wanted to blitz, and Josh wanted us to cover more, among other things. That created a conflict. Nolan was a guy who always wore a shirt buttoned up. Wore a tie on game days. Was clean-shaven. He was GQ, Jack. That's how he looked putting in the game plan, not just on game day. But as the season went on, he wasn't shaving. He wasn't dressing up. He was just wearing Broncos stuff, and he let other coaches put the game plan in. You didn't have to be a rocket scientist to know Mike wasn't going to be there much longer. And he was gone after the season.

He knew his stuff. We were 6–0. We were only allowing 11 points a game during that period. We were getting after people. But when you have one coach with one philosophy and another coach that has another, and one is the head coach, there will be problems. Josh was just learning who he was as a coach. I don't think he knew who he was yet. He tried to micromanage everything. It's one thing to have a blueprint and an understanding of how a team was going to work together, and another to micromanage every call. That's when we stopped blitzing as much. We would have a bunch of blitzes in the game plan, and we wouldn't use any of them. I was used to blitzing. I was used to lighting folks up.

When I first got to Denver, we were lighting folks up. And the second half of the season, we were only rushing three guys or even two. That's what they do in New England, where Josh had come from, and that wasn't Mike Nolan. So, it was clear they weren't on the same page. But one thing I did that year was have the most tackles (116) that I had in my career. I was a man possessed to show the Eagles that they messed up letting me go. My greatest accomplishment as a football player, aside from making it to the Hall of Fame, was going to Denver in my fourteenth year, making the Pro Bowl on the AFC side, making All-Pro at the age of 36.

When you go to another conference, you're not a household name. When I was in the NFC, and people started thinking about who they would vote for in the Pro Bowl, my name was in the mix. In the AFC, you have the other cats, like Troy Polamalu and Ed Reed. They are the significant names on that side. But in my first year with the Broncos, I was second on the team in tackles. I rushed the passer. I was still playing at a high level. Basically, the team was funneling the other teams' running backs to me, D. J. Williams, and Andra Davis, so we could clean 'em up. That was the game plan. They knew we could do it. So, when you think about it, to make that many tackles and to make All-Pro as a 36-year-old was perhaps my greatest accomplishment as a player.

That first year was a big change for me. I went to a new conference. I was far from Philadelphia. There was a lack of unity on the coaching staff, which hadn't ever been a problem for me with the Eagles. The culture was different. So were the fans. Denver fans are great fans. But they are more laid-back than Philly fans. They're passionate. They get loud, too. It was loud and lively on game day. But though it sounds crazy to say, I was used to the darkness that Eagles fans had. It sounds bad, but I say it with a smile on my face. For me there's a good edge to the fans in Philadelphia. When they go to a game, it's almost like they're playing in the game. They feel they are actually controlling what's going on in the game. It's a very knowledgeable fan base. I enjoyed my time in Denver, the fans welcomed me with open arms. Which that so-called washed-up safety greatly appreciated.

The second half of 2009 was tough, but the entire 2010 season was difficult. It was extremely frustrating because I went to Denver on the premise that it was a franchise that was on the rise. The owner, Mr. (Pat) Bowlen, was first-class, and I felt he understood what was necessary to get the players needed to have success on the field. We started the season 2–2 and then went the complete opposite direction. We had the league's worst defense, allowing 29.4 PPG. In week seven, we lost to Oakland, 59–17. It was the Broncos' worst loss since San Francisco beat them, 55–10, in Super Bowl XXIV. It was the most points given up by the team since 1963. And it was at home.

The brutal practices made everything worse. It was not fun at all. It's possible to lose some games and still have an enjoyment for the game. Now, I'm not talking about losing eight in a row, or nine out of ten like we did in 2010. But, believe me, you can lose a couple of games here and a couple of games there and still be enjoying the game. I can remember guys going into games still limping, because the practices were so long and drawn out. I would ask Josh if we could change things up and do things a little differently to help guys get their legs back.

That just meant for me, fifteen years into a career, that I had to spend more time on the massage table and in the training room. I can tell you that I was home very seldom. I was either in the training room, getting worked on, doing some extra stretching or getting something else done. They were using me basically as a linebacker. I kept getting put closer and closer to the line of scrimmage by that time in my career. They wanted me to blitz, even though I could still move and cover. It wasn't easy, because I wasn't just dealing with me. I was working with some young cats as well.

I kept telling them, "You have to fight through this. You have to put good stuff on film for other teams to see." I began to have many conversations like that, as the year went on.

What made things even more difficult were the injuries I suffered that year. I only played in eleven games. I tore my hamstring a little bit, and then I wound up spraining both my MCLs. I did one. Missed a few weeks, came back and sprained the other to a lesser degree. I came back too early from the hamstring. And I probably came back too early from my first knee sprain. But we were losing, and I felt I had to get back out there. I wanted to keep being a good example for my teammates. I was hoping they were ashamed to go half-speed if I was playing, because here was this 36-year-old dude running around to the ball. So, I felt like I had to be on the practice field so that I could help the defense focus better.

I felt it was important to show the other guys the significance of practicing the way you play. Of course, I already didn't move the

way I had been able to when I was younger, and I was still fighting
that hamstring.

While I was fighting injuries, Josh McDaniels was struggling
to keep his job. He didn't succeed. Mr. Bowlen fired him in early
December. The team was playing some of its worst ball in decades,
but that wasn't all of it. There was also the videotaping scandal when
we played in London. Our video operations guy filmed six minutes
of the 49ers practice over there, and Josh didn't report it. The league
found out, and since this was after New England's "Spygate," it was
a real problem. The Broncos even investigated not paying Josh the
remainder of his contract after they fired him, because they thought
he had committed a violation of the morals clause in his contract.
It was a mess, and it was a rough end of my first two years in Denver.

One of the interesting parts of the season was the arrival of
quarterback Tim Tebow. The Broncos drafted him near the end of
the first round, and the media jumped on him quickly. He had won
the Heisman Trophy and the national championship, and set a whole
bunch of records at Florida. So, everybody was wondering when he
was going to play. And he actually played in nine games that year
and started three.

Tim is a good dude. A quality guy. And from my vantage point
he really is like he comes across on TV. That's how he talks. I wasn't
in meetings with the offense, so I can't tell you completely how he
behaved in every situation, but I saw him in practice, and what people see is what I saw. He was a quality cat. He excelled at quarterback in college, because of the style that he played. It was perfect for
him. But when he had to play the NFL style, he had a lot of trouble.

The media attention Tebow received was nothing new to me.
I was used to it from playing with T.O. It wasn't a big deal. I was
still going to do my job, and I had already been in situations in
Philadelphia where the offense struggled to score. So in 2010, when
the Broncos didn't score a lot of points and used both Kyle and Tim
at quarterback, I knew it was about trying to turn up the intensity on defense and helping guys understand how to do that if they
didn't already know. It was about holding guys accountable because
we knew we couldn't give up points with Tim at quarterback. The
offense wasn't scoring a lot with him in there. We wanted to try to

get him to the fourth quarter, because that's when he became a different quarterback.

I'm not taking shots at him. I'm not beating him down. From what I saw of him in practice and during games, when he was out there late in games, he stopped thinking and just went with what he saw. You know, playing loose. Anticipating and reacting, instead of thinking. He became a better quarterback. You could see that in 2011 when he started eleven games.

◇◇◇

The 2010 season was brutal, but before we could get to '11, we had to deal with the lockout. When the Players Association's contract with the owners expired, the owners locked us out. This happened in March, and it lasted until July 25. There were no mini-camps or OTAs. We couldn't work out at team facilities. We weren't able to see team doctors. And we couldn't talk with our coaches. I was on the NFLPA Executive Committee, so I knew a lot more about what was going on than most players did.

The one thing that was pretty evident as we went through the negotiating process was that some owners did not like being across the table from us. They didn't feel like we belonged in the same room as they did. They didn't think the players should have a say in how they did business. That's the way I saw it.

But while I was interested in helping the players union get a good contract, I also had to focus on my off-season regimen. I didn't have a whole lot of time left in my career. I was on the back nine, the last couple of holes, and I had to make sure I would be in shape for the 2011 season. So, I connected with Loren Landow, who has been training folk in the Denver area for a long time. The Broncos hired him as their strength and conditioning coach in February 2018. I paid Loren to work out our team. Whoever was in town and didn't have a place to go could join us. Loren is one of the best, and that's why I wanted him to work with us. I wanted to win games in 2011.

We would get together at Valor Christian High School, where my son, Brian Jr., went. We could lift in the gym and use the fields and track. I didn't want guys just to go home and do things on their own or work with people who weren't good at training people. Some of the young guys didn't have anywhere to work out and didn't have the money to pay someone to train them. The disparity in the league between guys who have money and guys who don't is tremendous. That was a big thing about the labor negotiations. A lot of guys were worried they couldn't withstand a full season without a paycheck. It was going to get tough for them if there wasn't a contract.

But we settled in late July, in time for training camps to start up and with no danger to the 2011 season. It was time to go again.

One last time.

CHAPTER 15

Time to Say Good-Bye

I had gone through coaching changes before. It happened in college, when Clemson replaced Ken Hatfield with Tommy West. It happened in Philly, when Andy Reid took over from Ray Rhodes. If you take it back to my first days playing Pop Warner, I had a new coach after my first year. So, it wasn't a very difficult experience for me to adjust to John Fox, Denver's coach in 2011.

John is a straight shooter. He's going to give you a bunch of country sayings, too, like "Mosquitoes pulling the wagon." He's a funny man, with a real quirky sense of humor. I wish I could have played longer for Foxy, to be honest with you.

Our defensive coordinator was Dennis Allen, who was coming into his own at that time. He really liked to put pressure on other offenses. We did a lot more pressuring with him than we did when Josh was head coach, which I loved. Dennis is an extremely confident cat. And he liked to inflict pain on people. I'll just leave it at that. So, you can imagine we got along just fine.

One of the people that I loved playing with in Denver was Champ Bailey, the All-Pro cornerback who was named to twelve Pro Bowls during his fifteen years, the most ever for a Hall of Fame cornerback. He was a phenomenal player and athlete. I wish we could have met and played together on the same team in our primes. When I first got to Denver, and I lined up on defense, I looked at him and said, "Man, that's Champ Bailey. I'm going to be playing with Champ Bailey." He was another one of those outliers, guys who play the game at a high level for a long time.

Another real special player was Von Miller, who was drafted by Denver before the 2011 season. Everybody's saying it now, so just add me to the choir. I saw how great he was immediately. Anyone with eyes could see it. His movements his first year? Oh, my goodness. His ability to close on a running back and close on a quarterback or run somebody down from behind were off the charts. His ability to bend and get around offensive linemen his rookie year was amazing. He was light, and at the time, he didn't really know a lot about the game of football. He was extremely raw, but he had it. He was also extremely goofy. Raw and goofy. But he had IT.

There have only been a few guys who stood out to me as rookies, who could just flat out light it up like Von could. One was Brian Westbrook, even though he didn't play right away. Another was DeSean Jackson, who played wide receiver for the Eagles. Another was Chris Harris Jr. Chris not only had skill. Chris has a finish, a won't-back-down and infectious attitude about playing the game that is second to a short list of folks that I have played with. He stood out. But Von? My goodness. After the first couple of games, it was clear. He reminded me of the great Kansas City linebacker, Derrick Thomas.

The 2011 season was strange—even though we lost our last three games, we still made the playoffs, because the West Division was a mess. Three teams finished at the top with 8–8 records, and we won the division on a tiebreaker. Our offense wasn't very good. We scored more than 20 points only six times all year. We were really shutting people down on defense, and in my opinion, the MVPs for that year were the kickers. Punter Britton Colquitt was knocking the laces off the ball, pinning people down. And Matt Prater, our kicker, hit some really long field goals, consistently, with ease. Our defense was getting off the field that year.

Going into the season, I didn't think this would be my last in the NFL. I hurt my neck again, and that was a factor. But the thing is, I am always extremely honest with what I see on film. I am brutally honest with myself. I saw that I wasn't making the plays that I should be making. I was still making some plays. I still made the Pro Bowl that year, but I wasn't doing the things I felt I should be doing.

The game became much more of a test for me. The things that once took me no effort to do required a whole lot more effort, and I began to think about stuff a lot more. I wasn't anxious, but I was thinking about what I couldn't do.

I was still having a good time, but I never wanted to be a liability for my team. I knew that space was no longer my friend. That meant that whenever there was space between me and someone else on the field, like a running back in the open field, it could be problematic. So, it took a whole lot more work for me to do things. I could still do it, but I had always told myself I didn't want to be somebody who quit too late. I've seen too many guys in all sports who over the years who have waited too long.

I spent a lot of time praying and asking the Lord that when it's time, give me the peace to leave. That peace began to happen when I hurt my neck again. I hurt it the first time in 2007. In '11, I hurt it in "friendly fire." I was going to make a tackle on Chargers tight end Randy McMichael in a game in October, and the guy ducked. My teammate, D.J. Williams, hit me and pinched a nerve. No matter what I tried, I couldn't get back to full strength. I played in some games, but I didn't finish a lot. That's why I missed the playoffs. I tried to regenerate the nerve, but once it's damaged, it takes a long time to come back. There are techniques that can be used and an instrument that can make it come back quicker, but it just didn't happen quickly enough for me to play in the playoffs.

I wanted to play in the playoffs so bad, because I wanted to get back out there with my teammates. We had missed the playoffs my first two years in Denver, so I felt I had to get out there.

But things started to happen. I began to coach from the sideline. I began to coach in the meeting rooms more. And I enjoyed it. Before, when I was out with an injury, I would watch the games and go crazy because I wasn't out there, except for the time I worked with Clinton Hart. But now, I was watching the games and saying, "I'm going to help this guy do this better. I'm going to help that guy see that." My mindset was completely different than it had ever been in the past. I had a peace on game day that I hadn't had before when I was injured. It wasn't the same. When I walked off the field after the game against the Patriots in December because of my neck, a huge part of me knew that would be the last time I was on an NFL field.

But I still made the Pro Bowl that year, so I decided to take my family out to Hawaii for the last time. That was actually my last time on a field, but it wasn't a regular-season game. I played about 10–15 snaps in the Pro Bowl, but then I let the young cats have at it. I let them go out there.

It's always tough for an athlete to retire, because even if he has played a lot of years, like I did, he's still relatively young. I was only 38 and entering the prime of my life. But it wasn't my prime on the field. But it was cool, because I was someone who could say that I was blessed to be able to decide when I was done. I had some teams who wanted me to sign with them for a year, to be a mentor and to play a specific role on the field, but I didn't want to do that. I chose not to play anymore. For a lot of people, it's not a choice when they shut it down. It's injuries, or they're not wanted anymore. They feel like they should still be playing, that it was somebody else's fault. For me, it was nobody else's fault. I said, "That's it for me."

This was less about the injury. Instead, it was more that the desire to put forth the effort needed to get ready for a season, and the joy I felt going into the games, weren't there like they used to be. When I was young, I felt there was nothing I couldn't do on a football field. In my eyes, my ability to make plays was limitless. There was no position I could be in on the field that was a problem for me. As I got older, especially in the last couple years of my career, I knew that there were certain situations that weren't good for me to be in. It's not that I definitely couldn't succeed. It was just that getting to the point where I could be successful took a whole lot of effort, and there was no guarantee I was going to get it done.

In the last couple years of my career, I had to think a lot more on the field. Positioning myself and playing the angles were more important than ever for me. It wasn't always fun or successful. It was more like work. And I wasn't sure how my body was going to hold up from week to week. I could feel great one week, and all of a sudden, things weren't so good that next week. Then I could be great again and then not great. There was no way I could tell people whether I would be clicking on all cylinders week to week.

It wasn't about injuries. I'm talking about those signals from the brain to the body, that quick-twitch muscle reaction. If I had to do something in the moment, I might not be able to do it. There were times when I didn't have my legs up under me. Other times I could, because I had my juices really kicking, and my quick-twitch was really activated. In those circumstances, I knew I was probably going to have a good day. When that didn't happen, there was possible trouble.

◇◇◇

It was my decision to retire as an Eagle. I had spent too much time building up a great relationship with the fans to let the fact that the team let me go stop me from celebrating with the people of Philadelphia. I had so many wonderful teammates, and the fans had been so great that I had to finish up officially with the Eagles.

In an organization, people come and go—personnel, front office people, coaches. But that Eagle head will always be there, and the fans will be fans of the Philadelphia Eagles. I had to celebrate with them. And I can't leave out Jeffrey Lurie. He'll still be the owner of the team, even as others around him move in and out. So, I signed a one-day contract with the Eagles and retired as a member of the organization. That was important.

People might not believe this, but the decision to retire was not a hard one emotionally for me. I can honestly tell you that I gave 100 percent at all times. I was eating right. I was using a hyperbaric chamber. I was getting stretched. I gave everything I had every time my feet touched that field, for sixteen years. I feel good about that. So, when I knew it was time to go, there were no negative emotions about it.

And it was great to be just one of three safeties—Paul Krause and Eugene Robinson were the others—blessed enough to play sixteen seasons in the NFL. That's tremendous, man, because it takes me back to some of the conversations I had with myself when I started in the league. I set goals for myself, and one of them was to be one of the best safeties ever to play the game. I wanted to have a career that was consistently dominant from start to finish, and I did that by making the Pro Bowl in my last season. When I retired, I led the Eagles with 34 career interceptions. I was blessed to be the first player in NFL history to record a sack, interception, forced fumble and TD reception in the same game. I was elected to nine Pro Bowls and was first-team All-Pro five times.

I hadn't just wanted to play for sixteen years. I wanted to have a significant impact on my team's ability to win for sixteen years. By playing the way I did, I think I helped further the safety position. Jim Johnson and I helped further the way safety is played. Safeties are being used in a completely different way, on a consistent basis now than the way they were before I started, and that will continue to grow.

It's not just that I blitzed. It was everything. I'm not saying Jim and I were the first people to have safeties blitz as much as I did. Leroy Butler played for the Packers from 1990–2001, and he was doing that back in the day. And he did it well. I did that and just about everything else a safety could do for sixteen years. When you do it that well for that long, the significance of your work allows you to have a chance to get that jacket, to have the chance to be in the Pro Football Hall of Fame.

That's why I respect Darrell Green so much. He played twenty years with Washington. I wanted to be the kind of guy who could play at a high level that long, or close to it. I wanted to be that guy.

The Eagles retired my number during the September 30 game against the Giants in 2012. Before the game, they had a ceremony outside the stadium. Then, I put on my number 20 jersey and led the team out, just like old times. That was crazy hype. They had a big "20" on the field, and at halftime, they unveiled the banner of me.

It was an incredible moment. I was a kid who grew up in Jacksonville. I wasn't highly recruited. I had to fight to earn a way onto the football field and to play the position I wanted to play. I played center in Pop Warner. Clemson took me in as a throw-in. I got drafted and played sixteen years in the National Football League. And to get my number retired? That's amazing. I was so grateful, so blessed.

But it all started back in Jacksonville, Florida. Think about that young, energetic, little, angry, introverted dude. It was hard. My high school and college numbers haven't been retired. But the Eagles retired my number? Out of all the football I played and all the teams I played for? It was just unbelievable. You start thinking about other guys who have had their numbers retired. Magic. Jordan. Dr. J. Those are the guys who get their numbers retired, not me.

Unbelievable.

◇◇◇

Even though I had been at peace with my decision to retire, the juices still started flowing around the time training camp was supposed to begin before the 2012 season. My body was telling me that it was time to go. I would see guys were training, and those juices were flowing. But it wasn't like, "Oh, man, I wish that was me."

At that point, I was a fan. On Sundays, I was going to sit down with some chicken wings and watch the games. And I ended up working for ESPN. That was surprising because in my mind, there was no way I was going into TV. When I was playing, I wasn't a big fan of the media's ability to twist things around and only point out certain things that were part of a narrative. I wasn't happy with that. So, it wasn't something I considered when I was playing.

The speech coaches at ESPN saw something inside of me and helped me bring it out. It's just like all the other coaches in my life, like Coach Humph. He brought out the best in me, too. When I say "Blessed by the best," I mean Coach Humph and the others who helped bring out who I am. Somebody who saw something in me was the late, great ESPN broadcaster John Saunders. He brought me into his office one day and said—and I'll never forget this—"Son, you have an extremely unique voice. What you do when you speak is extremely unique. There's a genuineness about how you talk and how you communicate with people. That is extremely hard to do." I was so grateful. Then he began to talk about some of the people in the business that I reminded him of. One that he mentioned was

James Brown, the NFL Today host. I said, "Wow, really? That guy?"

When I heard that from John, it meant a lot. At the time, I was still trying to change some things in the way I spoke. I still have some trouble. Instead of saying "the" all the time, I said "da." It's not a big deal, but John was telling me that the ability to speak clearly, to control my breathing, and to slow my pace down was important. It was all right to make a mistake because it was live television, and not to panic. But he gave me some things to work on and showed faith in me. That was huge.

When some people teach little kids to swim, they throw them in the water and see how they do. That's what they did with me. They put me on the air without much training, and I did pretty well. I wasn't totally confident talking on the air. It was tough to remember all the stats and still be able to give my opinion. I felt like I messed up, and a sense of panic came over me. But we were on live so there was nothing I could do about it. Part of me wanted to get up and walk off the set. But I stuck it out. I took a couple deep breaths and finished my thought.

After that, the training started, and I became more and more comfortable in front of the camera being myself. Those early times on ESPN taught me about speaking and not being too hard on myself when I made mistakes. When I was a player, I was extremely hard on myself. You can't be that way on air. You're going to make mistakes. You're going to mess up every once in a while, and it's no big deal. I was taking everything really seriously at first. But that meeting with John was powerful for me because it allowed me to see that I had a gift. I had thought it was more for motivational speaking to teammates, not for the public or TV. And here was one of the best ever to do the job telling me this, so it meant a lot.

I really took what he said to heart, because it wasn't his job to boost me or encourage me. He saw something and wanted to tell me about it. So, I started doing the exercises the speech coaches gave me, and I took it very seriously because John's words had a big impact.

There were parts of that job that I enjoyed, but my role really wasn't about helping guys. It was more about rating them and talking about their strengths and especially their weaknesses. What made this offense good or bad? What was this quarterback doing well or poorly? It wasn't about helping people, so it wasn't a good match for me. I tried not to criticize people. I wanted to critique them. I didn't want to tear them down. And I'm not sure that's what ESPN wanted. I don't know if that's what fans wanted, but it wasn't me.

◇◇◇

I worked for ESPN for three seasons, but I felt a pull back to football, and not just on TV. When I was at ESPN, it was one of the first times in a long time that I allowed myself to get complacent. I wasn't really growing there as far as the job was concerned. I was improving as a speaker, but I wasn't growing as a person, to be honest with you. They let me know that some cuts were coming among the people who worked on the air, but they didn't announce it. I was still getting paychecks for a little while, but I wasn't going up to Bristol (Connecticut), ESPN's headquarters, to work. During that time, I was okay, and I was trying to see what I was going to get into next. I always believe that when the Lord closes a door, he leads you to something else. I wanted to see what I could use my gifts for next.

It had to come from my heart. It doesn't matter if someone calls you on the phone and asks. If you don't really want to do it, and you don't feel you can make a difference, then it doesn't matter whether you accept the offer. You won't be successful.

When I left the Eagles, I never thought I was going to be back in Philadelphia, other than to visit. When I went to Denver after the Eagles didn't re-sign me, that was it. When I came back and retired as an Eagle, that was cool. We made amends. I felt I would be back periodically, but not a lot more. But I never, never thought I could come back and live here.

In July 2016, I first accepted a spot in the Eagles scouting department as part of the Nunn-Wooten Scouting Fellowship, which was created to introduce retired players to the NFL personnel business and the life of a scout. At the time, I told the press that the football field provided a certain level of comfort for me. It was an opportunity to evaluate some guys. I was blessed to have the chance to do it. But it was tough. Yet soon after I was hired on as Football Operations Executive.

The work was not hard. It was the family part that was difficult, because I was gone quite a bit, and I was away from the family. And when you are talking about football and people who work in the sport, there is a lot of pride there, so you learn to work around that and not step on people's toes. When people asked me things about how I might do something as a player or how I might instruct someone on something, I didn't say, "You have to do it this way." I'd say that they should think about it in a certain way and see how that fits with what they have been doing. I was trying to be an asset to the organization and to add onto what was already there. I wanted to try to help.

I really enjoyed the opportunity to speak with some of the players. I can't go into many specifics, because I was working with the team at the time, and I don't want to violate any confidences. But I was able to go back to my playing days, even to when I was in high school, because what I have been doing since then is using my experience to help others. I was able to help people with goal setting and help them stay on track toward their goals. I would ask them what their daily scheduling was, and point out some habits that might have prevented them from growing in ways they could have. I was all about maximizing the moment for those guys and helping them make the most of the opportunities they had.

It was a lot of fun to be back on the field and in the locker room, although it was in a much different capacity. There will always be a strong connection between me and the franchise and the fan base. It's hard to explain to people. But I enjoyed being part of it again. I told somebody before I started with the Eagles that I thought my days of getting that police escort on the bus to hotels and the stadium were over, but there I was on the bus again, getting helped through traffic. It was a good time.

When the Eagles won the Super Bowl, I have to admit that it was bittersweet, for me and my teammates that went through all of those NFC championship games together. I was excited about winning, but part of me said, "That should have been us. That should have been us."

The parade was tremendous. I was so happy for the city. It had been through a whole lot. After the Super Bowl, I was talking to a police officer, and I asked him if he had seen a difference in people since we won the Super Bowl. He said, "Yes. I happen to know there's a difference. Things have been different in a lot of ways since then."

I worked with the Eagles for two seasons, and I left in March 2018, after the Super Bowl title and after the parade. I felt that some of the things I had been called to do had been done. It was time to move on to the next challenge. That's when I started to move toward Brian Dawkins Ventures and the Brian Dawkins Impact Foundation. It was time for the next chapter, and I was excited about it.

CHAPTER 16

Building Bridges, Bringing Hope

Every time I hear the late Sean Taylor's name, I smile, and not just because he could have been one of the best safeties ever. When he lost his life in 2007, he had it all together. He was playing so well. He seemed ready to make that big jump.

The previous year, he went to the Pro Bowl, but he hadn't been elected to the NFC team. I had been, but Connie was pregnant with the twins and having complications.

I saw a spoof one time about a gadget people can buy, that tells them what a woman really means when she says things. I didn't have to have one of those things that year. Connie was at home, miserable, and she said, "You go ahead and enjoy yourself at the Pro Bowl." Yeah, right. There was no way I was going to enjoy myself with her at home suffering. So, I called the NFL and said that I couldn't go. Sean Taylor went in my place, and he blew up Buffalo punter Sean Moorman with a big hit that people still talk about.

But that was the Pro Bowl. It was easy to make the decision not to go to that. It's an all-star game and a fun week. But what about the Super Bowl? Could I have stayed home with Connie and missed that? What about the playoffs? Those aren't easy decisions. That's where selfishness can creep in. That's where football might jump family and test faith. Early in my career, I was more selfish. I have worked hard to change that.

I have worked hard to make sure my priorities are right, beginning with the Lord.

◇◇◇

When I look at myself as a husband, I see a work in progress. I don't think there is ever a point where it's, "get it, got it, good." It's always a work in progress. During my time as a husband, there has been a lot of laziness and selfishness in me.

I have gone back and apologized to Connie, because there were many things over the years she shouldn't have had to do. I was gaining maturity on the fly, and I have learned how to swallow some pride and to work on getting more in touch with who I am. Notice I didn't say all pride, yeah, so still working indeed. One of the issues with swallowing pride though, is it's still in the body. We have to expel it out of us. I found journaling to be of great assistance. I am learning how to be more emotionally available, not just to Connie but also to my kids.

When you are a competitor, your competitiveness can come out at the wrong times. When you are talking to your wife, that is not a good time for it to come out. A better way to look at those tough discussions is to ask, "How can we move forward from this moment to the next?" That wasn't always the case for me. But I have more wisdom and growth now, and I am trying to control that anger.

I have tried to fall back on James 1:19–20:

"My dear brothers and sisters, take note of this: Everyone should be quick to listen, slow to speak and slow to become angry, because human anger does not produce the righteousness that God desires."

Human anger does not produce the righteousness God desires. But I didn't want to be the one to listen. That's where emotional availability comes in. It's okay to be emotional and available. A good husband is a great listener. It's important to hear what your wife is trying to tell you. I had to practice listening to Connie, and still do. To learn to filter through all the details to the root of the conversation. A similar principle to learning to filter bad language from coaches when I was younger. So the ability was in me, I just have to choose to use it. Even when I don't want to.

She would say to me, "How can you be so patient with other people, but not here with me?" That really hurt to hear. Because I knew it was true. It was a pride thing. I had to learn to listen to my wife and the details she was going to give. To do that, I couldn't be gritting my teeth. I have purposefully worked on keeping a blank face, so she can speak to a canvas that is open to her. She shouldn't feel that I am defensive. The canvas should be clear and not have a glimpse that would tell her where she should probably direct her message.

It takes work. I sometimes have to take a deep breath and bring myself down emotionally so she can speak to that blank canvas.

I owe that to her, because she really is a great woman. She has a certain smile that she gives and a certain laugh that she has where she closes one eye tighter than the other. I love that. She has a huge heart—sometimes to a fault. She gives of herself and gives of herself and wants to please other people, sometimes too much.

Over the years, I have found that I have a big heart. The thing that separates my heart from her heart is that I'm more accepting of things. She's not. She will ask questions to try to get to the bottom of everything. I will tell her that isn't what the average person does. Negotiation-wise, I'll put her up against anybody, Jack. When people start talking price, I say, "Let me get my wife on the phone." She's going to ask questions and get the best deal.

Connie's mom and dad separated when she was younger, and she was the big sister and mom to her sister, Marquette. She still has a protective nature about Marquette. She and her sister get into spats about that from time to time. Connie has been through a lot with the separation of her parents and the way things were handled. When parents divorce, it's so tough for the kids. One of the reasons she stuck around when I was having problems was that she didn't want our kids to go through divorce. She stuck around to preserve the family, and I'm so glad she did.

◇◇◇

Brian Jr. is my homeboy. I'm proud of the young man he's becoming. He has an idea of what he wants to do with his future and a good understanding of what he needs to get better at.

But when he was a baby, that joker wouldn't sleep. When he was a toddler, he was fighting people all the time, and even got kicked out of daycare. He was frustrated, because he didn't talk right away, and he had a boatload of energy. I know where that came from, but my goodness. He has dealt with a lot of things in his life, and he's a tough dude.

He has had to go through a lot because of his name. I believe I blessed him with that name, but it also has been tough for him. He has stood up strong. We joke around a lot. I always want him to have the opportunity to talk to me about anything and everything. We pray together, and I want him to see that prayer is powerful, and it's not only okay for men to pray together, but that is what is meant to happen.

All I can do is give him support about how he can be himself and his own man, but I can't tell him how to handle having a father with the same name.

While I have been able to build my relationship with Brian Jr., I have also committed to getting to know my daughters better. I have told myself that I have to do more silly things with them. I have to be more aware that I have to be goofy around them, so they can see that side of me. Of course, they say, "Oh, Dad!" when I do some of the stuff, but I know it's good for them. I was not always that way. When I was dealing with issues with my job and when I was in pain, not just mentally but physically, so much of my thought process was on what was happening then in my life. I wasn't able to let my goofy side come out. When I was in my fifteenth and sixteenth years in the NFL, and I was hurting, it wasn't like I could recover fast, like I could when I was young. I needed to take care of my body and didn't always have time for my children.

But I'm in a different place now, and I have more to give my daughters than I have ever had. And I need to spend as much time with them as I can.

I have a strong relationship with Brionni. She knew me before I got all beat up later in my career. But if Brionni had been like Brian Jr., we wouldn't have had any more kids, Jack. She was a lot easier as a baby than her brother was, and so we were able to think about having another after her. We always say we "had the storm before the calm." But we waited a long time between Brionni and the twins. There are three years between Brian Jr. and Brionni and eight between her and the twins. We wanted to have one more child, and we were blessed with two. It was a double blessing, and I try to let all of my children know that I think of them that way.

◇◇◇

There is a simple reason why I treat people the way I want to be treated: my faith. I don't just want to read the Word of God. I want to be a doer of God's word. I want that to take root in others and bless them. The foundation of my faith guides me and keeps me from being an individual who goes out and does what he wants to do, just because he feels like it. My emotions no longer run the roost.

My faith allows me to have wisdom in conversations with people. I can give them things they never went through, but I have. That blesses them and gives them an increase in an area they might be lacking. My faith tells me that life is a temporal existence. My faith tells me we are all going to leave here, and my faith tells me that we will spend an eternity in one place or another. I believe there is a heaven, and my faith puts me in a place where I am constantly living my life to help as many people as possible to join me for eternity there. But I also believe that we can create a place here on earth that is a reflection of the heaven that I believe in. I believe my thoughts, attitude, and action can help create heaven on earth.

I can look past this earth, and I want to bless as many people as possible with hope to increase their strength when they are having mental and physical struggles. I want to help them see that they can handle tough times and give them a mindset to achieve the results they want to achieve. I want them to see that there is another place to go, that they don't have to stay in that state of depression, that it will be better. As a matter of fact, it can already better. In the now. One of the main reasons we get depressed is because of the past, and one of the main reasons we have anxiety is because of the future. That's why the ability to live now, in the moments we are blessed to have, is so important. I want to help them get to a light that is much brighter than any gold jacket. That light blows it out of the water. A light that is on pilot-light mode in them. Waiting to be ignited and set ablaze.

Physically, I want to help people get up and start working out and eating right. Those are things that energize you. It helps release endorphins and testosterone and other feel-good chemicals, as I call them. It also gives you a routine that you begin to look forward to. So instead of having anxiety about the future, you replace it with something that you are excited about. And the fact that you will meet people that you will connect with, to get a smoothie or something afterwards. All of which puts positivity in your body and can help you get out of a spiritual dark place quicker and a mental dark place quicker, because of that energy that is coming through your body. When people are lacking in all three areas—mental, spiritual, physical—that's when suicide may creep into the mind as an option. I have been there, and it's a dark place.

The goal of the Brian Dawkins Impact Foundation is to provide people with hope. The goal of Brian Dawkins Ventures is to provide people with help. I have gone through a traumatic situation in my life, and I am still fighting and winning.

One of the things we want to do with the Foundation is to provide college scholarships. I understand how important education is, and learning to communicate is. The ability I had to speak on stage at the Enshrinement Ceremony was something I had to learn and something that I developed in part because I went to Clemson. If people can't articulate their thoughts, it makes it that much more difficult to get jobs. They can't get people to buy into their ideas. They can't get people to understand them. I want people in the types of communities like the one I grew up in to have that opportunity.

The Bible instructs us to be a beacon to the world. In Matthew, Jesus says, "You are a light of the world." You don't light a candle and cover it up. You put that candle on the hill. You want it to shine.

The light I shine won't bless everybody. It will bless those I am blessed to bless.

I want to do everything I can to allow those who see the light in me to experience the best lives they can. I want people to see where I came from and where I stand now. I want them to see the possibility to get up and achieve great things. It's up to them. The greatest things the Lord gave us are our minds and our thoughts. Both of which are able to shape our future, today. Our thoughts can become actions, because they can help us build good habits, or as I love to call them, disciplines.

I habitually think about the positive things in my life, and I give thanks for them. I see more and more how many things God has given to me. The purpose of my company and my foundation is to bless people. We want to help people by giving them scholarships and grants, and I want to inspire them in my motivational speaking engagements not just seek that better version of themselves, but to take the next steps to achieving it. The destination may seem like it's off at a distance, but the next step is not.

One person changed is a household changed. It can change the whole trajectory of a family for generations. If a person graduates college from a family that has never had a college graduate, it can become the new normal. If a person doesn't feel that anybody cares about them or that he or she doesn't get any breaks, and we can give that person a boost and push them out of that "stinkin' thinkin'" to do different things, then that has made a difference. People need to see hope is there. But we have to make hope affordable for people.

Some people think they can't afford hope. I want to bless people by letting them know there are others out there listening and that the Lord can help them in this thing they are going through. We want to give them a "John Stockton," an assist. That way, their families can see a different world.

Oftentimes, we as athletes understand the significance of what we gain from weight training. We are pushing ourselves past pain and limits. We understand what that feels like. We learn that in order to lift the heavier loads, sometimes we need a spot. We learn that even when we are tired yet look to help others, we gain more energy and strength. It's the same thing from a spiritual and mental standpoint. When you push through things, you build perseverance. You have to go through things to build something, brick after brick after brick. There are storms we must fight through. I am who I am because of the storms I fought through, yet I don't necessarily look like what I have come through.

◊◊◊

I expect good things to happen, not just for Brian Dawkins. I think differently. I believe differently. In tough times, I still know that you can't make decisions on things that are happening in the moment. You can't make a permanent decision on the momentary pain. I'm not the only one who has used this formula for success, and I won't be the last.

After my speech in Canton, different people emailed me and told me they were on the verge of harming themselves, but they got help because they heard me. My life has gone in a different direction. We don't know what the Lord has in store for us, but we have to be available when opportunities open up for us to connect with other people, and also available for the Lord to use us. When I say available, I'm speaking of when someone asks you can you meet them for lunch, or go to a conference or the like, and you say "Let me check my schedule." If you are not free to be used, because you got your plans and you got your own dreams, then you are missing an opportunity that was sent your way.

Many plans are in a man's mind, But it is the Lord's purpose for him that will stand [be carried out]." – Proverbs 19:21 (AMP)

It's a direction that's much needed in this world. Technology has flooded into the world, and people are less likely to look to have personal relationships with others. They become more isolated and lonely people. Think about it. We have the ability to speak to people around the world at the click of a button, yet people feel more isolated and lonely. I am blessed to think that I have the ability to let people know that somebody loves them. That goes a long way to helping people get out of the darkness of depression and those suicidal thoughts. I know that place. It's a place where you don't want to do anything. You want to sit in complete darkness, eat junk food, stare at the TV screen, and you don't want anybody to come into the room. You put on depressing music to push you further down. You fake that you're happy around other people, and that makes you more miserable after you leave them. You're not really that happy dude. You just keep more and more inside you.

When I felt like that in my early NFL career, the medicine I took numbed me just enough to let me get out of that dark place. I could let my faith take over. People think that once you overcome depression it's gone. Nope. That feeling is always there in me. And while I know depression is not just a feeling, it is those familiar feelings that are brought up out of our subconscious. Familiar feelings, sounds, smells, and everything else that could send us back to that dark place. I don't always feel it. But if enough negative things happen, that dark place is waiting there for you. It whispers, "You aren't this. You aren't that. But you are this (a loser), and you are that (incompetent)." It wants you to come back to it. And the enemy is always waiting for the opportunity to pile on to what we first start with our stinkin' thinkin'.

That's when you have to take a standing eight count. For me, that means praying a little more. Journaling a little more. Meditating a little more. Even exercising a little more. It's like a fighter. He gets woozy, and he takes a count to eight. That way, he can get back up and take the next positive step. When I was a younger man, and that feeling would come up, I would go into my room and stay away from people.

One of the worst things a person can do is build that man cave and to hide from people. I need to be around my family. My girls need a man's voice in their lives. If they see a man around them, they will look for a man to marry who will stay around them. I need to be around my wife and children. When Connie and I build our new house, it won't have a man cave. It will have a game room. That way, we can all be together.

I want each of my girls to see a guy who is not just married to their mom but a man who is also emotionally available to her. They see me kissing Connie, and they say, "Ew!!" But they need to see that.

One of the most powerful things we can do as men is to admit when we're not strong or capable. Our silence is killing us as men. Mentally, spiritually, and physically. We have to develop a better understanding of what a man is. Hollywood and television bring us some bad images of what a man is. I can tell a man how I feel about him without making it sound sexual or saying, "I love you, bro." We don't need the "bro." We don't have to toughen up love. We don't have to do it. We don't have to follow examples from the neighborhood, or even some of the households. We have to get rid of the toxins from our past, that are polluting our present and our future. We have to be available to all people to bless them, just like many of us have been blessed.

As I said in Canton, this journey of mine is far from over. During my speech, I thanked the Lord for "blessing me with the sense to know I didn't do it by myself." I have truly been "blessed by the best." As I continue down the road, there is so much to come.

I can't wait to see what the Lord is going to do with me next.

Acknowledgments

The Lord has done a work in me and through me. I acknowledge that it is by His guidance and grace that I've been blessed to be provided by so many wonderful folk that have helped me get to where I am, making it possible to go to where I'm going. I know I did not get here by myself, and I want to thank all those who have poured into this vessel. My Mom and Dad, my siblings, and Saint Dawkins (Grandma Dawk, my paternal grandmother). Furthermore, my coaches, teachers, trainers, doctors, and ministers. My close friends (Blessed Pack). My haters (my elevators).

I would like to thank Pat Waters for his efforts towards this book and he would like to dedicate his efforts to his beloved cousin Lisa McDowell, who left us the very same day I delivered by HOF speech, and his Dad, Jerry Waters.

Most importantly, my wonderful children Brian Jr, Brionni, Chonni and Cionni and of course, my HOF wife, gift from the Lord, Connie.

Thank you Lord, for what you have brought me through. Thank you for those you have placed in my path to help me grow. I thank you for where I now stand. And I thank you for where I am going.

Be Blessed.
—Brian Dawkins, Sr.

Many authors start a project like this believing that they are completely responsible for the final product and quickly realize how wrong they are. As this book progressed, I became more reliant on others for encouragement and assistance.

First, I want to thank my family for its continued support—my patient wife Meg and sons Bryan, Christopher and Ian.

I would like to thank former Eagles All-Pro running back Brian Westbrook for his valuable aid at this project's outset and throughout its journey.

Thank you to Greg Welsh, who worked tirelessly to transcribe the interviews I conducted with Brian and even learned how to use some old-school technology in the process.

Miriam Seidel, the editor of this book, deserves considerable praise and gratitude for her great work and tremendous patience throughout the process.

Finally, thank you to Pat Waters, who served as a great emissary between Brian and me and was extremely committed to this book from the beginning.

—Michael Bradley

Appendix

To learn more about the health professionals mentioned in this book:

Shawn Caldwell, DC
Chiropractic Medicine
Denver Sports Recovery
3490 Youngfield Street
Golden, CO 80401
www.denversportsrecovery.com

Kate Decker, USATF, CSCS, ART
Institute of Athletic Movements (IAM)
Chattanooga, Tennessee
www.instituteofathleticmovement.com

Brett Fisher, PT, ATC, CSCS, DN, Cert. ASTYM
Fischer Sports Physical Therapy & Conditioning
5730 S 32nd Street
Phoenix, AZ 85040
www.fischerinstitute.com

Ann Frederick
Stretch to Win – Fascial Stretch Therapy® (STW-FST®)
Stretch to Win Institute
580 N. 54th Street, Suite 1
Chandler, AZ 85226
www.stretchtowin.com

Steve Hamilton, CMT
Sports massage
Cync R' Nize Sports Therapy
Denver, Co
https://www.linkedin.com/in/steve-hamilton-616b8a54/

Jeff Higuera, BS Kinesiology, Performance Coach, SPRI, Master Trainer PES, Pn1, FMS, L1, CSAC
Competitor Performance Academy
1085 Belle Avenue
Winter Springs, FL 32708
www.coachjdh.com

Andrew Kirschner, DO
Osteopathic Medicine
Suburban Multispecialty
1 Belmont Avenue #416
Bala Cynwyd, PA 19004
www.suburbanmultispecialty.com

P. Michael Leahy, DC, ART, CCSP
Active Release Techniques® (ART®)
9240 Explorer Drive
Colorado Springs, CO 80920
www.activerelease.com

Brian Popiel, NMD
Naturopathic Medicine
Sonoran Naturopathic Center
9316 E Raintree Drive # 140
Scottsdale, AZ 85260
www.sncaz.com

Nelson Vetanze, DC
Chiropractic Extremity Practitioner
Omni Chiropractic
13710 E. Rice Place
Aurora, Colorado 80015
www.omni-chiropractic.com